Is Religion Natural?

Issues In
Science and Theology
This series is published under the auspices of the European Society for the
Study of Science and Theology

Series Editor
Dirk Evers

Advisory Board

Pierre Bourdon (Physics, Theology), Paris, France
Grzegorz Bugajak (Philosophy), Warszawa, Poland
Willem B. Drees (Philosophy of Religion), Leiden, the Netherlands
Dirk Evers (Theology), Halle-Wittenberg, Germany
Antje Jackelén (Theology), Lund, Sweden
Anne Kull (Theology), Tartu, Estonia
Javier Leach (Mathematics), Madrid, Spain
Hubert Meisinger (Theology), Mainz, Germany
Lluis Oviedo (Theology), Rome, Italy
Roger Trigg (Philosophy), Warwick, UK
Chris Wiltsher (Theology), Durham, UK

Published in this series:
Is Religion Natural? (2012)
How Do We Know? Understanding in Science and Theology (2010)
Creation's Diversity: Voices from Theology and Science (2008)
Wisdom or Knowledge? Science, Theology and Cultural Dynamics (2006)
Creative Creatures: Values and Ethical Issues in Theology, Science and Technology
(2005)
Design and Disorder: Perspectives from Science and Theology (2002)
The Human Person in Science and Theology (2000)

Is Religion Natural?

Editors

Dirk Evers
Michael Fuller
Antje Jackelén
Taede A. Smedes

t & t clark

Published by T&T Clark International
A Continuum imprint
The Tower Building, 11 York Road, London SE1 7NX
80 Maiden Lane, Suite 704, New York, NY 10038

www.tandtclark.com

British Library Cataloguing-in-Publication Data
A catalogue record for this book is available from the British Library

ISBN: 978 0 5672 2727 0 (Hardback)

Typeset by Fakenham Prepress Solutions, Fakenham, Norfolk NR21 8NN
Printed in Great Britain

Contents

Preface and Acknowledgments

Every other year, the *European Conference on Science and Theology* (ECST) is organised by ESSSAT, the *European Society for the Study of Science and Theology*. ESSSAT is a scholarly society that promotes the study of the interactions of science and theology, thus creating opportunities for scholars from a wide diversity of backgrounds, geographically und linguistically, and from different disciplines and confessions to engage in conversation and debate. From 7 to 11 April 2010, ESSSAT arranged the Thirteenth *European Conference on Science and Theology* (ECST XIII) in Edinburgh, Scotland. For the first time, the Edinburgh conference was a joint conference between ESSSAT and *The Science and Religion Forum* (SRF), and our host was the University of Edinburgh's *School of Divinity*. Many participants from both organisations and beyond were attracted by the conference, and ESSSAT members and other conference participants alike were inspired to present and discuss about 100 papers in the conference's paper sessions.

The theme of this conference was: *Is Religion Natural?* With this theme, ESSSAT turned towards the much debated Evolutionary Psychology of Religion and was able to invite some of the leading scholars in this field to attend. Central issues were the cognitive dimensions of religion, the theological relevance of scientific studies of religion and the meaning of naturalism with regard to religion. The wide range of themes covered by these sessions is reflected in this volume of *Issues in Science and Theology* with 13 selected articles written by authors from the fields of science, philosophy, and theology, who discuss the question of the naturalness of religion from different perspectives and with different voices. Some of the contributions are revised and edited versions of the plenary lectures at ECST XIII; others have been selected from the various short papers discussed at the conference. Some of the other papers of the conference will be published in Volume 12 of the yearbook of ESSSAT, *Studies in Science and Theology*, which all society members receive and which can be ordered directly from ESSSAT.

The publication of this volume is an opportunity to thank organisers and sponsors of our conference. We express our gratitude to the local organiser Neil Spurway (ESSSAT Vice-President for the conference) assisted by Alison Spurway (registration officer), whom we thank for all their efforts before and during the conference. Other members of the Organising Committee were Antje Jackelén (ESSSAT President), Peter Colyer (SRF), Michael Fuller (SRF), Marie Vejrup Nielsen (ESSSAT Secretary), Taede A. Smedes (Scientific Programme Officer) and Chris Wiltsher (ESSSAT Treasurer). Roger Paul (SRF Treasurer) gave support and advice. Particular thanks go to Professor David Fergusson of the University of Edinburgh's *School of Divinity* as the host of the conference.

Without sponsors and partners we would not be able to arrange conferences like these. ESSSAT wants to express its gratitude to the University of Edinburgh *Gifford Fund*, the *Thora Ohlssons Stiftelse* (Sweden) which provided substantial sponsorship, and the *Church of Scotland*. *Action of Churches Together in Scotland* sponsored one theological student from Eastern Europe to attend the conference. The ESSSAT prize was supported by an anonymous donation.

Johannes Schimming, Alexander Tiedemann, Samuel Hüfken and Conrad Krannich helped with the editorial work in different stages of the process. Finally we thank the staff of T&T Clark for their cooperation on this volume, now the seventh in this series.

Dirk Evers

Part I

Religion – From a Natural Point of View

1 The Naturalness of Religion and the Unnaturalness of Theology[1]

Justin L. Barrett

Some people have no particular musical talent. Some people are tone deaf. Some people enjoy music more than others. Yet, singing, drumming, rhyming and chanting appear in every culture. We show receptivity to music from early childhood and huge majorities of people practice music to some degree, whether it is only whistling or singing to oneself, or publicly performing. Essentially everyone enjoys music of some sort. Music appears to be a 'natural' part of human cultural expression. This naturalness of music does not entail that music is a biological adaptation or that we have a 'music gene' or a particular, specific musical part of the brain. In fact, given the diversity of forms of musical expression, the ways music varies in degree and type of elaboration from culture to culture, and the various social and personal functions it serves, it would be surprising indeed if there is a single cause, a biological one, for music. And yet, *prime facie*, it seems right to call music *natural*. Religion is comparably natural.

Although almost everyone enjoys music and even shows musical expression on occasion, very few people deliberately and devotedly study music: its history, its composition, its structure and its techniques. People who do so – musicologists, music theorists, expert musicians and the like – are doing something relatively unnatural. Theology is comparably unnatural.

In this chapter I argue for the naturalness of religion – that religion is a natural kind of human cultural expression because of how human minds naturally function in ordinary human environments. Religion is cognitively natural. I further argue that doing theology, in contrast, is relatively unnatural in terms of its moorings in

[1] This essay borrows heavily on the ideas of philosopher Robert McCauley who was a visiting fellow in Oxford's Centre for Anthropology and Mind in 2007 and gave a series of lectures on the naturalness of religion and the unnaturalness of science as preparation for a book-length treatment of the topic (forthcoming). His discussion of theology as a middle-ground case (more natural than science but more unnatural than religion) was inspiration for this essay. I refer readers to McCauley's forthcoming book for a more thorough and nuanced presentation with different emphases, evidence, and rhetorical strategy.

human cognition, and hence requires special cultural scaffolding, and will tend to have certain predictable tensions with ordinary religious practice. I end with some implications of this analysis.

Recognizing the broad and contested meanings associated with my three key terms, I will offer working definitions of *religion, theology* and *natural*. By *religion* I mean a shared body of ideas and practices related to the presumed existence of counterintuitive intentional agents. I will unpack the technical sense of counter-intuitive below. For now it is enough to note that it maps fairly closely onto the common sense meaning of supernatural, but avoids the ontological problems associated with specifying what is and is not natural. *Natural* will be used in a different sense here. *Natural* below refers primarily to ease, fluency or automaticity in thinking about or engaging in a particular domain of competence. In this sense *natural* will be shorthand for cognitive naturalness or ease of processing, generally marked by rapidity in generating actions or inferences and with little drain on conscious attentional resources. As will become clearer below, this primary sense of *natural* and *naturalness* will be closely associated with a secondary sense: *natural* meaning common, widespread or characteristic of humans. By *theology* I refer to the scholarly, reflective study of religious ideas and practices, but I will also use *theology* to mean the resulting body of thought.

I. The Naturalness of Religion Thesis[2]

The vast majority of humans have natural cognitive predispositions that make them receptive to religious thought and behaviour. That is, people have psychological inclinations that collaborate to encourage the acceptance of supernatural agency and subsequent actions in response to this acceptance. Such cognitive predisposi-tions or biases might be thought of as extra-cultural in the sense that they are not products of specific cultural arrangements, but of some interaction between human biological endowments and the sorts of environments (natural and social) in which humans typically find themselves.

Below I sketch some of the most directly relevant cognitive systems for such an account of religious recurrence. Before I do, I offer some justification for two premises of the naturalness thesis: (1) that the cognitive level is the right level of analysis for accounting for the widespread recurrence of religious thought and behaviour, and (2) that some aspects of human cognition might be considered extra-cultural.

1. Why the Cognitive Level?
We often focus on questions such as 'Why do some people (either individuals or groups) like rugby whereas others like basketball?' or 'Why do some people

---

[2] The (cognitive) naturalness of religion thesis has been developed numerous times elsewhere (Boyer 1994; Atran 2002; Barrett 2004; Bloom 2009, 2007; Boyer 2001, 2003; McCauley forthcoming; Tremlin 2006).

like opera whereas others prefer folk music?' For questions such as these, the answers are likely to lie on the level of culture, perhaps in interaction with cultural psychology of the individual. Why do some people think care for the poor is an essential value whereas others think ensuring individual liberties is most important? Why do some people become Muslims whereas others become Buddhists? For these questions, the most powerful explanatory factors surely will be found in the cultural environment. Here, however, I am focusing on a different type of question. Why is it that people tend to be religious everywhere and in every time or age? For this question we need to look down a level to something about human psychology that might be largely invariable across cultural contexts. We would not answer the questions 'Why does music appear in every culture?' or 'Why does sport appear in every culture?' with 'Because every culture promotes music and sport'.

Scholars of religion have not missed this basic explanatory strategy, but have often appealed to the level of social dynamics, arguing that pan-cultural phenomena are explainable in terms of their social functions. For instance, sport, music and religion are common across societies because they serve to create and sustain social groups in one way or another. A full evaluation of the merits and limitations of such approaches is beyond the scope of this chapter. I will only insist that cognitive approaches are not incompatible with such social-functional explanations, which have been resuscitated by evolutionary studies of religion (Bulbulia 2008; Sosis 2006), but do shore up a weakness of social-functional explanations. Explanations on the level of social dynamics often fail to specify the psychological mechanisms by which sport, music or religion create group cohesion and to address the question why, if so many such forms of cultural expression do the job, do we have them all? Further, why religious content (focusing on supernatural agency, as I have circumscribed) instead of, say, the importance of irrational numbers or immaterial particles? Clearly some kinds of ideas-actions clusters are more mutually reinforcing and more likely to facilitate social group formation than others, but which ones and why? As my concern here is with why thought-action systems concerning counter-intuitive/supernatural agency are so recurrent, an explanation that has nothing to say about the particular content (counterintuitive agency) is insufficient even if otherwise helpful. For content, we must turn to underlying cognitive systems that bias us toward some kinds of content – some ways of thinking – as opposed to others. But, of course, this tack assumes that there are cognitive systems that bias us toward some kinds of thought as opposed to others. Do we have any reason to believe this is the case?

2. Evidence of Natural Cognitive Predispositions
Philosopher Robert McCauley has helpfully identified several rules-of-thumb for identifying motor or cognitive capacities as what he terms 'maturationally natural'

– i.e. cognitively natural, widely recurrent capacities that nearly everyone acquires as a normal part of development regardless of culture (McCauley forthcoming). In addition to a high degree of fluency, automaticity or ease in using the capacity, maturationally natural cognition is marked by (1) little or no need for explicit tuition, (2) no need for culturally specific artefacts, (3) typically developing early in the lifespan (so early that we usually do not remember not having the capacity), (4) very little intra-group variation in the capacity, and (5) little inter-group variation. McCauley also notes that if one does not acquire the capacity, we would generally regard this as a developmental deficit or abnormality. I add to McCauley's list of indicators (6) that these capacities typically have an ancient appearance in our species – in the order of tens of thousands of years.[3]

Speaking one's native language is a good example of a capacity that bears all six marks of a maturationally natural capacity. (1) Children do not need to be told the grammar of their native language or otherwise receive explicit 'language training' to acquire it. They pick it up by being immersed in a linguistic environment. (2) No artefacts are required to learn your native language. (3) We learn to speak our native language in the first three years of life, early enough that we do not remember not being able to speak. (4) By-and-large, all people of any given cultural group are roughly equal in their native language fluency (compared with, say, algebraic fluency or musical fluency). (5) It is strange to suggest that one cultural group is more fluent in their native language than is another group, whereas it would be perfectly justifiable to suggest that some cultural groups are better at chess playing or doing calculus than others. (6) Language has probably been a part of human natural capacities for tens of thousands of (Mithen 1996).

McCauley's pointers suggest several empirical strategies for discovering evidence of natural cognitive predispositions. First, as those cognitive systems that are natural would be those that have little inter-group variation, cross-cultural evidence of a capacity's existence would be an important piece of evidence. For example, if we find that in all cultures sampled we find similar recognition of basic emotions (e.g. fear, anger, sadness, happiness, surprise, disgust), then we have evidence that such emotion recognition is cognitively natural. Unfortunately, getting such a broad, cross-cultural sample that has not been importantly 'contaminated' by historical contact is very costly and difficult (if not impossible). Fortunately, other supporting evidence can be discovered.

A second type of evidence relevant to claims of cognitive (maturational) naturalness is that gathered through developmental psychology. As McCauley observes, capacities that normally emerge early in development – especially before the sixth year – tend to be maturationally natural. Developmental psychologists use techniques that can investigate the minds of even pre-verbal infants. If a baby characteristically does something in the first year of life, this is strong evidence that

---

[3] McCauley notes that one may achieve a high degree of fluency, automaticity, and ease in other ways (as we see in chess masters or concert pianists), but these cases require special cultural conditions and lots of practice. He calls these forms of naturalness 'practiced naturalness' and their profile is the flip side of the maturationally natural.

the capacity is natural for humans generally. We might also suspect a trait as having maturationally natural origins if it appears in children more strongly than in adults of the same population. For instance, if children have firmer and more elaborate beliefs in the natural world being purposefully designed than what their parents or other adults give evidence for (Kelemen 2004), then it may be that this tendency enjoys some maturationally natural impetus. Cultural factors may serve to tamp down a natural bias instead of only serving to develop new biases.

Similarly, as maturationally natural capacities typically arose early in human evolution and do not require special artefacts (that might only have become common with various technological revolutions), species-comparative and archaeological evidence might be leveraged to make claims regarding cognitive naturalness. If chimpanzees can be shown to have a degree of self-awareness (e.g. through recognizing themselves in a mirror) or early humans can be safely inferred to have such awareness (e.g. through discovery of polished obsidian mirror stones) and even a fairly narrow human sample (such as Western university students) can be shown to have similar self-awareness, it would be unreasonable to venture that such a capacity is culturally specific. A safer assumption is that it is maturationally natural in light of this evidence (until some compelling evidence arises to the contrary).[4]

Given these evidential criteria (cross-cultural recurrence, early childhood development, and earlier peoples or other related species similarities), many cognitive domains appear to have a strong maturationally natural composition. Much as other species have 'instincts' to perform certain problem-solving in characteristic ways, humans have cognitive 'instincts' that inform and constrain their ways of thinking and acting. Below I briefly sketch only a few examples that have been raised as particularly important to religion.

a. Naïve physics
Well before babies' first birthdays, they have a number of expectations about the properties and movement of bounded physical objects. This collection of expectations has alternatively been called 'naïve physics', 'folk mechanics' or 'intuitive physics' to stress the idea that such reasoning is non-reflective and automatic. This naïve physics system delivers intuitions about physical objects. Using looking-time measures, babies have been experimentally shown to expect that physical objects move as coherent wholes, must move continuously in space and time, cannot pass through other solid physical objects, and must be contacted in order to be launched or for their trajectory to be modified (Spelke and Kinzler 2007). Upon this foundation other knowledge about physical objects is built such as knowing that solid objects generally must be supported or else they fall, and that they

---

[4] Occasionally anthropologists, who rightly fear uncritical application of Western psychology on non-Western populations, will suggest that a given group of people do not show a cognitive capacity (such as Theory of Mind) that Westerners have. Such a claim becomes untenable – if not offensive – when evidence emerges that chimpanzees or bonobos have the same 'Western' cognition.

are tangible and visible. This early developing maturationally natural cognition structures, informs and constrains further learning. Tell me about a novel object and I'll assume all of these properties unless otherwise specified. They need not be explicitly communicated. If you tell me about an invisible body or a body that walks through walls, you will capture my attention immediately because you have violated my maturationally natural intuitions. Note that whether these intuitions are 'learned' from environmental regularities or in some sense 'innate' is irrelevant. Children (and other primates) acquire naïve physics as part of normal maturation.

b. Agency Detection

Not all objects follow all of the expectations of naïve physics. One particularly important class, intentional agents, routinely violate the 'contact principle': that an object needs to be contacted in order to be launched or have its path of movement modified. Agents (such as people or animals) launch themselves. They are 'self-propelled' (Premack 1990). Numerous researchers have demonstrated that infants reason differently about agents than other physical objects, allowing them to launch themselves and expecting them to act consistently with perceived goals. That is, they are 'goal-directed' (Gergely and Csibra 2003; Csibra 2008). When babies see something that is self-propelled and goal-directed, they reason about it differently than other sorts of objects (Gergely and Csibra 2003; Leslie 1994; Scholl and Tremoulet 2000). In addition to non-contact, contingent or goal-directed action, another cue for detecting an agent is whether it has a human-like face. From birth babies selectively attend to human faces in their environment and give evidence of imitating a range of facial expressions (Meltzoff and Moore 1989). Upon this cognitive foundation, an agency detection system develops that not only detects objects as agents, but also registers whether events are actions of an intentional agent (Lawson and McCauley 1990), and whether states-of-affairs in the natural world are products of intentional agency (Guthrie 1993; Barrett 2004). Experimental evidence suggests that this agency detection system is easily activated and appears to be a default interpretive scheme for actions that are not readily explainable in terms of other intuitive causal cognition (such as naïve physics). When adults see a disk 'chasing' another disk on a computer screen, they tend to attribute agency to the disk as well as mental states and sometimes genders and personalities (Heider and Simmel 1944; Scholl and Tremoulet 2000). When shooting stars are registered as a sign from the gods, we attribute a good harvest to divine action, or we see a ghost in the graveyard, we are using our agency detection system (sometimes called ADD for agency detection device, or HADD for hyper-sensitive agency detection device) (Barrett 2004).

c. Theory of Mind

As social beings, humans have early developing cognitive capacities that enable reasoning about other humans' behaviours: why they act the way they do. From birth, it seems, we recognize other humans as agents and our agency detection system typically triggers our developing 'Theory of Mind' system (ToM) to generate inferences about the mental states of the agent in question whether it be a human, animal or god. A mature ToM helps us explain and predict others' behaviours in terms of unseen internal states – mental states – including beliefs, desires, percepts and emotions. For instance, we act in order to satisfy our desires, and if we satisfy a desire we experience positive affect. Beliefs are impacted by precepts and shape how we act upon our desires. Although seemingly absent in most animals, a rudimentary (at least) ToM may be present in chimpanzees. In humans across cultures it has a characteristic developmental pattern (Wellman et al. 2001). As we generally regard agents as minded, insofar as a god is an agent, reasoning about it will tend to activate ToM.

d. Teleofunctional Reasoning Biases

When asking children about why some rocks are pointy or why there are rivers or whether tigers are for doing something (as opposed to just capable of doing things), children have been found to gravitate toward teleological or functional explanations. Tigers are for living in zoos, rivers are here so that people can go boating on them, and rocks are pointy so that animals will not sit on them and crush them (Kelemen 1990; DiYanni and Kelemen 2005). Children tend to associate purpose with intentions so, unsurprisingly, when asked about where first things came from (such as animals or mountains), children prefer intentional explanations (DiYanni and Kelemen 2005; Kelemen and DiYanni 2005), and creationist origins of animals over evolutionary explanations even if their parents and teachers endorse evolutionary accounts (Evans 2000, 2001). Kelemen has recently shown that these teleofunctional reasoning biases persist into adulthood and appear to be only tamped down to a degree by formal education (Kelemen and Rosset 2009).

e. Other Cognitive Domains

These maturationally natural cognitive systems and dispositions by no means exhaust the domains of content-rich intuitive cognition that appears to inform and constrain cultural learning and expression. Language is probably the most rigorously studied domain, and it is now conventional wisdom that humans are not equally good at learning just any logically possible symbolic communication system, but are naturally biased to acquire the kinds of 'natural' languages such as English, Spanish, and Mandarin and not 'unnatural' communication systems such as binary code (whereas our personal computers have just the opposite language-use biases). Science has shown us that we more readily form some types of associations more readily than others, such as becoming afraid of snakes or spiders. It takes little encouragement for a child (or a monkey!) to become afraid of snakes compared to, say, becoming afraid of flowers. Many snakes pose hazards for us today and probably would have in our ancestral past as well, and so being disposed to be cautious about them would have been adaptive. Similarly, our disgust system can be easily conditioned: one good bout of illness after eating something iffy and we'll probably not want to even think about it for years to come. Likewise, seeing our parents recoil with disgust at certain substances during our early years can readily cement food avoidance within certain parameters. We may have a related 'hazard precaution' system for many unseen environmental hazards, such as germs, contaminants and intruders, that has a characteristic range of inputs and outputs. This system has been implicated as a critical player in normal ritualized behaviours seen in young parents and children, in people with Obsessive-Compulsive Disorder, and in cultural rituals, including religious ones pertaining to ritual purity and marking offsacred spaces (Lienard and Boyer 2006; Boyer and Lienard 2006).

f. The Relationships between Natural Cognition and Culture

What many, if not all, of all of these maturationally natural, extra-cultural cognitive systems have in common is that they all appear to have certain natural parameters (acquired through some combination of pan-cultural environmental factors and species-wide biological endowment) that are then 'tuned-up' by culturally specific inputs. For instance, the kinds of things regarded as disgusting in one cultural context versus another will vary, although within certain parameters; such associations will be acquired in predictable ways and during predictable periods of development. Similarly, just what range of 'minds' becomes the concern of the Theory of Mind system for a particular person will be different for the subsistence hunter who has to reason about the movement of predators and prey compared to the urban dweller who only has to meaningfully consider other humans. Cultural particulars matters to how most of these cognitive capacities develop, but do not account for their appearance or determine them.

That said, as these natural cognitive capacities have characteristic parameters and tendencies regardless of cultural context, and because they typically predate any particular cultural form (naïve physics, agency detection and some kind of theory of mind were probably present in pre-human species) and emerge early in an individual's life, they are going to shape what and how cultural material is acquired. One might think of cultural expression as boats floating on the water with anchor-lines. Maturationally natural cognition provides conceptual anchor points, and the closer some kind of cultural knowledge or action is to the relevant anchor point(s) the less stress on its successful acquisition and persistence. Or think of maturationally natural cognition as providing a number of 'sticky spots' on a wall: stickiest in their centres with decreasing stickiness the further away from the centres. Individuals in any cultural setting will creatively generate lots of different ideas and practices and 'throw them' against the wall. Those closest to the sticky spots will be most likely to 'take' and become widespread enough to become recognized as 'cultural' as opposed to merely idiosyncratic or a transitory innovation.

This cognitive 'anchoring' of culture helps to explain cross-cultural recurrence including the recurrence of religious ideas and practices, but it also makes predictions regarding some areas of cultural diversity: those ideas or practices that deviate from natural cognition (are some distance from anchor-points) will require special conditions to be culturally successful. A given individual might be able to maintain 'unnatural' ideas or practices (in the sense of deviating from the deliverances of maturationally natural cognition) because of special cognitive abilities, genius or impairment, but as such special cognitive abilities are always only manifest in a small proportion of a population, special cultural conditions would be required for relatively unnatural cultural expression. What might these special conditions be?

Various forms of 'cultural scaffolding' could assist in the acquisition and transmission of relatively unnatural cultural expression. These include writing and other symbolic systems that can serve as mnemonic aids for ideas too cumbersome for accurate preservation by human memory. Artefacts and specially designed spaces can also serve as cognitive prosthetics – the most dramatic being calculators, computers and other IT systems that vastly extend human computational abilities and give ready access to information. Institutions designed to support cultural transmission can also promote less-than-natural ideas and practices. Schools, laboratories, museums and special societies serve this function. They create space for deliberate, systematic and repetitive communication of unnatural ideas, often employing a certain division of labour such that expertise is distributed across an expert faculty, so that no one person has to maintain the entire corpus of ideas. This kind of 'distributed cognition' is another form of cultural scaffolding that allows for more complex problem solving than what would be available to any given individual (Hutchins 1995). Above all, acquiring relatively unnatural ideas or practices (think mastery of calculus, chess or the violin) requires time, effort and (often) material wealth – luxuries not available to everyone and, hence, limiting factors in their accessibility.

3. The Naturalness of Religion

Religion – or any type of cultural expression – can be said to be natural to the degree that it does not deviate far from the deliverances of (maturationally) natural cognitive systems and is, in fact, encouraged by this ordinary cognition. Of course, this claim is a relative one: some forms of cultural expression are more or less cognitively natural. Verbal fluency is more natural than literacy, which is more natural than computer programming fluency. Music appreciation and production (e.g. singing, drumming) is very natural, more so than being a concert musician or musicologist. Religion, I argue, is more natural than theology.

Religion's claim to naturalness gains some *prima facie* support from its relatively strong agreement with the six indices of maturational naturalness and the general ease, automaticity and fluency with which people engage in religious thought and action. (1) Although religious instruction is helpful, many people engage in religious thought and practice with little or no explicit tuition. They hear the gods talked about, and observe the related actions, and think and do likewise. (2) Culturally specific artefacts are frequently incorporated into religious practice, although they are not necessary. (3) People often acquire religious beliefs and practices so early in life they do not remember not having them. (4 and 5) While devotion or zeal may vary, the general capacity to 'do religion' is not terribly variable within or between cultural groups. Admittedly, variability here is much greater than with language, for instance, but it is much less than literacy, mathematics, science or technological sophistication. It may be more comparable to music in variability. (6) Archaeological evidence such as ritualized burials suggests that religion has been with us for upwards of 30,000 years (Mithen 1996). Religion then bears many of the marks of being natural.

Additionally, scholars in the cognitive science of religion (CSR) area have begun specifying just how natural cognition supports and encourages religious thought and action, without appealing to culturally specific factors to account for its recurrence. The success of this academic project adds additional support to the naturalness of religion thesis, and so I sketch an exemplary account below by appealing to the natural cognitive capacities introduced above.

Two of the factors above – agency detection and teleofunctional reasoning biases – may both provide impetus for entertaining the existence of supernatural agents. If, as experimental evidence suggests, the agency detection system is a bit hair-triggered and often detects agency given only slight and ambiguous evidence, then people may experience a detection of intentional agency that is not readily labelled as human or animal. This dynamic is a primary driver in Stewart Guthrie's cognitive account of religion: people experience 'false positives', detecting agency where there may in fact be none, and then use such experiences to postulate the existence of spirits, ghosts or gods (Guthrie 1993). Guthrie argues that this enthusiastic attention to any signs of human-like agency is a product of selective pressure: in our ancestral past, humans and other large animals would have posed our greatest threats and promises for survival and reproduction. Failing to detect them would have carried greater costs than over-detection, and so our cognitive-perceptual systems are tuned to be permissive instead of stringent. Placing aside whether this agency detection system produces *false* positives in the case of detecting supernatural agency, certainly a liberal agency detection system would encourage the positing of agency (accurately or not) in a wide range of circumstances compatible with spirits and gods as opposed to humans or animals. The system creates conceptual space that is readily filled by gods. Similarly, the teleofunctional reasoning biases that Kelemen has documented appear to produce a conceptual gap in our minds regarding the apparent design and purpose in the natural world. We have natural cognitive biases that make us open to the idea that someone (or many someones) caused or causes the world to be the way that it is, and yet we know that human or animal agents are unsuitable candidates for this designing and creating role. Spirits that manage the forest ecosystem or created the first plants, animals, rivers and mountains readily fill a general conceptual gap. In these ways, the agency detection system and teleofunctional reasoning biases may provide natural impetus for people to suspect that there are kinds of intentional agency about beyond humans and animals.

Gods, however, are not just creators or managers of the natural order. Gods (broadly construed) are frequently regarded as having other superhuman attributes such as being super knowing and super perceiving. Such attributes may receive natural impetus from another natural cognitive system, the Theory of Mind system (ToM). Experimental developmental psychologists have provided evidence that when it comes to attributing knowing and perceiving to others, two- to three-year-old children appear to have a bias toward over-attribution. That is, if they understand something as know-able and perceptible, they tend to regard others as knowing and perceiving those things. My research group has extended these findings to reasoning about gods: whether the gods in question are culturally elaborated as super-knowing or highly fallible, three-year-olds tend to attribute super-knowledge to them (Knight 2008; Knight et al. 2004; Barrett et al. 2001; Barrett and Richert 2003; Barrett et al. 2003). If the god in question is a super-knowing god (as in the Abrahamic traditions), then children answer questions correctly about God's knowledge or perception one to two years *earlier* than they are accurate on the same questions when asked about people. It is not until around age five that a majority of children fully recognize that humans have false beliefs and failures to perceive things accurately, but by this age they can already conceptualize gods differently than people on these dimensions. Learning the fallibility of humans appears to be a greater developmental accomplishment than learning about the super knowledge of a deity. In this way, natural cognitive biases may prepare children to learn about gods, making them relatively natural. Gods, then, are not all that super-natural.

Another class of agency that features prominently in many cultural systems is the agency of the deceased, as ghosts, spirits or ancestors. That some aspect of a human's identity and agency can survive death is cross-culturally recurrent, but it is elaborated in different ways and to different degrees. Why such ideas appear to be so natural is enthusiastically debated by cognitive scientists of religion, but Paul Bloom (2004) offers one prominent view. Bloom has argued that in reasoning about fellow humans we have to use at least two different conceptual systems that must be brought to bear: one concerned with physical bodies (the naïve physics system) and one concerned with minded agents (ToM). Because these two systems have different evolutionary histories, developmental pathways, and input-output conditions, they are not easily zippered together and can be readily dissociated. The consequence of this dynamic is 'intuitive dualism', a natural tendency to reason about minds as distinct and causally separable from bodies. Given this intuitive dualism, the divorcing of mind from physical body at death is readily accommodated. Indeed, it has been suggested that ToM doesn't have the same 'off switch' as the cognition surrounding bodies, and so the idea that the mind continues to function after death presents very little strain on our ordinary cognition (Bering et al. 2005; Bering 2006; Boyer 2001; Bering and Bjorkland 2004). Some kind of afterlife, then, may be relatively natural and it is only the particular cultural elaborations that require culture-based explanation.

By no means are all religious ideas wholly intuitive or natural. The claim here is only that religious ideas, as recurrent folk beliefs, tend to be well-supported by ordinary cognition. But even slight deviations from natural anchors are accommodated by cognitive accounts of religion. Pascal Boyer's very influential account argues that slight deviations from intuitive cognition actually help advance religious and other folk concepts (Boyer 1994, 2001; Boyer and Ramble 2001; Atran 2002). The reasoning runs this way: if an idea is too counterintuitive (i.e. violates the automatic deliverances of maturationally natural cognition) it is difficult to mentally represent, to remember, to communicate and to generate inferences from. Consider a dog statue that is invisible (in violation of naïve physics), can pass through solid walls (in violation of naïve physics), listens to people's conversations (a transfer of ToM to an inappropriate target), acts to frustrate its own desires (violation of ToM), gives birth to kittens (in violation of transferred folk biology) and only remembers things that didn't happen (in violation of ToM). Such a concept is too counterintuitive to be a strong candidate for cultural success. On the other hand, a wholly intuitive idea such as a brown, floppy-eared dog just is not very interesting. No novel or important inferences are generated from the concept and so it is unlikely to be talked about and spread within a population. Boyer has argued for a cognitive optimum: concepts that are largely intuitive with good potential to generate useful inferences will be readily remembered and communicated, and hence are more likely to become culturally shared. Gods fit this profile. They are largely intuitive (natural) but with just a small number of counterintuitive tweaks that boosts their inferential potential. Gods, then, can be referred to as modestly or minimally *counterintuitive agents* in Boyer's technical sense. In the sense of 'natural' I have been using, gods are only slightly super-natural.

Other theorists in the cognitive science of religion area have considered how ordinary, natural cognition can be used to inform and constrain religious actions once existence of these counterintuitive agents is assumed. For instance, E. Thomas Lawson and Robert McCauley have argued that ordinary cognition dealing with how people understand actions (as distinct from non-agentive events) structures our intuitions surrounding religious rituals (Lawson and McCauley 1990; McCauley and Lawson 2002). Brian Malley has considered how ordinary cognitive dynamics impact the use of sacred texts (Malley 2004). Emma Cohen has shown that ordinary assumptions about mind–body relations can impact how spirit possession is conceptualized: a point I return to below (Cohen 2007).

II. The Unnaturalness of Theology

Theology, the scholarly, reflective study of religious ideas and practices and the resulting body of thought, clearly is less natural than religion. A simple nose-count of people who are engaged in doing 'religion' versus 'theology' would undoubtedly reveal that theology is a rare pursuit and, hence, likely to be cognitively unnatural. Ticking through the six indices of naturalness reinforces the same point. (1) Theology requires explicit tuition, careful explication of doctrine, justification of practices and the like. (2) Theology, at least as it has been practised for millennia, makes heavy use of culturally specific artefacts, particularly writing and writing materials, and books. Biblical, historical and archaeological theology may also make use of ancient artefacts, works of art, writings, buildings and the like. (3) Although young children may impressively express musings and wonderment resonant with theology, it would be overly generous to suggest they do theology. Those who have engaged in reflective theological work can probably remember when they first began such activities. (4) Intra-group variability in theological prowess is relatively high as instructors of undergraduate theology courses can readily attest. (5) Inter-group variability is likewise high. It isn't the least bit absurd to argue that some cultural groups have stronger, more active histories of doing theology than others. (6) As theology is heavily dependent upon external conceptual aids such as writing systems, it is unlikely that theology (at least as we recognize it today) vastly predates literacy or other elaborate symbolic systems. Hence, theology, even by the most generous accounts, is likely many millennia younger than religion. These reflections collectively suggest that theology is a much less natural form of cultural expression than is religion, but just how unnatural theology is varies considerably by kind.

Theology occupies a range of degrees of naturalness depending upon the type of theology and the cognitive tools required to exercise it. The minister-theologian may suffer pressure to keep theology relevant and accessible to a broad swath of parishioners and, hence, may trade primarily in relatively natural theology. Preachers, teachers and evangelists quickly learn that keeping things simple is key to successful oral communication. Traditionally, members of the clergy, as official representatives of particular theological orthodoxies, have the ballast of their heritage keeping them from floating too far from ancient teachings – teachings likely to have been relatively natural or they would not have survived and spread well (unless they developed special mechanisms to aid their preservation, as discussed below). As McCauley writes: 'Theology, like Lot's wife [Gen. 19:26], cannot avoid the persistent temptation to look back – in the case of theology to look back to popular religious forms" (forthcoming). McCauley contrasts this theological 'looking back' with the drive in science to produce increasingly counterintuitive and counter-commonsensical explanations. Theologians may feel some need to demonstrate that their teachings are consonant with The Prophet or with St Paul's Epistles, but scientists feel no such pressure to be Newtonian or Mendelian.[5]

Eduardo Cruz (2010), however, notes that this 'looking back' can be overstated in the contemporary practice of theology. Increasingly theologians of various stripes draw upon fairly counterintuitive, unnatural philosophical and scientific timber to do their craft. In discussing biblical theology he notes: 'Despite the hermeneutical side of this discipline, most biblical scholars pride themselves in reaching their conclusions in an independent (and even opposite to) way from the faithful' (2010: 8).[6] Cruz notes that contemporary theologians often employ the specialized, academic and unnatural resources of linguistics, archaeology and history. At points these disciplinary products are undergirded by use of geology, palaeontology, astronomy and psychology. The contemporary theologian, then, may participate in

[5] Being a faithfully Darwinian may be an exception in this regard, but note that Darwin's theory included at least two radically unnatural, counterintuitive ideas at its core: apparent design does not require a designer, and one natural kind can have offspring of a different natural kind.

[6] One may wonder if even theologians wishing to remain orthodox in a particular tradition would, as academics seeking to make a contribution to their field, suffer professional pressure to innovate and, hence, deviate from this more cognitively natural orthodoxy.

sophisticated, reflective, scholarly pursuits that deviate considerably from natural cognition and are much more comparable to the unnaturalness of modern science.

The relative unnaturalness of theology has not received great attention by cognitive scientists of religion (who typically focus on folk religious beliefs and practices). Work on *Theological Correctness* (Barrett 1999; see also Barrett 1998; Barrett and Keil 1996) and *Theological Incorrectness* (Slone 2004) are notable exceptions.

We might hear Christians, Muslims or Jews talk about the utter transcendence of the Divine, but in the next moment confess to thinking of God as having beliefs, desires and attention much like a human. Similarly, while reflectively affirming that karma is impersonal, in 'real-time', more reflexive circumstances it may be (mis)represented as some*one* punishing or rewarding, or instead as something akin to dumb luck (Slone 2004). The gap between the stated, reflective beliefs and the on-the-hoof, automatic representation has been termed Theological Correctness or the TC effect: analogous to political correctness, people know the right thing to say theologically even if their intuitions aren't consistently in line with it. Through a series of experiments with religious believers and non-believers in the United States and India, Barrett and colleagues demonstrated that adults' god concepts can function in markedly divergent ways depending on the conceptual demands of the context (Barrett 1998, 1999; Barrett and VanOrman 1996; Barrett and Keil 1996). These studies capitalized on earlier psychological findings that in any narrative gaps are automatically filled by the audience's relevant expectations, often resulting in 'intrusion errors': something is remembered as having been in the narrative that was not actually there (Bransford and McCarrell 1974). In these Theological Correctness studies, participants read narratives that included God (or Vishnu, Krishna or Brahma for Indian participants) but also included many inferential gaps. Comprehension questions were scored for intrusion errors reflective of anthropomorphic divine attributes that were denied by participants when asked directly by questionnaire. For instance, participants that regarded God as capable of attending any number of things at the same time erroneously remembered stories saying that God was interrupted, distracted or completed one task before turning to another task. Overall, participants in these studies tended to use a fairly abstract, non-anthropomorphic conception of God when answering explicit belief questions but used a more crudely anthropomorphic conception when comprehending stories about the god. It appears that some divine attributes are too counterintuitive or unnatural to easily generate inferences in on-line tasks.

A corollary of Theological Correctness is *Theological Incorrectness*: the tendency for people to systematically misunderstand or simplify theological ideas that they have been taught because they deviate too far from natural, intuitive cognition. Jason Slone illustrates Theological Correctness in action in a number of historical case studies from Chinese Buddhism to Calvinism and the Great Awakening (Slone 2004). For instance, in discussing how Arminian ideas rapidly displaced Calvinism during the Great Awakening (sometimes even at the hands of Calvinist preachers such as Jonathan Edwards), Slone observes:

Minimally counterintuitive ideas are easy to learn, and more important, they are easier to recall than maximally counterintuitive ideas, which are cognitively burdensome. In the case in question, Calvinism proves to be less likely to survive over the long run because it is a burdensome idea that precludes the role of human agency. Arminianism, in contrast, maintains the same inferential potential about superhuman agency as Calvinism – Arminianists also believe that God has divine sovereignty – but supplements it with human agency. (2004: 97)

Slone's broader point is that theological ideas which deviate too greatly from maturationally natural cognitive deliverances will suffer in terms of uptake by the masses, resulting in either extinction or distortion.

The experimental evidence on Theological Correctness and Slone's historical case studies concerning Theological Incorrectness provide further evidence that theology is relatively unnatural from a cognitive perspective. If theology as a whole were more cognitively natural there would be no reason for distinctions between what we profess in the reflective mode and how we think on-the-fly, or between what theologians teach and what is received by the folk.

1. Implications of the Naturalness of Religion and Unnaturalness of Theology
These considerations of the cognitive naturalness of religion on the one hand and the unnaturalness of theology on the other spawn a number of implications. To conclude this chapter I mention five such implications. My intention in this concluding section is only to gesture toward the sorts of implications and lines of further inquiry that a cognitive perspective on the naturalness of religion and unnaturalness of theology might suggest.

a. Religion is Resilient
The naturalness of religion almost guarantees its persistence over time. Until our cognitive architecture changes dramatically or until our general environmental conditions are radically altered, human beings will tend to be religious in one way or another. It may be that unusual cultural conditions will reduce or modify traditional religious practices (as can be seen in some parts of Europe, for instance), but various relatively natural forms of religion are likely to leak out even in systematically anti-religious cultural contexts (as the history of religion in the Soviet Union can attest). To make the point from the other side, strict and consistent naturalistic materialism that denies any and all counterintuitive/supernatural agency will always have difficulty supplanting religious thought and action, a topic I discuss more fully elsewhere (Barrett 2004, 2010).

b. Theology Requires Special Conditions to Thrive
Similar to what is required for the success of modern academic disciplines, theology requires special cultural scaffolding – special conditions and resources – in order to spread and thrive. The use of literacy and other external mnemonics, access to the insights from other disciplines and other special resources have already been mentioned above. Behind the use of these resources is a presumption

that those engaging in theology have the time and material resources to do so. Doing theology requires the luxury of careful, measured reflection. Further, not unlike other intellectual pursuits, theology thrives in collegial communities that intellectually challenge and support each other and distribute the burden of maintaining large, complex bodies of knowledge. Similarly, forums for systematic teaching and dissemination are required for transmission of these complex, cognitively unnatural bodies of knowledge. Consequently, institutions of various sorts are required for theology to develop and spread. Eliminate theological institutions – faculties, schools, orders – and the practice of theology would be seriously hamstrung.[7] Religion, in contrast, will persist without formal institutions as can be seen in small-scale traditional societies.

c. Taught and Received Theology Will Be in Tension

As the discussion of Theological Correctness/Incorrectness illustrates, as long as theology seeks to develop perspectives that deviate from the natural conceptual anchor-points where religion dwells, what gets taught by theologians and what gets received and used by the folk will always be at odds. Pascal Boyer has referred to this condition as 'the tragedy of the theologian': 'It is very difficult for literate groups [e.g. theological experts] to counter people's tendency to make their religious concepts more *local* and more *practical*. People are never quite as 'theologically correct" as the guild would like them to be' (2001: 283).

The ethnographic work of Emma Cohen (2007) illustrates this tension nicely. Studying Afro-Brazilian spiritualists in northern Brazil, Cohen observed how the house leader (*pai-de-santo*) resolved a theological problem with the group's central spiritual exercise: spirit possession. In these trance possessions in which the ancestor or other spirit temporarily inhabits the host's body, anomalies sometimes arise. For instance, a particular spirit may have a different character in one host as opposed to another host, being a polite, well-spoken, teetotaller in one case, but a rowdy, foul-mouthed, drunk in another. Or a spirit has a conversation with an individual while in one host, but seems to have forgotten it shortly afterward when inhabiting a different host that was not previously present. How can these dynamics be accounted for? The house leader's solution was to reason that the possession episode is a blending of spirits in a single body for its duration. Each possession trance produces a unique, fused individual in that moment. Hence, the character of the invading spirit takes on some features of the host and cannot be expected to remember everything that took place when fused with a different host during a later possession episode. This fusion model was the authoritative theological position on spirit possession that Cohen observed being taught on multiple occasions. Nevertheless, all of her lay informants reported a different conception of what happens during spirit possession. Rather than a fusion of the host and the ancestor (or other spirit), the possessing spirit fully displaces the agency of the host. The folk were taught one thing and came away with something

---

[7] McCauley (forthcoming) makes a similar point about modern science's dependence upon institutions.

else. Why? Cohen interprets the displacement model as more cognitively natural than the fusion model (Cohen 2007; Cohen and Barrett 2008).

As this case illustrates, just because it is taught repeatedly from up front does not mean it will penetrate if a more natural conception is available. The Christian doctrine of Grace may be another case in point. The idea that we get what we deserve/tit-for-tat may be more natural than unmerited favour and so Christian preachers find they spend an enormous amount of time on Grace.[8]

d. Some Theologies Are More Natural Than Others

As Slone's observations about Arminianism versus Calvinism suggest, some theological claims and their surrounding systems of thought will be relatively more natural than others. It follows that those that are more unnatural will require more effort and resources to survive and spread. Conversely, part of why some religions seem to out-compete others may be their relative naturalness. I have suggested elsewhere that children's bias to attributions of super knowledge to all agents (until they learn otherwise) and related biases may advantage religions with super-god theologies, such as we find in the Abrahamic traditions, above religions with less-super gods (Barrett 2004). Similarly, given teleofunctional reasoning biases, we might expect gods that suitably fill the 'who dunnit?' question regarding purpose in the natural world to out-compete gods that inadequately fit the profile. Once introduced, more natural theologies would be likely to out-compete less natural theologies, all else being equal. For less natural theologies to compete, they would need additional cultural scaffolding.[9]

e. Some 'Revelations' Have to Wait

If one is doing theology within a tradition that includes periodic divine revelation through prophets, visions, incarnations and the like, a theological question that may arise is: why is it that the god(s) are incremental in their revelation? Why not give it all at one time? Similarly, someone concerned with the orthodoxy of a given tradition might have to answer why it is that theology shows signs of development within a given tradition. I do not pretend to offer a comprehensive and generalizable answer to these hoary questions, but perhaps a cognitive perspective can play in to such discussions in the following way: if humans have increasing 'cultural scaffolding' including cognitive prosthetics such as books at their disposal as time goes on, and if more complex and unnatural theologies require additional cultural scaffolding to be successfully adopted and spread, then some aspects or versions of a given theology would have to wait for the requisite cultural scaffolding to be available.

---

[8] I thank Nicholas Gibson for this suggestion.

[9] McCauley and Lawson (2002) similarly suggest that some combinations of religious rituals in a given system are more 'balanced' or optimal than others because of their cognitive and motivational dynamics. Unbalanced systems will fail or evolve to become more balanced.

III. Conclusion

Religion, a shared body of ideas and practices related to the presumed existence of counterintuitive intentional agents, is largely natural in the sense of being strongly undergirded and encouraged by the extra-cultural cognitive capacities that humans have. These conceptual systems bias people to acquire religious ideas and practices, making religion relatively independent of explicit tuition, culturally specific artefacts, or other forms of cultural scaffolding to aid its acquisition and spread. I have identified several content-rich cognitive systems that have been implicated as contributing to the naturalness of religion. Theology, the scholarly, reflective study of religious ideas and practices and the resulting body of thought, bears few marks of this cognitive naturalness. Consequently, theology requires special cultural factors – not available to all humans – in order to be developed and transmitted. Theologians will always be faced with challenges in transmitting their discoveries successfully because of this relative unnaturalness.

Acknowledgement

The author thanks Michael Burdett for comments on a draft of this manuscript.

References

Atran, S. (2002), *In Gods We Trust: The Evolutionary Landscape of Religion*. Oxford: Oxford University Press.

Barrett, J. L. (1998), 'Cognitive constraints on Hindu concepts of the divine'. *Journal for the Scientific Study of Religion, 37*, 608–19.

—(1999), 'Theological Correctness: Cognitive constraint and the study of religion'. *Method and Theory in the Study of Religion, 11*, 325–39.

—(2004), *Why Would Anyone Believe in God?* Walnut Creek, CA: AltaMira Press.

—(2010), 'The relative unnaturalness of atheism: on why Geertz and Markússon are both right and wrong'. *Religion, 40*, 169–72.

Barrett, J. L. and F. C. Keil (1996), 'Anthropomorphism and God concepts: conceptualizing a non-natural entity', *Cognitive Psychology, 31*, 219–47.

Barrett, J. L., R. M. Newman and R. A. Richert (2003), 'When seeing does not lead to believing: children's understanding of the importance of background knowledge for interpreting visual displays'. *Journal of Cognition & Culture, 3* (1), 91–108.

Barrett, J. L. and R. A. Richert (2003), 'Anthropomorphism or preparedness? Exploring children's God concepts'. *Review of Religious Research, 44*, 300–12.

Barrett, J. L., R. A. Richert and A. Driesenga (2001), 'God's beliefs versus mom's: the development of natural and non-natural agent concepts'. *Child Development, 72* (1), 50–65.

Barrett, J. L. and B. VanOrman (1996), 'The effects of image use in worship on God concepts'. *Journal of Psychology and Christianity, 15* (1), 38–45.

Bering, J. M. (2006), 'The folk psychology of souls'. *Behavioral and Brain Sciences, 29*, 453–62.

Bering, J. M. and D. F. Bjorkland (2004), 'The natural emergence of reasoning about the afterlife as a developmental regularity'. *Developmental Psychology, 40*, 217–33.

Bering, J. M., C. Hernández-Blasi and D. F. Bjorkland (2005), 'The development of "afterlife" beliefs in secularly and religiously schooled children'. *British Journal of Developmental Psychology, 23*, 587–607.

Bloom, P. (2004), *Descartes' Baby: How Child Development Explains What Makes Us Human.* London: William Heinemann.

—(2007), 'Religion is natural'. *Developmental Science, 10*, 147–51.

Bloom, P. (2009), Religious belief as an evolutionary accident. In M. J. Murray and J. Schloss (eds), *The Believing Primate: Scientific, Philosophical, and Theological Reflections on the Origin of Religion.* New York, NY: Oxford University Press, pp. 118–27.

Boyer, P. (2001), *Religion Explained: The Evolutionary Origins of Religious Thought.* New York, NY: Basic Books.

—(2003), 'Religious thought and behavior as by-products of brain function'. *Trends in Cognitive Sciences, 7*, 119–24.

—(1994), *The Naturalness of Religious Ideas: A Cognitive Theory of Religion.* Berkeley, CA: University of California Press.

Boyer, P. and P. Lienard (2006), 'Why ritualized behavior? Precaution systems and action-parsing in developmental, pathological, and cultural rituals'. *Brain & Behavioral Sciences, 29* (6), 595–613.

Boyer, P. and C. Ramble (2001), 'Cognitive templates for religious concepts: cross-cultural evidence for recall of counter-intuitive representations'. *Cognitive Science, 25*, 535–64.

Bransford, J. D. and N. S. McCarrell (1974), 'A sketch of a cognitive approach to comprehension: some thoughts about understanding what it means to comprehend'. In W. B. Weimer and D. S. Palermo (eds), *Cognition and the Symbolic Processes.* Hillsdale, NJ: Lawrence Erlbaum, pp. 189–27.

Bulbulia, J. (2008), Meme infection or religious niche construction? an adaptationist alternative to the cultural maladaptationist hypothesis. *Method and Theory in the Study of Religion, 20*, 67–107.

Cohen, E. (2007), *The Mind Possessed: The Cognition of Spirit Possession in an Afro-Brazilian Religious Tradition.* New York, NY: Oxford University Press.

Cohen, E. and J. L. Barrett (2008), 'Conceptualising possession trance: ethnographic and experimental evidence'. *Ethos, 36*, 2, 246–67.

Cruz, E. R. (2010), 'Lot's wife temptation, or the unnaturalness of theology'. Unpublished manuscript presented at the 13th *European Conference on Science and Theology*, Edinburgh.

Csibra, G. (2008), Goal attribution to inanimate agents by 6.5-month-old infants'. *Cognition, 107*, 705–17.

DiYanni, C. and D. Kelemen (2005), 'Time to get a new mountain? The role of function in children's conceptions of natural kinds'. *Cognition, 97*, 327–35.

Evans, E. M. (2000), 'The emergence of belief about the origins of species in school-aged children'. *Merrill Palmer Quarterly, 46*, 221–54.

—(2001), 'Cognitive and contextual factors in the emergence of diverse belief systems: creation versus evolution'. *Cognitive Psychology, 42*, 217–66.

Gergely, G. and G. Csibra (2003), 'Teleological reasoning in infancy: the naive theory of rational action'. *Trends in Cognitive Sciences, 7* (7), 287–92.

Guthrie, S. E. (1993), *Faces in the Clouds: A New Theory of Religion*. New York, NY: Oxford University Press.

Heider, F. and M. Simmel (1994), 'An experimental study of apparent behavior'. *American Journal of Psychology, 57*, 243–49.

Hutchins, E. (1995), *Cognition in the Wild*. Cambridge, MA: MIT Press.

Kelemen, D. (1990), 'Why are rocks pointy? Children's preference for teleological explanations of the natural world'. *Developmental Psychology, 35*, 1440–53.

—(2004), 'Are children "intuitive theists"? Reasoning about purpose and design in nature'. *Psychological Science, 15*, 295–301.

Kelemen, D. and C. DiYanni (2005), 'Intuitions about origins: purpose and intelligent design in children's reasoning about nature'. *Journal of Cognition & Development, 6*, 3–31.

Kelemen, D. and E. Rosset (2009), 'The human function compunction: teleological explanation in adults'. *Cognition, 111*, 138–43.

Knight, N. (2008), 'Yukatek Maya children's attributions of beliefs to natural and non-natural entitites'. *Journal of Cognition & Culture, 8* (3–4), 235–43.

Knight, N., P. Sousa, J. L. Barrett and S. Atran (2004), 'Children's attributions of beliefs to humans and God: cross-cultural evidence'. *Cognitive Science, 28*, 117–26.

Lawson, E. T. and R. N. McCauley (1990), *Rethinking Religion: Connecting Cognition and Culture*. Cambridge: Cambridge University Press.

Leslie, A. M. (1994), 'ToMM, ToBy, and agency: core architecture and domain specificity'. In L. A. Hirschfeld and S. A. Gelman (eds), *Mapping the Mind: Domain Specificity in Cognition and Culture*. Cambridge: Cambridge University Press, pp. 119–48.

Lienard, P. and P. Boyer (2006), 'Whence collective ritual? A cultural selection model of ritualized behavior'. *American Anthropologist, 108*, 814–27.

Malley, B. (2004), *How the Bible Works: An Anthropological Study of Evangelical Biblicism*. Walnut Creek, CA: AltaMira Press.

McCauley, R. N. (forthcoming), *The Naturalness of Religion and the Unnaturalness of Science*. Available at http://www.google.de/search?sourceid=chrome&ie=UTF-8&q=mccauley+the+naturalness+of+religion+and+the+unnaturalness

McCauley, R. N. and E. T. Lawson (2002), *Bringing Ritual to Mind: Psychological Foundations of Cultural Forms*. Cambridge: Cambridge University Press.

Meltzoff, A. N. and M. K. Moore (1989), 'Imitation in newborn infants: exploring the range of gestures imitated and the underlying mechanisms'. *Developmental Psychology, 25*, 954–62.

Mithen, S. (1996), *The Prehistory of the Mind: A Search for the Origins of Art, Religion and Science*. London: Thames and Hudson.

Premack, D. (1990), 'The infant's theory of self-propelled objects'. *Cognition, 36,* 1–36.

Scholl, B. and P. D. Tremoulet (2000), 'Perceptual causality and animacy'. *Trends in Cognitive Sciences, 4,* 299–308.

Slone, D. J. (2004), *Theological Incorrectness: Why Rreligious People Believe What They Shouldn't.* New York, NY: Oxford University Press.

Sosis, R. (2006), 'Religious behaviors, badges, and bans: signaling theory and the evolution of religion'. In P. McNamara (ed.), *Where God and Man Meet. How the Brain and Evolutionary Sciences are Revolutionizing Our Understanding of Religion and Spirituality.* Westport, CT: Praeger, pp. 61–86.

Spelke, E. S. and K. D. Kinzler (2007), 'Core knowledge', *Developmental Science, 11,* 89–96.

Tremlin, T. (2006), *Minds and Gods: The cognitive Foundations of Religion* (New York, NY: Oxford University Press.

Wellman, H., D. Cross and J. Watson (2001), 'Meta-analysis of theory of mind development: the truth about false-belief'. *Child Development, 72,* 655–84.

2 Are Religious Experiences Natural? Biological Capacities for Religion

Marjorie Hall Davis and Karl E. Peters

This chapter explores natural, biologically based capacities for two major features of religion. The first is the inner experience of being in a calm, centred state of consciousness that has been called religious or spiritual, and the second is the experience of connectedness, often expressed in love and compassion. We attempt to show how these two features are related.

The words 'natural' and 'religion' have many meanings (e.g. Cavanaugh 2003: 765). For example, 'natural' can refer to the world of nature beyond humans, or it can include the totality of everything in space and time, including humans, human technology and culture. It is sometimes contrasted with that which is beyond space and time, or 'supernatural'. It is also used to mean that which is biologically natural for humans. An example of this is 'what comes naturally', as in Bernard Malamud's 2(003) baseball novel *The Natural*. Another example is 'natural law' that underlies morality in Roman Catholic thought. We will be using the term 'natural' in the limited sense of human biological capacities, especially brain capacities that have evolved in the human species. This includes brain capacities for the development of culture in general. However, these capacities are further developed in human inter-action and influenced by particular, culturally transmitted beliefs and practices, including religious beliefs and practices.

'Religion' also has many meanings. Religion can signify the system or structure of a complex cultural tradition of beliefs, moral codes, ritual practices and religious experiences. If one looks at religion functionally, one can draw on the common etymological meaning, used by Augustine and rooted in *religare*, of being bound together or connected. While recognizing the importance of beliefs, moral codes and rituals, we will be focusing on how religion functions in relation to the experience of connectedness. A feeling of connectedness is present in the mystical experience of union with the ground of all that is the 'oceanic experience'. We suggest that the feeling of connectedness is also an aspect of an everyday version of this experience – that of being in a calm centred state, with full awareness in the present moment of all that is going on within and without.

To understand this experience more fully we turn to the approach of marriage and family therapist Richard C. Schwartz and his model of the human psyche, the Internal Family Systems (IFS) model (Schwartz 1995, 2001). Effective in the practice of psychotherapy, it is a perspective that can also enhance one's everyday living. This therapeutic process has qualities that have been experienced and described as 'spiritual'.

Schwartz's model suggests that we have aspects of our personality which are like sub-personalities. These aspects or 'parts' operate with relative autonomy and interact internally in ways that are similar to the ways that people interact externally in relationships within families and communities (Breunlin et al. 1997: 64). All of these parts of our inner ecology are valuable. In their various roles they serve a protective function, and they can work together harmoniously for our benefit. However, in times of severe stress and trauma they can be forced out of their valuable roles into extreme roles, take over our internal system, and get us to act in ways that are harmful to ourselves and others.

At the core or centre of our being is a different state which Schwartz calls the Self (with a capital 'S'). This concept of the Self differs from other uses of 'self' such as the total person or the 'ego'. It resembles some aspects of the 'ideal executive self' described by Patrick McNamara (2009: 257–8). For Schwartz, 'being in Self' is an experience which can be universally recognized. We feel centred, calm and peaceful. We have confidence, clarity, curiosity, creativity and courage. We feel compassion and seek to understand, not to judge. We sense connection with that which is both within and beyond us. We seek to be present, and to be in the present. In the words of Schwartz:

> Once you've attuned with your client, the session begins to flow, and there's an almost effortless quality to the work, as if something magical were unfolding almost by itself. I don't even think about what I'm going to say – the right words just come out, as if something were speaking through me. Afterward, I'm full of energy, as if I've been meditating for an hour rather than doing hard, demanding, clinical work. In a sense, of course, I've been in a state of meditation – a state of deep mindfulness, full-bodied attention, centered awareness, and inner calm. And even after all these years, I still have the sense of being witness to something awe inspiring, as if the client and I both were connected to something beyond us, much bigger than we are. (Schwartz 2004: 43)

In the therapeutic relationship the therapist's presence in Self facilitates healing, irrespective of the particular therapeutic theory or process. This spiritual aspect of persons connects us with compassion and curiosity to others and to all parts of ourselves.

While called the Self in secular language, in religious traditions this spiritual experience has been named in many ways, including *sacred centre, soul, spirit, God within, mind of Christ, Buddha nature, atman* (Hindus), the *Beloved* (Sufis), and the *inner light* (Quakers). Many people have the experience of 'being in Self' in prayer or meditation, or when quiet and focused on breathing. When we are active, the experience may feel like a sense of 'flow'. It may occur in the presence of another person, an aesthetically beautiful scene, or a particular quality of music. The capability for this experience seems to be universal across cultures.

Although present in all of us, the Self can be eclipsed by parts in extreme roles, preventing us from having this spiritual experience more often.

Many other theoretical constructions of the human psyche or internal system have used the concept of multiplicity. In the psychological literature Sigmund Freud used the terms *id, ego,* and *superego.* Carl Jung used the terms *anima, animus, persona, shadow* and *archetypes.* Psychosynthesis uses *sub-personalities;* Object Relations theory uses *internal objects;* and other theories have used various terms to describe different kinds of inner states. The Internal Family Systems model uses the terms *exiles, managers,* and *firefighters* (see Figure 2.1).

Exiles are parts that hold emotions we don't like to feel, such as fear, grief, worthlessness, powerlessness, loneliness, shame and hopelessness. Their protective role is to isolate these feelings from consciousness.

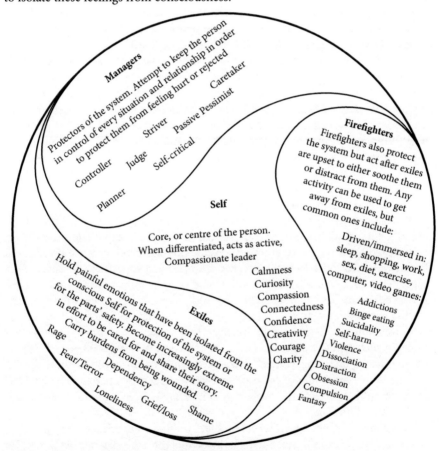

Figure 2.1 The internal system (Mullen 2001–2)
Adapted from Richard C. Schwartz, *Internal Family Systems Theory* (1995)
Graphic by Janet R. Mullen

Manager parts function to keep order and control over events and relation-ships in an attempt to avoid provoking hurt and rejection. Striving for perfection, pleasing, caretaking, judging, criticizing self and others, intellectualizing, rational-izing and denying are characteristic of *managers*.

But *Exiles*, like any who are oppressed, imprisoned or exiled, want to have a voice, to have their suppressed feelings witnessed and understood, and to be cared for. When *exiles* are activated by painful memories or present events, the feelings they are carrying can come pouring out and threaten to overwhelm the inner system.

Firefighter parts then spring into action to extinguish the inner flames of painful feelings, override them, or disconnect the person from them. They may use alcohol and drugs, food binges, sex binges or shopping binges. Sometimes it is by too much exercising, too much sleeping or by suicidal thinking and violence to self, others and relationships. Acting suddenly and impulsively, *firefighters* can be very destructive, activating *managers* to attempt to gain control.

The arrows in Figure 2.2 show interaction patterns among the parts. When parts are in extreme roles, the interaction resembles a tug-of-war, as parts strive to protect the internal system. The Self is hidden or eclipsed.

The IFS therapeutic process is a collaboration between therapist and client. As the process is facilitated by the therapist's being 'in Self', the client is able to separate from parts and access the presence, healing power and compassionate energy of his/her own centred Self. The Self is able to be present to all the life experiences, memories, feelings and beliefs that the parts have experienced and help them to heal. When the painful feelings carried by the *exiles* are healed and transformed, other parts are released from their extreme roles, and inner harmony is restored under Self-leadership.

Changes in the internal system are in turn reflected externally in the person's behaviour and relationships (Schwartz 2008).

What might be the biological bases for the inner states that are metaphorically described in Schwartz's model? We hypothesize that such experiences are natural because biologically evolved brain systems provide capacities for these experiences. Biological evolution selects for survival qualities and capacities. However, these capacities have developmental potential which can be influenced, diminished and enhanced by life experience, states of health, changes in the environment, and culturally evolved practices including spiritual and religious practices and rituals.

Neuroscience is beginning to uncover the multitude of brain systems that underlie such types of experiences. There are as yet no available research studies of persons experiencing various states specifically in the IFS psychotherapeutic process. However, evidence from other brain research points to particular areas of the brain that seem to be involved when we subjectively experience *Self, exiles, managers* and *firefighters*.

For example, it has been observed that when we experience fear (a feeling characteristic of *exiles*), brain circuits involving the amygdala are working. The amygdala is part of the limbic system, which is sometimes referred to as the 'emotional brain' (Newberg 2008; for more detail see Carter 2010: 93–9). Manager parts in the IFS model may be related to circuits in the frontal lobes, especially

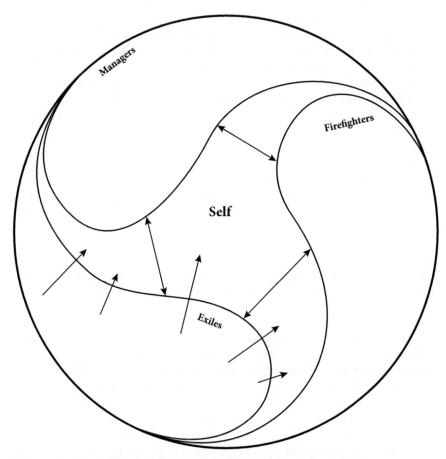

Figure 2.2 Internal system interactions (adapted from Figure 2.1)

the ventro medial (lower middle) prefrontal cortex. This area of the brain is regarded as the locus of executive functions such as imagining the consequences of actions and planning for the future. It also is an area involved in controlling emotions. Lack of development of the prefrontal cortex, that can be partly genetic, as well as damage to this area of the brain because of accidents or strokes, are correlated with people having a difficult time controlling emotions such as anger (Carter 2010: 89–93). Andrew Newberg states that there is a 'push–pull' between the frontal lobe and limbic system (more specifically between the lower central frontal lobes and the amygdala). This push–pull balancing 'can get out of whack sometimes. If we get overly emotional, our frontal lobes shut down, and if we become over-logical, our emotional areas shut down' (Newberg 2008). This is consistent with the subjective experience of conflict among parts as described by Schwartz (Figure 2.2).

A 2004 study by Darin Dougherty and colleagues used PET (Positron Emission Tomography) scans to compare, among other things, the regional blood flow in brains of healthy individuals and in depressed and angry individuals. When healthy individuals re-imagined anger-provoking autobiographical incidents, brain images showed that their lower-central prefrontal cortex was active, signifying frontal lobe control of the anger. However, when depressed and angry individuals re-imagined anger-provoking incidents, images showed that the frontal lobe was not in control (Dougherty et al. 2004). This also is consistent with the subjective experience of polarized interaction among parts.

It can be postulated that some fears, self-control and anger (and their supporting neurological systems) have biologically evolved as part of overall physiological strategies for self-defence and survival. Other feelings and behaviours (and their biological substrates) also have evolved – especially those that are pro-social – which are related to religious connectedness. These feelings and behaviours are especially important because the long period of dependency in human development requires a nurturing environment that is first established in mother–infant bonding. The neurotransmitters and hormones oxytocin and vasopressin, with receptors in the nucleus accumbens and the ventral pallidum of the brain, have been shown to facilitate bonding between mates and with offspring (Lim et al. 2004; Fisher 2006). Further, oxytocin evokes feelings of contentment, calmness and security around a mate (Meyer 2007). Other studies have shown a correlation of oxytocin with trust and generosity (Zak 2008).

Mirror neurons are another biologically evolved feature of the brain supporting pro-social behaviour. They were discovered in 1995 in the premotor area of monkeys in the lab of Giacomo Rizzolatti and Corrado Sinigaglia (2008). In humans they seem to extend into areas of the frontal lobes and are involved with intentions and emotions. Mirror neurons are activated both when a person does a particular act, as well as when that act is observed in others. 'A similar effect occurs with neurons that code for emotions and thoughts – some of the brain cells that would normally be activated when a person feels a particular emotion, or thinks a particular thought, also become active when emotion or thought is discerned in others.' Knowing, 'intuitively, what another person is feeling or thinking is thought to be the basis for mimicry and empathy' (Carter 2010: 141).

Oxytocin and mirror neurons illustrate that there are biological bases for affiliative feelings and behaviours that are at the core of what makes us human and enable us to survive as social beings. However, according to evolutionary science, this biologically based sociality is limited to those with whom we feel most connected, family and kin (kin altruism), and those with whom we engage in direct give-and-take relationships (reciprocal altruism). As human societies become larger and more complex, a significant problem is how to extend feelings and behaviours of connectedness (such as love and compassion) from those with whom we are most biologically and socially connected to all human beings, especially to strangers or those who are different from us. Newberg states that 'when you're looking at somebody from the opposite party, or thinking about them, it tends to activate the amygdala, the limbic areas, again, that tend to trigger more of an emotional response, whereas when you're looking at people who are concordant with your views and beliefs, that tends to activate some of the areas of the frontal lobe and also that the anterior cingulate that helps you mediate your conflict-resolution powers' (Newberg 2008).

To move beyond our biological limits and enhance pro-social capacities, the influence of culture is important. Learning through family, friendships, education, neighbourhoods, civic organizations and religious communities helps to develop biological potentials. What we learn through repetition in a nurturing social environment, starting with early childhood, facilitates the physical development of the neuron connections in our brains. This applies to learning language, daily habits and core social, political, and religious beliefs and practices. Newberg states '[t]hat the practices and rituals that exist within both religious and non-religious groups become a strong and powerful way to write these [core] ideas into our brain. … When you go to a church or a synagogue or a mosque, and they repeat the same stories, and you celebrate the same holidays that reinforce that, you do the prayers, and you say these things over and over again, those are the neural connections that get stimulated and strengthened. That is a strong part of why religion and spirituality make use of various practices valuable for writing those beliefs strongly into who you are" (Newberg 2008).

There is a great variety of religious beliefs and practices that have culturally evolved and continue to be influenced by language, geography, science and world views. Although we have biological capacities for religious connectedness, and although the process itself of cultural evolution is natural for humans, the particular forms and content (theology, practices and rituals) of religions are culturally evolved. No one form or system of religion is natural – that is, determined by our biology.

Religions and their core beliefs can either limit, contract or expand feelings of connectedness. Examples of expansion include: the belief system of Confucians in ancient China that extends filial piety from immediate family relationships to the wider community, the empire and even to ultimate reality that is called 'Heaven and Earth'; the Muslim belief that all are brothers and sisters because all are children of Allah; the teachings of Jesus on universal and undiscriminating love that extend the idea of 'neighbour' to all regardless of their cultural or social group; and the Buddhist concept of compassion for all living beings. A contemporary scientifically grounded understanding that also extends connectedness to all is 'the evolutionary epic', which claims that we are all kin in the sense that we share the energy from the big bang, the atoms created in the explosions of earlier massive stars and the molecules of all life on earth.

Is the conceptual extension of connectedness, established through learning, also supported by religious experience? Are there brain systems that enable universal love and compassion? How might the brain be functioning when we are what Schwartz calls 'in Self'?

In recent years a number of imaging studies have been done on brain activity associated with meditation and prayer, by people such as Mario Beauregard at McGill University (Beauregard and O'Leary 2007; Beauregard and Paquette 2006), Richard Davidson at the University of Wisconsin (Davidson and Harrington 2001;

Lutz et al. 2008), and Andrew Newberg at the University of Pennsylvania (Newberg et al. 2001; Newberg and Iversen 2003; Newberg et al. 2003). Some of this work is summarized in Patrick McNamara's discussion of the neurology of religious experience (McNamara 2009: 106–30).

To illustrate the possibility that the practice of meditation helps extend connectedness, love and compassion to all, we draw on some of Newberg's work with Tibetan meditators and Franciscan nuns doing centring prayer. Using SPECT (Single Photon Emission Computed Tomography) scans, Newberg imaged blood flow to regions of the brain in a baseline state before meditation and prayer, and during meditation and prayer (see Newberg undated for images). In both cases there was an increase in activity in the frontal lobes in the area that focuses attention and in the thalamus, which is a relay centre that allows sensory information to come into the brain. At the same time there was a decrease in the activity of the right parietal lobe. Newberg writes:

> The parietal lobe, when active, gives us a sense of self in relation to time, space, and other objects in the world. … Our brain-scan studies of contemplative forms of Buddhist and Christian meditation show that when activity in the parietal areas decreases, a sense of timelessness and spacelessness emerges. This allows the meditator to feel at one with the object of contemplation, with God, the universe, peacefulness, or any other object upon which he or she focuses. (Newberg and Waldman 2010: 51–2)

This feeling of oneness, of unity, and of connectedness is very similar to that of being in Self reported by Schwartz (quoted earlier):

> In a sense, of course, I've been in a state of meditation – a state of deep mindfulness, full-bodied attention, centered awareness, and inner calm. And even after all these years, I still have the sense of being witness to something awe inspiring, as if the client and I both were connected to something beyond us, much bigger than we are. (2004: 43)

Combined with cultural beliefs that hold that all things are connected, such a natural experience of being in Self, resembling those experiences observed in brain imaging, can provide a sense of universal connectedness (*religare*) and help motivate love and compassion toward all.

References

Beauregard, M. and D. O'Leary (2007), *The Spiritual Brain: A Neuroscientist's Case for the Existence of the Soul*. San Francisco, CA: Harper Collins.

Beauregard, M. and V. Paquette (2006), 'Neural correlates of a mystical experience in Carmelite Nuns'. *Neuroscience Letters*, 405, 186–90.

Bruenlin, D. C., R. C. Schwartz and B. Mac Kune-Karrerk (1997), *Metaframeworks: Transcending the Models of Family Therapy*. San Francisco, CA: Jossey-Bass.

Carter, R. (2010), *Mapping the Mind* (Revised and Updated edition). Berkeley, CA: University of California Press.

Cavanaugh, M. (2003), 'Is nature enough: introduction to the symposium: is nature enough? The thirst for transcendence. *Zygon: Journal of Religion and Science, 38* (4), 763–7.

Davidson, R. J. and A. Harrington (2001), *Visions of Compassion: Western Scientists and Tibetan Buddhists Examine Human Nature.* New York, NY: Oxford University Press.

Dougherty, D., S. L. Rauch, T. Deckersbach, C. Marci, R. Loh, L. M. Shin, N. M. Alpert, A. J. Fischman and M. Fava (2004), 'Ventromedial prefrontal cortex and amygdala dysfunction during an anger. induction positron emission tomography study in patients with major depressive disorder with anger attacks'. *Archives of General Psychiatry, 61,* 795–804.

Fisher, H. (2006), 'The drive to love: the neural mechanism for mate selection. 'In R. J. Sternberg and K. Weis (eds), *The New Psychology of Love.* New Haven, CT: Yale, pp. 87–115.

Lim, M. M., A. Z. Murphy and L. J. Young (2004), 'Ventral striatopallidal oxytocin and vasopressin V1a receptors in the monogamous praire vole (microtus ochrogaster)'. *Journal of Comparative Neurology, 468,* 555–70.

Lutz, A., J. Brefczynski-Lewis, T. Johnstone and R. J. Davidson (2008), 'Regulation of the neural circuitry of emotion by compassion meditation: effects of meditative expertise'. *PLoS ONE, 3* (March), 1–10.

Malamud, B. (2009), *The Natural.* New York, NY: Farrar, Straus and Giroux.

McNamara, P. (2009), *The Neuroscience of Religious Experience.* New York, NY: Cambridge University Press.

Meyer, D. (2007), 'Selective serotonin reuptake inhibitors and their effects on relationship satisfaction'. *The Family Journal,* 15 (4), 392–7.

Mullen, J. R. (2001–2), 'IFS Mandala'. *Self to Self, 5* (Fall–Winter), 13.

Newberg, A. (2008), 'How our brains are wired for belief'. *Pew Forum for Religion and Public Life.* Available from: http://pewforum.org/events/?EventID=185.

—(undated), 'The effect of meditation on the brain activity in Tibetan meditators: frontal lobes.' Available at: http://www.andrewnewberg.com/research.asp

Newberg, A., A. Alavi, M. Baime, M. Pourdehnad, J. Santanna and E. d'Aquili (2001), 'The measurement of regional cerebral blood flow during the complex cognitive task of meditation: a preliminary SPECT study'. *Psychiatry Research, 106,* 113–22.

Newberg, A. and J. Iversen, 2003 'The neural basis of the complex mental task of meditation: neurotransmitter and neurochemical considerations'. *Medical Hypotheses, 61,* 282–91.

Newberg, A., M. Pourdehnad, A. Alavi and E. G. d'Aquili (2003), 'Cerebral blood flow during meditative prayer: preliminary findings and methodological issues'. *Perceptual Motor Skills, 97,* 625–30.

Newberg, A. and M. R. Waldman (2010), *How God Changes Your Brain.* New York, NY: Ballantine Books.

Rizzolatti, G. and C. Sinigaglia (2008), *Mirrors in the Brain: How Our Minds Share Actions, Emotions, and Experience* (trans. F. Anderson). New York, NY: Oxford University Press.

Schwartz, R. C. (1995), *Internal Family Systems Therapy*. New York, NY: Guilford Press.

—(2001), *Introduction to the Internal Family Systems Model*. Oak Park, IL: The Center for Self Leadership.

—(2004), 'The larger self'. *Psychotherapy Networker*, May/June, 37–43.

—(1999), 'Releasing the soul: psychotherapy as a spiritual practice'. In F. Walsh (ed.), *Spiritual Resources in Family Therapy*. New York, NY: Guilford, 1999, pp. 223–39.

—(2008), *You are the One You've Been Waiting For: Bringing Courageous Love to Intimate Relationships*. Oak Park, IL: Trailheads Publications.

Zak, P. J. (2008), 'The neurobiology of trust'. *Scientific American*, June, 88–95.

3 'Gene Theology and Folk Biology': Is Religion a Natural Context for the Opposition of Genetics?

Jussi E. Niemelä

Introduction

In this article I will examine the challenge that recent findings in cognitive science present to theological bioethics. During the past few decades cognitive science has unearthed some very profound elements about natural human thought tendencies concerning the biological world. These tendencies are typically called 'folk-biological thought', and it is argued that human beings universally share some spontaneous predispositions concerning the biological world.

This is not to say that all people think alike when it comes to biological issues. On the contrary, scientific education can significantly alter the way in which people perceive the biological world. However, what remains after the best possible education and what all people share is the spontaneous and automatic tendency to react to certain biological things in a certain way. Distaste reactions (pathogen avoidance), certain automatic classifications and essentialistic inferences, incest avoidance (kin recognition and selection) and the like are examples of folk-biological thought. Religious and (to an extent) theological conceptualizations of the biological world can be seen to be based on these same cognitive mechanisms.[1] There exists some research that points towards a direct relation between an adopted system of complex religious concepts and the prevalence and persistence of essentialistic reasoning.[2] It is argued here that the findings of cognitive science establish an important point of possible interaction between theology and science, and that this interaction especially impacts bioethics.

---

[1] This is an argument that I hope to test further. Some supportive evidence can be found in my Doctoral thesis (Niemelä 2007).
[2] See, for example, Lawson and Worsnop (1992), Evans (2001), Poling and Evans (2004), Shtulman and Schultz (2008).

I. Theological Bioethics

There is some difficulty in precisely defining just what 'theological' bioethics is in comparison to philosophical or religious bioethics. There seems to be some consensus that these three types exist, but their boundaries are slightly vague.

Philosophical bioethics is probably the easiest of the three to delineate. In a nutshell, philosophical bioethics is not based on any form of religious doctrine or tradition, but builds instead on secular moral philosophy. Philosophical bioethics can and often does engage in dialogue with religious or theological views, but often arrives at different conclusions.[3] Philosophically oriented bioethical assessment can be called 'contractual' bioethics or 'principalism'.[4]

Christian religious bioethics is any bioethics that emphasizes doctrinal authority, Biblical inerrancy and/or infallibility, and extensively utilizes transcendental assumptions as the basis of argumentation. Hence, by definition, religious bioethics discusses matters of faith in bioethical language, and thus belongs outside of the scope of scientific debate. Theological bioethics stands somewhere in between its philosophical and religious cousins:

> … the presence of discerning and modest theologians …can bring beneficial results in the field of bioethics. These results may not be characterized as theological conclusions, yet in essence, they are imbued with the knowledge and influence of theology. In many cases it is better that we present and analyze theological views as if they were covered up with a philosophical garment, instead of seeing two separate or antagonistic entities, that of philosophical bioethics and that of the religious or theological bioethics … Theology must produce challenges for working out decisions, not of religious, but of theological character. (Griniezakis and Symeonides 2005: 10–11)

Theological bioethics draws from the Christian tradition of ethical and moral codes and reasoning, as well as from the Bible as the root of this tradition, while abandoning the transcendental position of religious bioethics as the basis of argumentation. Courtney S. Campbell, for example, defines theological bioethics by two broad types of practical reasoning. The first of these is a form of moral casuistry, which means that theological bioethics examines the extent to which a given moral dilemma is relevantly continuous with ethical contexts and issues already familiar within the Christian tradition. Since sacred texts such as the Bible do not, for obvious reasons, offer direct advice on matters such as the ethical complexities of modern genetics, a form of casuistical and analogical reasoning is required (Campbell 2010: D-6). In this sense, for example, what has been said before from a theological point of view concerning family and procreation, impacts on discussion on cloning.

The second mode of practical reasoning that Campbell discusses involves the application of the moral and anthropological norms of the faith tradition to generate an ethical assessment of the given moral dilemma (Campbell 2010: D-6).

---

[3] See, for example, Holland (2003: 57, 62–5, 152).
[4] See, for example, Beckwith (2010).

These norms might include such conceptualizations as humans being created in the image of God, humans as 'created co-creators', stewardship ethics concerning ecology and so on. Campbell continues to list seven normative factors that arise out of the idea of *Imago Dei*, which include human freedom, human fallibility, division into spiritual essence and corporeal embodiment, the sacredness of sex and dominion over the natural world (Campbell 2010: D-10–D-11).

The existence of God, ensoulment, the sacredness of the human sexual act and a view of human fallibility as having a transcendental link (in the meaning of sin or sinfulness) appear to be rather generally accepted tenets in theological bioethics. So, pending a precise definition of theological bioethics, it seems safe to say that it retains an inferential backbone that clearly separates it from the foundations of scientific biological assessment. Consequently, inferential structures conforming to psychological essentialism as well as folk-biological thought appear to hover in the background of several of the core assumptions of theological bioethics.

II. Psychological essentialism and folk-biological thought

1. Psychological essentialism[5] in natural thought

Simply put, psychological essentialism refers to any set of non-scientific ideas positing that entities belonging to a given category have an invisible core property or attribute that causes them to belong in that particular category.[6] In everyday inference, the inclusion of a given member in a given category allows for significant inferential economy: since the members of the category share important identity-defining characteristics, a lot can be inferred about their behaviour by the category membership alone. This is a normal function of human cognition: since extensive inferential elaboration is often counter-productive in everyday situations, people act (and indeed must act) as 'cognitive misers'.[7] Psychological essentialism and the quick, spontaneous inferential structures it enables are a natural way for human cognition to structure the immensely complex world surrounding it. It can be said that essentialistic assumptions streamline the cumbersome cognitive process of making sense of the natural world. In the words of Medin and Atran:

> To get along in the world, people need to be able to understand and predict the general properties and behaviors of physical objects and substances (physics), the more specific

---

[5] For further information concerning psychological essentialism see Gelman 1999, 2003). For more information concerning essentialism and 'folk biology' see Gelman and Hirschfeld (1999), Strevens (2000), Sousa et al. (2002), Gelman and Bloom (2007).

[6] Cognitive tendencies to essentialize the natural world should not be mixed with classical varieties of philosophical essentialism. While the two are similar in many respects, there is an all-important difference: the theory of natural cognitive tendencies aims to explain the way people are inclined to understand the world surrounding them, not to explain what the world actually is (Gelman 1999: 283). A good discussion on philosophical essentialism as utilized in bioethical discussions is presented by Häyry (2003).

[7] See Fiske and Taylor (1991), Fiske (2004).

properties of plants and animals (biology), and the particular properties of their fellow human beings (psychology). (Medin and Atran 2004: 960)

Psychological essentialism is one of the most overarching and important inferential tendencies that enable the different aspects of natural human thought. What is important in the context of this article is that human tendency to infer in an essentialistic way greatly affects folk-biological reasoning processes. In the realm of biological inference, essentialism causes the human tendency to think that the hidden, identity-determining aspect of an organism that remains unchanged through growth, morphological transformations and reproduction determines the category to which the phenomenon belongs (Gelman and Hirschfeld 1999: 404). In other words, a dog is a dog because it was given birth by a dog that had the essence of a dog. The dog will continue being a dog no matter how much its outer appearance might change over the years of its existence. According to essentialist inference, a human baby, an adult and an elderly person with a prosthetic leg and one lung removed are all equally human, no matter how different they are morphologically. Essentialistic inference even tends to categorize blastocysts in the same essentialistic category.

2. 'Folk-biological' inference

'Folk biology' is a domain of natural and spontaneous human cognition, which is usually divided into several categories by researchers. The most commonly used groupings for these natural thought tendencies are folk mechanics, 'folk biology', folk psychology and folk sociology.[8] Each of these domains is cross-culturally recurrent and the inferential tendencies driven by these predispositions are fairly automatic. The theory of the domains of spontaneous cognition is well documented and tested, and there seems to be little reason to doubt the theory in general.

The domain that is of interest in this context is that of 'folk biology', which means the natural cognitive tendencies that people have developed in order to be able to reason about nature in a quick and effective manner.[9] There are two central elements in folk-biological thought: folk taxonomy and the spontaneous induction automatically applied to taxa. Humans everywhere classify animals and plants into species-like groups that are hierarchical and allow for quick and complex inferences. Folk-biological taxonomies are universal to a degree, but are also culturally adjusted:

---

[8] For more information on folk mechanics see, for example, McCloskey et al. (1983), Proffitt (1999). For more information on folk psychology see, for example, Greenwood (1991), Davies and Stone (1995), Boonzaier et al. (2005), and for folk sociology see, for example, Ostrom (1984), Yzerbyt, Judd and Corneille (2004), Hirschfeld (1999).

[9] The scope of this chapter does not allow for extensive discussion concerning research on 'folk biology'. Readers interested in obtaining more information should see, for example, Atran (1998, 1999a, 1999b), Medin and Atran (1999, 2004), Atran et al. (2004), Gelman and Raman (2002), Gelman and Bloom (2007).

The universal character of folkbiological taxonomy does not mean that folkbiological categories are culturally irrelevant. On the contrary, insofar as they reflect a cognitively biased, phenomenal appreciation of the surrounding environment, they help to set the constraints on life that make a culture possible … folkbiological taxonomies tend to be among the most stable, widely distributed, and conservative cognitive structures in any culture. (Atran 1999b: 120)

Cognitive anthropologist Scott Atran describes four different ways of folk-biological thinking. First, people in all cultures classify plants and animals into species-like groups that biologists generally recognize as populations of inter-breeding individuals that have adapted to an ecological niche. Second, there is a recurring common sense assumption that each generic species has an underlying causal nature, or essence. This essence is perceived as being uniquely responsible for the typical appearance, behaviour and ecological preferences of the kind. The hidden essence is crucial for the organism, as it maintains the organism's integrity even as it causes the organism to grow, change form and reproduce (Atran 1998: 547–51).[10]

The third element of folk-biological thought is that of folk taxonomy. The classification of generic species into higher- and lower-order groups is not arbitrary, but has a definite and recurring structure. Finally, as his fourth element of folk-biological thinking, Atran discusses the inferential frameworks of folk-biological thought. Folk taxonomies not only organize and summarize biological information, they also provide a powerful inductive framework for making systematic inferences about the likely distribution of organic and ecological properties among organisms. To quote Atran's example, given the presence of a disease in robins one is "automatically" justified in thinking that the disease is more likely to be present among other bird species than among non-bird species (Atran 1998: 548).

Genetics causes all sorts of problems for folk-biological essentialistic inference. First and foremost, if it is an universal tendency of human cognition to classify plants and animals into species-like groups of interbreeding individuals that have adapted to an ecological niche, then what about hybrids and transgenic organisms? These organisms are manufactured to specifically transcend the limits of natural interbreeding and their respective ecological niches. In essentialistic cognition 'natural' plants and animals are postulated as belonging to a certain environment and to behave in a certain manner because they share an inner 'essence' that causes the behaviour. Now, to natural human cognition this manipulation appears as something that seriously violates the basic rules of 'how-things-should-be'. Religiously motivated people would probably say (and often do say) that species are as they are and behave as they do because God made them so. So, to religiously contextualized natural cognition the transgenic manipulation of organisms can easily appear as megalomanic and blasphemous scientists 'playing God'.

---

[10] Also see Richert and Harris (2008) for psychological test account that links essentialistic inference to human ensoulment.

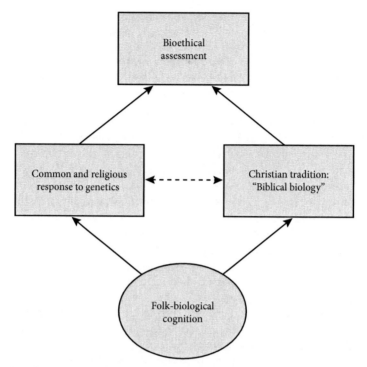

Figure 3.1 Cognition, cultural context and bioethics

Finally, if there is a natural tendency to create a hierarchical taxonomy and to draw specific essentialistic inferences based on an organism's taxonomy and, on its place on the biological hierarchy, genetic manipulation violates natural inferences concerning the biological world. Despite running the risk of oversimplification, it can be said that genetics makes folk-biologists unsure of what to think and how to conceptualize genetically altered organisms. Where there is uncertainty, fear of the unfamiliar is easy to bring forth with a rhetorical manipulation that suitably incorporates structures that correspond to what people naturally think. That is, the unfamiliarity of genetics to natural human thought creates a 'rhetorical niche' where (for example) a Christian rhetoric based on Biblical biology can offer an easy but not very justified response to biological prejudice.

It is claimed here that folk-biological inference has a great impact on how people conceptualize genetics. Furthermore, folk-biological thought has had an effect on Christian tradition and consequently on bioethical assessment. Figure 3.1 shows roughly how folk-biological thought enters bioethical assessment and argumentation.

First, the things the Bible and the Christian tradition say about biological reality mostly follow the rules of essentialistic inference and folk-biological thought (as probably is the case with any unscientific thought concerning biological reality).

This is only natural because biology as a field of systematic scientific enquiry was formed much later than most doctrines were decided upon. Of course, recently there has been a growing amount of dialogue between the Christian tradition and biology (theological bioethics being the most important of these developments), but no amount of dialogue will alter the basic tenets of Christian biological thought. This is not to say that it necessarily should: after all, Christianity is a religion, not a biological science, and the Bible is a sacred text, not a biology textbook.

Second, folk-biological inference has an effect on common (and religiously motivated) response to genetics. When people are not biologists, they tend to go with folk-biological thought.[11] This means that argumentation which is in line with what feels natural to people tends to gain support. Third, the Christian tradition, being based on folk-biological inference (when it comes to biological matters), creates a dialogical context for religious people to strengthen and cultivate their folk-biological conceptualizations. Thus, according to Evans:

> The idea that species are inherently immutable was hypothesized to be a crucial factor in the attractiveness of creationist ideas and the resistance to evolutionary ideas for all children in their early-to-mid elementary school years, and for both children and adults from Christian fundamentalist communities. With creationism the essentialistic beliefs of the early elementary school years are not only maintained, they are deified, at least in these Christian fundamentalist contexts. (2001: 253)

Finally the effects impact bioethical assessment and theorization in two ways. First, religious bioethics arises from religiously motivated folk-biological thought and evaluation. Second, through the effect of 'Biblical biology' and tradition, the folk-biological inferences enter theological bioethics. Furthermore, since at least a part of the issues theological bioethics assesses are motivated by the general concerns the people have, issues based on folk-biological thought gain prevalence.

III. Theological bioethics is partially based on psychological essentialism and folk-biological inference: ensoulment and human dignity

This section presents a brief example of how folk-biological thought tendencies can be seen as affecting bioethical discussion. Unfortunately, given the limits of the chapter it is not possible to give a comprehensive overview of this discussion. The themes of ensoulment and human dignity have caused a lot of discussion, but here the focus will be on few points central to these themes and on their relation to folk inference.[12]

---

[11] As a matter of fact, even specialists often have a hard time resisting their spontaneous inference systems.

[12] Both of the themes will be discussed from the viewpoint of folk inference in separate articles in the future.

One of the most common objections to cloning, be it for stem cell harvesting or for the hypothetical live birth purpose, is that it is an affront to 'human dignity'. When the term 'human dignity' is utilized in an ontological sense[13] it bears a great resemblance to religious concept of 'ensoulment'.[14] Folk-biological inferential tendencies can be seen as an 'essentializing background noise' that informs reasoning that humans are both unique within the biological world, and that this uniqueness is automatically transferred to offspring in the procreative process. Consider the following examples:

> It should be noted however that, should the extension of cloning to the human species be desired, this duplication of body structure does not necessarily imply a perfectly identical person, understood in his ontological and psychological reality. The spiritual soul, which is the essential constituent of every subject belonging to the human species and is created directly by God, cannot be generated by the parents, produced by artificial fertilization or cloned. (Pontifical Academy for Life, Statement on Cloning 1997)

> Created in the image of the one God and equally endowed with rational souls, all men have the same nature and the same origin. Redeemed by the sacrifice of Christ, all are called to participate in the same divine beatitude: all therefore enjoy an equal dignity. (Catholic Catechism, section 1934)

The idea of a 'soul' can be seen as a textbook example of psychological essentialism at work. 'Dignity' in this sense is a doubly hard concept, because in bioethical discussions it is often used in a non-essentialistic manner. 'Dignity' can refer to, for example, a certain set of properties or functions people have agreed on to be dignified. In this case, we have agreed that certain types of action in interpersonal relationships generate dignity for both the subjects and the objects of actions as well as for the actions themselves. Thus, dignity in this case becomes something that is done, generated, in actions that both subjects and objects have agreed upon as (for example) desirable as well as ethical and hence can identify as dignified. This type of relational or 'contractual' dignity is often referred to as 'principalism'.[15]

When Christians, Catholics for example, talk about 'inherent human dignity', they are not referring to a concept that derives from certain functions in interpersonal relationships. They are (at least often) referring to an extension of human createdness, to an extension of an essentialist conceptualization of a human being. In the essentialistic version, 'dignity' is not primarily generated in actions (although Christian philosophers probably wouldn't totally reject the idea), but actions themselves are required to be dignified because of the inherent dignity that

---

[13] Compared, for example, to functional and relational accounts. See, for example, Lawler (2009), Birnbacher (2004).

[14] See, for example, Niemelä (2007). The discussion concerning ensoulment connects with many interesting new projects within CSR. Among these are the idea of natural dualism (see Bloom 2004, also Bering 2002) and cognitive accounts of possession (see Cohen 2008, Cohen and Barrett 2008).

[15] See, for example, Fletcher (1995), Beckwith (2010).

human beings have because of their createdness. So, by its definition, the concept 'inherent human dignity' is as essentialistic a concept as 'the soul', and very different from contractual dignity, as in principalism. Consider the following examples from recent bioethical journal articles:

> Because human dignity is not a degreed property, it cannot develop and/or atrophy. For that reason, it is not a material property that has mass or extension. Moreover, because human dignity is intrinsic to every being that exemplifies human nature, it is not the sort of property that is local, in the sense that it depends on the actualization of particular human powers and properties, such as intelligence, good looks, rational faculties, etc. Rather, human dignity is a global property, one that applies to the human being as a whole. That is, human dignity is the property had by the unified entity of a particular sort that maintains absolute identity through change, including the development, growth, and flourishing, as well as the decline and diminishing of her numerous properties and powers. (Beckwith 2010: 98)

> Human dignity is, therefore, objective, transcendent, intangible and thus normative, and thus always valid value in the realm of experimentation. No human being, regardless of whoever he or she is or whatever his or her condition, can ever be reduced to the status of means. This is what is meant by human dignity from the practical perspective. (De Koninck 2009: 24)

From these examples it is quite obvious that it is not wholly uncommon to utilize the concept of 'human dignity' in a manner that is entirely compatible with the theory of psychological essentialism.[16] The reason such arguments have appeal and are quite easy to relate to is precisely because they resonate with natural human cognitive tendencies. In the issue of human cloning or, more precisely, stem cell harvesting, the inferential process proceeds (roughly) as in Figure 3.2.

Folk-biologically it is natural to think of human beings as being categorically separated from other intentional members of the biological world. It is equally natural to think that in procreation, biological species pass on to their offspring some essential core property that makes them what they are. In the case of human beings, religiously or theologically this core property can be expressed as either a 'soul' or as inherent 'in-built' human dignity. In this manner tradition provides a framework, or 'substance', to articulate the folk-biological intuitions. The arguments against cloning that follow are a direct result of the interaction between natural thought dispositions and tradition.

All would be much simpler if it were not for science. Consider the bewildering amount of problems modern embryonic science has caused to the biblical idea of ensoulment. When everything that had to do with human reproduction was the sole property of folk-biological inference (i.e. no-one really knew what was going on), the concept of ensoulment fitted the whole process like a glove. Now, with

[16] I would like to thank Uku Tooming for pointing out that my claim that 'human dignity' is sometimes used in line with psychological essentialism needs some flesh on its bones.

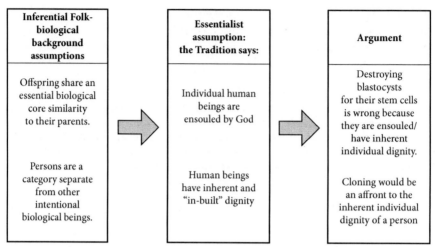

Inferential Folk-biological background assumptions	Essentialist assumption: the Tradition says:	Argument
Offspring share an essential biological core similarity to their parents.	Individual human beings are ensouled by God	Destroying blastocysts for their stem cells is wrong because they are ensouled/ have inherent individual dignity.
Persons are a category separate from other intentional biological beings.	Human beings have inherent and "in-built" dignity	Cloning would be an affront to the inherent individual dignity of a person

Figure 3.2 Folk-biological cognition, tradition and stem cell harvesting

(more or less) precise knowledge of embryonic development, all kinds of problems arise.

Consider this, for example: religious opponents of stem cell harvesting say that an embryo is ensouled from the moment of fertilization. The blastocyst (before the formation of the primitive streak) implants into the uterus at around ten days after being formed. It contains embryonic stem cells and tropoplastic cells that at this point start forming the placenta and the embryonic membranes. Until this point, ten days after fertilization and ensoulment, all these three were basically one same cell mass; so are the placenta and embryonic membranes also ensouled or was the soul somehow squeezed out of these cells before the implantation? Of course, being omniscient, God could direct the soul to only inhabit those cells that will actually continue dividing and differentiating into fetal period, but was that how it happened? Or were only the embryonic stem cells ensouled in the first place?

This may all sound simplistic for a theologian who is used to thinking of 'Christian mysteries', which denotes all those instances where God acts in a way that the mechanism of the act cannot be known. However, this type of 'simplistic' folk-biological pondering is not so uncommon for laypeople. This type of reasoning can be seen as an attempt to unite the essentialist assumptions that are set into motion by folk-biological inference and given substance by theological tradition with the knowledge of mechanisms supplied by modern science. And whatever the answers to the questions above are, we can be certain that the Church Fathers did not have to wrestle with these problems.

This is not to say that all theological bioethics, or popular thinking for that matter, concerning human dignity is folk-biologically essentialising. Natural folk-biological inferential tendencies, however, explain why such thoughts come to people so readily, and why they feel so persuasive for so many. This also explains why it takes strenuous effort of thought to be able to shift one's biological reasoning in the direction of, for example, relational or functional accounts of human dignity.

Hence there are further implications for theological bioethics. First, casuistical reasoning: if biblical principles concerning the biological world are functionally extensions of 'folk biology', then inferences based on them are just a form of theologically justified folk-biological thought. Second, the same goes, at least provisionally, for analogical reasoning based on faith traditions.

IV. Conclusion – the challenge of Cognitive Science

Theological bioethics is not a naturalistic project or based on naturalistic view of the world, nor does it need to be. However, as a normative project it has a great and severe responsibility of being aware of *what it is being normative of*. If there is evidence that human biological cognition is driven, or at least greatly affected, by certain automatic tendencies, then bioethicists should be aware of these tendencies.[17] This is important for two different reasons. First, the negative public response to several genetic technologies may not automatically mean that they are ethically suspect; it may mean that human cognition is just not naturally equipped to handle them. Second, it may be that these same cognitive tendencies have deeply pervaded the very theological tradition bioethics holds allegiance to. To quote Bernard E. Rollin in discussion concerning the Christian response to chimaeras: 'Two common types of bad ethical thinking are (1) confusing whatever disturbs people with genuine ethical issues and (2) confusing religious issues with ethical ones' (2007: 643). In both of these senses, being aware of one's inherent biases may result in better ethical assessment of complex issues that contradict what is easily accepted as 'normal'.

This is not to say that all questions dealt with by theological bioethics are faced with this problem. Casuistical and analogical reasoning works much less problematically when considering, say, the socio-economical aspects of biotechnology. Here theological bioethics can easily draw from stewardship ethics and not stumble upon cognitive challenges. However, there is a problem when Biblical biology, or biology based on a faith tradition, is utilized to try to solve the problems people have when wrestling with biotechnology using their folk-biological minds. In these cases, it may be that bioethics serves only to deepen the natural (and misplaced) negative dispositions people have because the faith tradition is partially based on the same cognitive mechanisms.[18]

It seems that advances in the understanding of human cognitive tendencies concerning biology present a challenge to those who would decide what is good

---

[17] There is some experimental evidence that this indeed is the case (Richert and Harris 2008, also Cohen and Barrett 2008), but further testing linking Christian essentialistic conceptualizations (soul-essentialism, etc.), their theological elaborations (doctrines regarding soul, etc.) and their combined effect on reaction towards biotechnology is definitely required. I hope to be able to carry out some of this testing in the near future.

[18] For more thorough discussions concerning the relation between theology, science and cognitive mechanisms see McCauley (2000, 2009), Pyysiäinen (2002, 2009), Wiebe (1991).

and what is not when it comes to biological manipulation. Philosophical bioethics will no doubt sooner or later include cognitive factors in the analysis of public and religious responses to biotechnology. It remains to be seen whether theological bioethicists will see it necessary to incorporate human cognitive tendencies as a building block of their analysis and as a point of reflection for their tradition.

References

Atran, S. (1998), 'Folkbiology and the anthropology of science: cognitive universals and cultural particulars'. *Behavioral and Brain Sciences, 21*, 547–609.

—(1999a), 'Folk biology'. In R. A. Wilson and F. Keil (eds), *The MIT Encyclopedia of the Cognitive Sciences*. Cambridge, MA: MIT Press, pp. 317–18.

—(1999b), 'Itzaj Maya folkbiological taxonomy: cognitive universals and cultural particulars' In D. L. Medin and S. Atran (eds), *Folkbiology,* Massachusetts Institute of Technology, pp. 119–203.

Atran, S., D. Medin, and N. Ross (2004), 'Evolution and devolution of knowledge: a tale of two biologies'. *Journal of the Royal Anthropological Society, 10* (2), 395–420.

Beckwith, F. J. (2010), 'Dignity never been photographed: scientific materialism, enlightenment liberalism, and Steven Pinker'. *Ethics & Medicine, 26* (2), 93–110.

Bering, J. M. (2002), 'Intuitive conceptions of dead agents' minds: the natural foundations of afterlife beliefs as phenomenological boundary'. *Journal of Cognition and Culture, 2* (4), 263–308.

Birnbacher, D. (2004), 'Human cloning and human dignity'. *RBM Online, 10* (Supp. 1), 50–55. Available from http://www.rbmonline.com/Article/157I

Bloom, P. (2004), *Descartes' Baby: How the Science of Child Development Explains What Makes us Human*. New York, NY: Basic Books.

Boonzaier, A., J. L. McClure and R. M. Sutton (2005), 'Distinguishing the effects of beliefs and preconditions: the folk psychology of goals, fantasies, and actions'. *European Journal of Social Psychology, 35*, 725–40.

Campbell, C. S. (1997), *Cloning Human Beings. Religious Perspectives on Human Cloning* (Commissioned Paper. Available from http://bioethics.georgetown.edu/nbac/pubs/cloning2/cc4.pdf)

Cohen, E. (2008), 'What is spirit possession? Defining, comparing, and explaining two possession forms'. *Ethnos, 73* (1), 101–26.

Cohen, E. and J. Barrett (2008), 'When minds migrate: conceptualizing spirit possession'. *Journal of Cognition and Culture, 8*, 23–48.

Davies, M. and T. Stone (eds) (1995), *Folk Psychology: The Theory of Mind Debate.* Blackwell Publishers.

De Koninck, T. (2009), 'Protecting human dignity in research involving humans'. *Journal of Academic Ethics, 7*, 17–25.

Evans, M. E. (2001), 'Cognitive and contextual factors in the emergence of diverse belief systems: creation versus evolution'. *Cognitive Psychology, 42*, 217–66.

Fiske, S. T. (2004), *Social Beings: A Core Motives Approach to Social Psychology.* New York, NY: Wiley.

Fiske, S. T. and Taylor, S. E. (1991), *Social Cognition* (2nd ed.). New York, NY: McGraw Hill.

Fletcher, D. B. (1995), 'Response to Nigel de S. Cameron's bioethics and the challenge of a post-consensus society'. *Ethics & Medicine: An International Journal of Bioethics,* 11 (1), 1–12.

Greenwood, J. D. (ed.) (1991), *The Future of Folk Psychology: Intentionality and Cognitive Science.* Cambridge: Cambridge University Press.

Gelman, S. A. (1999), 'Essentialism'. In R. A. Wilson and F. Keil (eds), *The MIT Encyclopedia of the Cognitive Sciences.* Cambridge, MA: MIT Press, pp. 282–3.

—(2003). 'The essential child: Origins of essentialism in everyday thought'. New York, NY: Oxford University Press.

Gelman, S. A. and Hirschfeld, L. A. (1999), 'How biological is essentialism?' In D. L. Medin and S. Atran (eds), *Folkbiology.* Cambridge, MA: Institute of Technology, pp. 403–6.

Gelman, S. A. and L. Raman (2002), 'Folk biology as a window onto cognitive development'. *Human Development,* 45, 61–8.

Gelman, S. A. and P. Bloom (2007), 'Developmental changes in the understanding of generics'. *Cognition,* 105, 166–83.

Griniezakis, M. and N. Symeonides (2005), 'Bioethics and Christian theology'. *Journal of Religion and Health,* 44 (1), 7–11.

Häyry, M. (2003), 'Philosophical arguments for and against human reproductive cloning'. *Bioethics,* 17 (5–6): 447–59.

Hirschfeld, L. A. (1999), 'Naïve sociology'. In R. A. Wilson and F. Keil (eds), *The MIT Encyclopedia of the Cognitive Sciences.* Cambridge, MA: MIT Press, pp. 579–81.

Holland, S. (2003), *Bioethics: A Philosophical Introduction.* Cambridge: Polity Press.

Lawler, P. A. (2009), 'The human dignity conspiracy'. *The Intercollegiate Review,* 1, 40–50.

Lawson, A. E. and W. A. Worsnop (1992), 'Learning about evolution and rejecting a belief in special creation: effects of reflective reasoning skill, prior knowledge, prior belief and religious commitment'. *Journal of Research in Science Teaching,* 29, 143–66.

McCauley, R. (2000), 'The naturalness of religion and the unnaturalness of science'. In F. C. Keil and R. A. Wilson (eds), *Explanation and Cognition.* Cambridge, MA: MIT Press), pp. 61–86.

—(2009), 'How science and religion are more like theology and common sense explanations than they are like each other: a cognitive account'. Unpublished manuscript. Available at http://userwww.service.emory.edu/~philrnm/publications/article_pdfs/How_Sci_and_Reli.pdf

McCloskey, M., A. Washburn and L. Felch (1983), 'Intuitive physics: the straight-down belief and its origin. *Journal of Experimental Psychology: Learning, Memory, and Cognition,* 9, 636–49.

Medin, D. L. and S. Atran (eds) (1999), *Folkbiology.* Cambridge, MA: Massachusetts Institute of Technology.

—(2004), 'The native mind: biological categorization and reasoning in development and across cultures'. *Psychological Review, 111* (4), 960–83.

Niemelä, J. E. (2007), 'The Catholic internet discussion on cloning: a study in cognitive rhetoric'. Unpublished Doctoral dissertation. Available from http://urn. fi/URN:ISBN:978-952-10-4220-1

—(2007), *The Catholic Internet Discussion on Cloning. A Study in Cognitive Rhetoric*. Helsinki: Helsinki University Press. Full e-thesis available at http://urn. fi/URN:ISBN:978-952-10-4220-1

Ostrom, T. M. (1984), 'The sovereignty of social cognition'. In R. Wyer and T. Srull (eds), *Handbook of Social Cognition* (vol. 1). Hillsdale, NJ: Lawrence Erlbaum, pp. 1–38.

Poling, D. A. and M. E. Evans (2004), 'Religious belief, scientific expertise, and folk ecology'. *Journal of Cognition and Culture, 4* (3), 485–523.

Pontifical Academy for Life (1997), Statement on Cloning, 25 June. Available from http://www.vatican.va/roman_curia/pontifical_academies/acdlife/documents/ rc_pa_acdlife_doc_30091997_clon_en.html

Proffitt, D. (1999), 'Naive physics'. In R. A. Wilson and F. Keil (eds.), *The MIT Encyclopedia of the Cognitive Sciences*. Cambridge, MA: MIT Press, pp. 577–8.

Pyysiäinen, I. (2002), 'A theory of ideology: implications for religion and science'. *Method and Theory in the Study of Religion, 14*, 316–33.

—(2009), *Supernatural Agents: Why We Believe in Souls, Gods, and Buddhas*. Oxford: Oxford University Press.

Richert, R. A. and P. L. Harris (2008), 'Dualism revisited: body vs. mind vs. soul'. *Journal of Cognition and Culture, 8*, 99–115.

Rollin, B. E. (2007), 'On chimeras'. *Zygon, 42* (3), 643–7.

Shtulman, A. and L. Schulz (2008), 'The relation between essentialist beliefs and evolutionary reasoning'. *Cognitive Science, 32*, 1049–62.

Sousa, P., Atran, S. and Medin, D. (2002), 'Essentialism and folkbiology: evidence from Brazil'.*Journal of Cognition and Culture, 2* (3): 195–223.

Strevens, M. (2000). 'The essentialist aspect of naïve theories'. *Cognition,74*: 149–75.

Wiebe, D. (1991), *The Irony of Theology and the Nature of Religious Thought*. Montreal: McGill-Queens University Press.

Yzerbyt, V., C. M. Judd and O. Corneille (eds) (2004), *The Psychology of Group Perception: Perceived Variability, Entitativity, and Essentialism*. New York, NY: Psychology Press.

4 Context Sensitivity and the Folk Psychology of Souls: Why Bering et al. Got the Findings they Did

K. Mitch Hodge

I. Context Sensitivity and the Folk Psychology of Souls: Competing Perspectives[1]

Bering's investigations into afterlife beliefs (Bering 2002, 2006, 2008a; Bering and Bjorklund 2004; Bering et al. 2005) have shown that humans intuitively believe that others 'survive' death. Moreover, his findings suggest that humans are more likely to affirm the continuity of mental states (i.e. emotional, desire and epistemic states) than physical states (i.e. biological, psychobiological and perceptual states) after a fictional character's death, to whom the participants were introduced through a narrative.[2] Thus, the responses participants gave about which states continue after death are context sensitive to whether the participants' attention is focused on the mental aspects of the decedent rather than the physical aspects of the decedent. Replications (Astuti and Harris 2008; Harris and Gimenéz 2005) of Bering's studies, however, have demonstrated that such affirmations are also context sensitive to secular versus religious priming – that is, they depend on whether the narrative in which the fictional character dies is presented secularly (e.g. the death is announced by a doctor) or religiously (e.g. the death is announced by a priest).[3] Participants presented with a secular narrative gave *fewer* continuity responses (i.e. responding that states continue after death) than those presented with a religious

---

[1] Bering (2006) is the first to introduce the phrase 'folk psychology of souls' to describe humans' intuitive belief that others 'survive' death.

[2] The use of 'mental' and 'physical' here are following one of the more prominent ways that Bering makes the distinctions between the two categories, and should not be taken to implicitly affirm a dualist interpretation of his results.

[3] The studies conducted by Harris and Gimenéz (2005), Astuti (2007b, 2007a) and Harris (Astuti and Harris 2008) were not replications of Bering and colleagues' (Bering 2002; Bering and Bjorklund 2004) studies in the strict sense, but nonetheless did delve into the same concerns about intuitive afterlife beliefs as Bering.

narrative, although the pattern of prevalence of mental states over bodily states continuing for the deceased remained remarkable in both contexts.[4]

The fact that mental states are claimed to be more likely to continue than physical states, has led many to claim that humans are intuitive Cartesian substance dualists (Bering 2006; Bloom 2004; Dennett 2006; Nichols 2007). For instance, Bering (2002, 2006, 2008b) argues from his findings that humans hold a 'common-sense' dualist perspective toward the death of an individual – that is, death of the body does not entail death of the mind.[5] The deceased continue to exist as disembodied minds; thus, it is not truly a conception of death, but rather of mental immortality. The experimental context sensitivity by this view is that humans believe and understand that the body ceases to function and that it perishes, but the mind of the individual continues to exist without the body and beyond the grave. This is why, in each of the experiments discussed above, participants responded that bodily functions, processes and states ceased at death, and that mental states continue.[6]

In contrast, the experiments of Harris and Gimenéz (2005) and Astuti and Harris (2008) suggest that the context sensitivity lies between the secular conception of death and the religious, metaphysical, conception of death. This latter conception entails that the deceased continue to exist with their mental, spiritual and agentive properties intact. Harris and Gimenéz (2005: 143, emphasis added) describe the former conception as follows: 'From a secular perspective, death is typically conceived as a terminal point when the bodily machine stops working. On this view, *the life of any given individual ends* irreversibly and completely at death.' Here they are initially describing the biological conception of death, but because they have added the additional component of the end of the life of the individual, they call it the secular perspective rather than the biological conception. The biological conception itself (Barrett and Behne 2005; Cox et al. 2005; Speece and Sandor 1984) does not include the intension of the terminus of the individual, but only

---

[4] It has often been objected to me that the studies carried out by Harris and Gimenéz (2005) and Astuti and Harris (2008) demonstrate that belief in the afterlife is not intuitive in the sense of an innate predisposition, but rather is a belief gained through enculturation. I have found no such arguments in their studies, however. Both studies argue against two aspects of Bering and colleagues' (Bering 2002; Bering and Bjorklund 2004) conclusions: first, that the secular conception of death (where all states, processes and functions cease) overrides the intuitive conception of death (where at least some mental states, processes and function continue) as one gets older; and second, that Bering's (2006) 'common-sense dualism' is the intuitive stance. In contradistinction to both of these conclusions, Harris, Gimenéz and Astuti suggest that enculturation may actually enhance an intuitive belief in the afterlife as one gets older and that the youngest children, even though their responses reflect those states, processes and functions continue for deceased individuals, do not respond as one would expect if they were 'common-sense dualists'.

[5] Bering (2008a, 2006, 2008b; Culotta 2009) aligns his 'common-sense' dualist view with, and endorses, Bloom's (2004, 2007) strong view of intuitive Cartesian substance dualism.

[6] It is not clear that there really is a clean distinction in reasoning about the mental. The problem is where one draws the line between the body and its functions, processes and states and the mind and its functions processes and states.

focuses on the effects of death on the body. The concept of biological death includes the intensions of inevitability, irreversibility and permanence, and the cessation of bodily processes and of agency in that body. To claim that death is the terminus of the individual requires an additional 'scientific' assumption that the life of the individual is an epiphenomenal manifestation arising from the processes, functions and states of the body. In other words, this scientific understanding carries with it the belief that, when the body dies, the individual connected with that body dies as well. Thus, the secular and religious conceptions of death for Harris and Gimenéz (as well as Astuti and Harris (2008), who follow these conceptions for their studies) are mutually exclusive. One cannot affirm the secular conception of death while at the same time affirming the continued existence of the deceased individual.[7]

I will argue that both contexts proposed suffer from a confound in their experimental methodology. This confound is that in each of the aforementioned experiments, the mental state questions contained social elements that the bodily state questions lacked. I propose that it is the inclusion of social elements in the mental state questions which increased their continuity responses; this inclusion shifts the focus – or rather the stance – that the participants take in reasoning about the decedent. On the one hand, when the questions focus the participants' attention on the dead body, the participants deploy the biological conception of death in reasoning about the decedent – in particular, the decedent's body. On the other hand, when the questions focus the participants' attention on social relationships held by the decedent, the participants utilize offline social reasoning and the intentional stance when thinking about the decedent. The context sensitivity I will propose here is between the biological conception of death versus the social conception of death. I will argue that through beliefs in the afterlife, humans accept the former while ameliorating the impact of the latter. In other words, the individual's body is very much dead, but the individual herself remains socially very much alive. Moreover, I will argue, that it is this context sensitivity that better explains the experimental results of Bering and colleagues, Astuti, Harris and Gimenéz.

II. Problems for the Intuitive Cartesian Substance Dualist Context Sensitivity

I have challenged the intuitive Cartesian substance dualist interpretation of the folk psychology of souls on several grounds (Hodge 2008). First, the intuitive Cartesian substance dualist interpretation is not faithful to cultural representations of deceased individuals. I offered evidence that when one examines representations of deceased individuals cross-culturally from funerary rites, mythologies,

---

[7] This is not to say that a person who at one point affirms the secular conception of death could not also affirm, at a different time, the religious conception of death. Research into mental models demonstrates that it is commonplace for people consciously to hold incompatible, even contradictory, models about the same thing (Gentner and Gentner 1983; Gentner and Markman 1997), as long as they are not invoked at the same time (Caws 1974).

iconography and doctrines, one finds that the decedents are not represented as disembodied. On the contrary, cultural representations of the deceased are usually embodied. Second, I argued that given the philosophical and intricate nature of the belief (intuitive or otherwise) in Cartesian substance dualism, it is unlikely that most humans would be able to hold, in any consistent manner, the representation of a disembodied mind as is necessary for this position to be an accurate description of folk representations of decedents. Third, I argued that the intuitive Cartesian substance dualist interpretation was not a good interpretation of the mounting empirical findings regarding how humans view the relationship between the mind and the body. For instance, following the studies conducted by Richert and Harris (2006) and Mahalingam and Rodriguez (2006), I argued that the evidence demonstrates that humans do not see the mind and the soul as intentionally identical, as is required by the intuitive Cartesian substance dualist position. Empirical evidence (Astuti and Harris 2008; Richert and Harris 2008) gathered since my initial analysis has further confirmed this problem.

The challenge I set forth in that same work that is most pertinent for our present purposes, however, was a problem with the experimental methodology of Bering and colleagues (Bering 2002; Bering and Bjorklund 2004; Bering et al. 2005). I argued that one of the reasons that mental state questions received more continuity responses than physical state questions was because of an asymmetry between the formats of the physical state versus the mental state questions. Physical state questions lacked a social context which was included in the mental state questions. Physical state questions took the form 'Can subject S still do activity A?' whereas mental state questions took the form 'Can subject S still do activity A with person P?' For instance, a question such as 'Can the deceased hold hands with his also deceased wife?' would be more telling toward continued embodiment than 'Can the deceased still see?'

III. Problems for the Secular versus Religious Context Sensitivity

As previously stated, Astuti, Harris and Gimenéz (Astuti and Harris 2008; Harris and Gimenéz 2005) claim that the extent to which the participants give continuity responses for a decedent's physical and mental states depends on whether they are primed with the secular or the religious conceptions of death.[8] Again, the secular conception of death according to these researchers entails the complete annihilation of the individual such that no physical or mental states should continue for the decedent. In contrast, the religious conception of death leaves the decedent's mental, spiritual and agentive states intact. Thus, participants who were primed with the religious vignette were significantly more likely to attribute continuing states to the decedent.

---

[8] It should be noted that Astuti, Harris and Gimenéz (Harris and Gimenéz 2005; Astuti and Harris 2008) all reject the intuitive Cartesian substance dualist view in favour a tripartite division of body, mind and soul (following, Richert and Harris 2006, 2008).

The first problem that this context sensitivity between the secular and the religious conceptions of death encounters is that even under the secular condition the participants were significantly more likely to attribute continuing mental states to the decedent than physical states. If the participants really were endorsing the secular conception of death as stated by Harris and Gimenéz, then all states should have ceased completely. Yet, none of their studies revealed this trend. What they demonstrated was that participants in the secular condition were significantly less likely to give continuity responses – not that such responses were eliminated.

The second problem with this context sensitivity position is that each of the studies followed the problematic asymmetric formatting of Bering and colleagues' mental and physical state questions. In other words, a social context was provided in the mental state questions but not in the physical state questions. This is problematic, for the reasons I stated above in my discussion of Bering and colleagues' experiments, and for reasons that will become even more apparent in the next section.

Third, given the amount of evidence accumulated above for the intuitiveness of afterlife beliefs (even by Astuti, Harris and Gimenéz), it appears that it is not required either that humans hold a religious belief regarding death (as demonstrated in Bering 2002), nor that they have specific religious instruction as demonstrated by Bering and colleagues (Bering et al. 2005). In the 2002 study, Bering found that even extinctivists who explicitly endorsed the secular conception of death were still significantly more likely to state that mental states continue for the decedent. In their 2005 cross-cultural study, Bering and colleagues found that while secularly schooled children gave fewer continuity responses for the decedents' activities than religiously schooled children, the same trend was found for both groups – namely that mental state questions were more likely to receive continuity responses than physical state questions. Thus, while religious and cultural views do affect the way that humans conceive of death, the context sensitivity cannot be as clearly demarcated by religion and enculturation as Astuti, Harris and Gimenéz claim it to be.

IV. Biological versus Social Conceptions of Death

There are two other well-documented conceptions of death that should be considered here: biological death and social death. As mentioned previously, *biological death* includes the intentions of inevitability, irreversibility, permanence, cessation of bodily processes and cessation of agency by the body. This is a concept that is developmentally sensitive – in fact, it is estimated that it is not until somewhere between the ages of 7 to 10 years of age that children have fully grasped this conception of death (Barrett and Behne 2005; Cox et al. 2005; Norris-Shortle et al. 1993, Speece and Sandor 1984). The biological conception of death focuses attention on the corpse of the deceased creature, and it stands in contradistinction to Harris and Gimenéz's (2005) secular conception of death in that it does not include the intension of the annihilation of the individual. To get to the annihilation of the individual from the biological conception of death, as argued above, requires the additional 'scientific' assumption that the individual is an epiphe-nomenal manifestation of biological functions, states and processes.

Even if, however, the biological conception of death did include the intension of terminus of the individual, or entail it, it is not clear that humans have the conceptual capability of intuitively representing non-existence in the manner which researchers suggest by the notion of secular death. As the research of Lakoff and Johnson (1999: 205) demonstrates, underlying the folk understanding of existence is a location metaphor, 'existence is being located here'; whereas the folk conception of nonexistence (as expressed cross-culturally through metaphor) does not have the intension of annihilation, but rather the intension of 'not being located here, now'. Most importantly for our purposes, ceasing to exist is under-stood by the location metaphor 'going away'. Humans treat death as an absence and talk about decedents as if they are not here (e.g. 'he is gone', 'she has departed', 'he passed away').[9] Because existence is understood in terms of location, death is not understood as an annihilation of an individual, but rather as a change in that individual's location (see also Kim 2001). The individual is gone, although the body remains. In fact, it is the word 'remains' that we use to refer to the body because that is what is located here. The person, our loved one, is absent – that is, not located here.

There is another conception of death, *social death* (Palgi and Abramovitch 1984) – that is, the person with whom we could carry out our normal social interactions has been extricated completely from our life. It is the loss of these potential future social interactions with the deceased loved one that is the more emotionally salient aspect of death, and it is this emotional impact that our intuitive and religious beliefs concerning the survivability of death serve to ameliorate. The intuitive belief (and religious beliefs that are cognitively supported by our intuitive belief) allows for recognizing the biological death of the individual and its implications (including nonexistence, metaphorically understood) while also allowing that same individual to escape a social death – that is, to remain socially active with respect to both the living and her fellow deceased. Thus, our intuitive belief about the afterlife allows the person to remain socially alive while still being biologically dead. In a review of his findings, Bering (2006: 2) allows for this: he writes, 'intuitive reasoning about dead agent's minds seems to leave open the possibility for continued social relation-ships with the dead'. Social relationships with the dead, according to Boyer (2001: 138), are carried out in a concrete manner:

> Also what is a constant object of intuitions and reasoning are situations of *interaction* with these agents. People do not just stipulate that there is a supernatural being somewhere who creates thunder or that there are souls wandering about in the night. People actually interact with these beings in the very concrete sense of doing things to them, experiencing them doing things, giving and receiving, paying, threatening, protecting, placating and so on.

---

[9] My use of the words 'humans' and 'we' here is meant to mean all of us who are susceptible to folk-reasoning processes, which I take to be the vast majority of humans.

Humans fear social death (also called the 'death after death': see Schmidt 2000). This was a major theme in mythologies and rituals in the ancient world, and a social death was considered far worse than a biological death. Ostracism, in the ancient world, was considered a greater punishment than (physical) death – it eliminated all social connections for the banished and it became taboo even to speak their name. They were considered dead *and* forgotten. This is why Socrates, in *The Apology*, when given the choice chose hemlock over being banished from Athens never to return (Cooper 1997). Even though ancient cultures had beliefs in an afterlife (often quite elaborate ones at that), the focus for the living was not only that they should not be forgotten once they were dead, but that they should commemorate the previously deceased for their deeds and contributions to their respective societies (a religious behaviour called *geneomyny*). The people in the ancient world were more concerned with being kept alive through the memories of their loved ones and their communities than they were with their personal fate after death: this is the immortality for which Gilgamesh strives, and which he finds in the end (Dalley 2000). It was the fear of eternal anonymity (*athazagoraphobia*) that motivated the elite and the commoners alike to commemoration cults in ancient Ugarit (Schmidt 2000); it is the knowledge that he will have imperishable glory (*kléos*) that consoles Achilles as his death approaches (Zeitlin 1991); and it was fame and glory (*fama gloriaque*) for which the legions and gladiators served and died for Rome (Rose 1995).

Yet, it is not simply the case that we fear our own eternal anonymity. A common (and quite strong) fear among those who have lost loved ones is that they will begin to forget the decedent (Norris-Shortle et al. 1993; Northern Arizona Healthcare 2010; Wilkin and Powell 1996). Thus, it is not merely that *we* want to be remembered after our passing; we want to be able to remember *others* that mattered to us after they die. We cling to their memories to keep alive their social significance to us – to keep them in *our* life socially after *their* biological death. We accomplish this through our memories and our imaginations.

These two conceptions of death, the biological and social, fall out naturally from two well established domains of intuitive human knowledge: folk biology and folk psychology. On the one hand, our intuitive knowledge from folk biology allows us to understand that *this* life depends on the proper functioning of the body, and, on the other hand, our intuitive knowledge from folk psychology allows us to understand our conspecifics as intentional and social creatures (Lawson 2007; Horst 2010), who remain alive as long as they can (potentially) socially interact with others. In addition, it is dependent on which of these domains of intuitive knowledge is activated whether we take the physical, design or intentional stance to understand and predict interactions with our environment and our conspecifics (Dennett 1990a, 1996, 2006, 2007). With respect to understanding the functions, processes and states of the body, humans naturally take the physical and design stances, but to understand and predict the social behaviours and interactions of our conspecifics themselves – as persons – we take the intentional stance. The intentional stance focuses our attention on our conspecifics' beliefs, desires, emotional states and goal-directed behaviour, and it is these functions, processes and states that were demonstrated from the experiments above to continue for the decedent. I take up how this stance arises for the living in thinking about the decedent in the next section.

V. Offline Social Reasoning and the Intentional Stance

As mentioned above, humans do not conceive of death as the annihilation of the individual, but rather as the decedent being absent. It is this conception of the decedent, according to Bering (2006), which activates a well-known cognitive system in the person thinking about the decedent, namely, *offline social reasoning*. Offline social reasoning is our ability to imagine, think about and plan social inter-actions with absent individuals. Out-of-sight is not out-of-mind for humans. In our everyday interactions with our conspecifics, we are accustomed to their periodic absences, but this in no way inhibits our ability to reason about their on-going (and upcoming) social interactions with others and ourselves. We think about where they are and what they are doing. With regard to the deceased, according to Bering's account, humans do not readily update their social registry when it comes to the death of individuals – in other words, they stay present in our minds and we continue to think about where they are and what they are doing. This is why, Bering argues, the afterlife is conceived of as a place.[10]

Thus, built into the offline social reasoning process, even in our reasoning concerning the deceased, is the presumption that the absent person is *somewhere doing something*. This presumption infects all of our subsequent reasoning about the decedent. This presumption can be overcome, but only with cognitive effort and not always successfully as found in Bering's (2002) experiment. As mentioned previously, extinctivists who explicitly believed that all processes ceased at death – that is, they accepted the secular concept of death – nevertheless asserted that the decedent was still capable of some states, such as the epistemic state of knowing that he is dead. This is interesting in that it shows that a process more primitive than belief is influencing the answers of participants. I suggest (following Gendler 2008a, 2008b) that when the offline social reasoning processes are activated in the case of reasoning about dead agents, that these processes activate the *alief* in the respondents that the decedent is somewhere doing something, which may or may not coincide with their explicit beliefs. Whereas beliefs are evidence sensitive, aliefs are not; aliefs are recalcitrant in nature and thus may be belief-discordant. An alief as defined by Gendler (2008a: 634) is:

> …[C]haracterized as a mental state with associatively-linked content that is representa-tional, affective and behavioral, and that is activated – consciously or unconsciously – by

---

[10] Although Bering (2006) is the first to introduce offline social reasoning as part of the explanation for afterlife beliefs, he sees this as having a non-causal role with regard to those beliefs. Instead, offline social reasoning supplements his novel cognitive mechanism, the simulation constraint. In contrast, I hold that offline social reasoning is the primary cognitive and causal mechanism for afterlife beliefs.

features of the subject's internal or ambient environment. Alief is a more primitive state than either belief or imagination: it directly activates behavioral response patterns (as opposed to motivating in conjunction with desire or pretended desire.)

In her discussion of alief, interestingly, Gendler (2008b, following Hume from *A Treatise on Human Nature*, 1739) appeals to the same sort of anecdotal evidence in the case of death as Bering (2006). Both describe how the decedent's survivors still *act as if* they believe the decedent were still alive, whether that be picking up the phone to call the decedent only to realize she cannot answer the call, or wandering the house looking for the decedent only to realize she will not be found. Even though the survivors believe – even understand – that their loved one is dead, they *alieve* that the decedent is still somewhere doing something; the decedent remains very much alive in their social registries and their imaginations.

I have argued (Hodge, 2011a), that the imagined *somewhere* for the deceased individual is the afterlife, and that the imagined *something* that the deceased individual is doing is continuing to fulfil his social obligations to both the living and the dead (see also, Bering 2006; Boyer 2001). It is the decedent's social role(s), and possible social interactions between the decedent and the living and other deceased individuals, that are the focus of our offline social reasoning concerning the decedent.

It is this focus which prompted my earlier (Hodge 2008) criticisms of Bering and colleagues' methodology. While Bering (2006: 6) did point out that afterlife beliefs 'leave open the possibility of continued social relationships with the dead', he fails to take into account that only the mental state questions of his experimental methodology exploit this possibility, whilst the physical state questions ignore this possibility. In other words, if Bering's physical questions had included a social element, I suggest that the results would have differed greatly; especially since it is offline social reasoning – that is, simulating possible social interactions – which allows us to think about dead agents at all.

Support for the hypothesis that adding social relationships to such questions will make a substantial difference comes from an unrelated study conducted by Sytsma and Machery (2009) concerning attributions of behaviour and functional states which entail attributing phenomenal consciousness to group agents. This study was intended to stand in contrast to a study conducted by Knobe and Prinz (2008), which suggested that the states which could be attributed to groups were much more limited than those that could be attributed to individuals. Sytsma and Machery, however, countered that one of the liabilities of the Knobe and Prinz studies was an asymmetry between the questions asked of participants concerning attributions of feelings to group agents. For instance, Knobe and Prinz's studies asked participants to evaluate which sentences sounded natural to them: (the 'feeling condition') 'Acme Corp. is *feeling* upset', versus (the 'the non-feeling condition') 'Acme Corp is upset about the court's ruling'. Knobe and Prinz's study revealed that participants found the former to sound 'weird' whereas the latter was acceptable. From this, Knobe and Prinz concluded that participants were not willing to attribute feeling to a group agent because that would require phenomenal consciousness. In contrast, however, Sytsma and Machery demonstrated that if they moved the prepositional phrase 'about the court's ruling' to the feeling condition (i.e., 'Acme Corp. is feeling upset about the court's ruling'), participants claimed that the sentence seemed natural (i.e. not weird). Sytsma and Machery suggest that the difference between the comfort levels of the two sentences was due to the addition of the prepositional phrase.

I suggest, however, that it is more than simply the addition of a prepositional phrase. The state in question must have the appropriate social connection between the agent and the intentional object of that state. For instance, while it seems natural to say, 'Acme Corp. is *feeling* upset about the court's ruling', it seems unnatural to say 'Acme Corp. is *feeling* upset about little Tommy spilling his coke on his mother'. The difference here is the appropriate social connection between the agent and the intentional object of its state.

The inclusion of social relationships in Bering and colleagues' mental state questions and their exclusion in physical state questions, I suggest, are in part responsible for the significantly greater frequency of continuity responses by participants for the former over the latter. Thus, from the positing of only offline social reasoning processes (without the need to posit any novel mechanisms) we have the first reason why Bering and colleagues found the result that humans are more likely to attribute mental states to deceased individuals over physical states. But this is not the only reason.

I previously argued (Hodge 2008) that Dennett's intentional stance was a better interpretation for Bering and colleagues' findings than intuitive Cartesian substance dualism. I have also suggested (Hodge, 2011b) that Bering and colleagues' findings are not surprising given the implications of humans taking the intentional stance toward agents. What I wish to spell out here is exactly why I think this is the case. Offline social reasoning, in part, allows us to predict and understand social interactions with our conspecifics. But the way that we predict and understand those social interactions is *constrained* by how we think about our conspecifics. Our reasoning is constrained in that we treat them, *ceteris paribus*, as agents who behave according to beliefs, desires, goals and rationality (Dennett 1990b, 1996, 2006; Griffin and Baron-Cohen 2002; Meltzoff and Moore 1995). We are, therefore, more interested in another agent's reasoning and goal-directed behaviour than we are with their mundane biological and perceptual functions.

The point is that we naturally focus on, and communicate to others about, other agents' intentional mental states in order to both understand and predict those others' behaviour. Unless the others' biological and perceptual functions directly affect their reasoning and goals in social interaction, we do not, *ceteris paribus*, use those functions to reason about what those other individuals are doing or are going to do.[11] This is perhaps an even greater constraint when thinking about imagined

---

[11] To illustrate the point of how mundane perceptual processes might affect our offline social reasoning about a decedent in exceptional circumstances, I offer a related anecdotal account provided by a friend and colleague (whom I will leave to anonymity given its personal nature, but nevertheless I have consent to use):

agents such as fictional characters. We are not concerned, when in the throes of a story, about the fictional agent's biological and perceptual functions, but rather with how the fictional agent *thinks, feels and acts.*

I have argued (Hodge, 2011a) that it is our imagination that preserves the presence of deceased loved ones in the afterlife.[12] But it is also important to recall that these imaginings are context sensitive. Questions asked of participants such as 'Can he still see?' and 'Do his eyes still work?' focus on biological functions (as opposed to states) of the decedent's physical body, as opposed to questions such as 'Does he still love his mother?' which focus on an intentional state. The former focuses the participant's attention on the reality of the dead body, whereas the latter allows the participant to entertain his imagined representation of the now deceased through offline social reasoning and the intentional stance. Thus, there are indeed two different representations of the deceased at work, one present in the physical reality of death, and the other with the decedent alive and well in the imagination. What I am suggesting, however, above what Bering and colleagues, Astuti, Harris and Gimenéz have argued, is that the context sensitivity is far more subtle than merely giving a secular and religious context, or distinguishing between mental and physical states. It is highly sensitive to which representation the question focuses the participant's attention upon. Mere functional questions focus the participant's attention on the reality of the corpse, whereas state questions, which include social relationships, intentional and goal-directed behaviour, allow the participant to focus on his imagined representation of the decedent. This helps us to understand why the former types of questions received more discontinuity responses than the latter.

VI. Conclusion

I have argued, in line with the findings of Bering and his colleagues, Astuti, Harris and Gimenéz, that affirmations of intuitive afterlife beliefs are context sensitive. In contrast to their suggestions as to what that context sensitivity may be, however, I have argued for a 'deeper' context sensitivity that better explains their experimental findings. Rather than participants invoking a Cartesian substance dualist

> My grandmother died last week, so I've been thinking about death a lot lately. For the last 2 years of her life, she was blind due to glaucoma, and all she could talk about was how terrible it was to be blind and how she wished she could see again. Her short-term memory had started to go, too, so I'm not sure if she was aware of how often she complained. When my mom called to tell me that Grandma was dead, one of the first things she said was, 'Well, at least she can see now'. Intellectually, it struck me as a little strange. What is she seeing with, after all? But the statement felt right intuitively. And it made me think of [Bering's] studies which showed that people are less likely to think that biological [perceptual] states continue, but everyone at the funeral unanimously agreed that she could now see. It's the one thing everyone kept mentioning. I'm not sure what to make of it.

[12] This is not meant to argue for or against the ontological status of an afterlife.

philosophy, or invoking mutually exclusive conceptions of death by secular or religious priming, this deeper context concerns whether the attention of the participant is focused on the reality of the dead body of the decedent through mere functional questions, or focused on the intentional and social actions of the decedent through questions including a social element. I have argued that the former invokes the participants' biological conception of death while the latter invokes the participants' offline social reasoning and treats the deceased as if she were absent but still socially active, thus allowing the decedent to avoid a social death.

By treating the deceased as if she were absent, the participant holds an imaginative representation that the decedent is somewhere doing something. This representation, or alief mandated through offline social reasoning, prompts the participants to take the intentional stance toward the decedent such that they treat her as an agent who behaves according to beliefs, desires, goals and rationality – especially in the case of imagined social interactions.

The afterlife, after all, is *a social realm*. Humans believe it to be a place in which their loved ones watch over them and take care of them (as well as threaten and scare them from time to time!). Moreover, the deceased continue to enjoy the same social relationships with both the living and their fellow deceased as they did in this life. And when the time comes that we too shall die, we believe (or maybe just hope) that they will greet us with open arms and welcome us to our new home.

Acknowledgements

I would like to thank the organizers and participants of the 13th Annual ESSSAT Conference in Edinburgh, Scotland. In particular, I would like to thank Steven Horst, Natalie Emmons, Uku Tooming and Helen de Cruz for the excellent feedback I received on my presentation of these ideas there. I would also like to thank Tracy Orr for her help in preparing this manuscript and Graham Macdonald for his on-going help throughout this research and project.

References

Astuti, R. (2007a), 'Ancestors and the afterlife'. In H. Whitehouse and J. Laidlaw (eds), *Religion, Anthropology, and Cognitive Science*. Chapell Hill, NC: Carolina Academic Press, pp. 161–78.

—(2007b), 'What happens after death?' In R. Astuti, J. P. Parry and C. Stafford (eds), *Questions of Life and Death*. Oxford: London School of Economics Monographs, p. 227–47.

Astuti, R. and P. L. Harris (2008), 'Understanding Mortality and the Life of the Ancestors in Rural Madagascar'. *Cognitive Science, 32*, 713–40.

Barrett, H. C. and T. Behne (2005), 'Children's understanding of death as the cessation of agency: a test using sleep versus death'. *Cognition, 96*, 93–108.

Bering, J. (2002), 'Intuitive conceptions of dead agents' minds: the natural foundations of afterlife beliefs as phenomenological boundary'. *Journal of Cognition and Culture, 2,* 263–308.

—(2006), 'The folk psychology of souls'. *Behavioral and Brain Sciences, 29,* 1–46.

—(2008a), 'The end? Why so many of us think our minds continue after we die'. *Scientific American Mind, 19,* 34–41.

—(2008b), 'Death as an empirical backdoor to the representation of mental causality'. *Interdisciplines.* Available from http://www.interdisciplines.org/causality/papers/11/3

Bering, J. and D. F. Bjorklund (2004), 'The natural emergence of reasoning about the afterlife as a developmental regularity', *Developmental Psychology, 40,* 217–33.

Bering, J., C. H. Blasi and D. F. Bjorklund (2005), 'The development of "afterlife" beliefs in religiously and secularly schooled children'. *British Journal of Developmental Psychology, 23,* 587–607.

Bloom, P. (2004), *Descartes' Baby: How Child Development Explains what makes us Human.* London: Arrow Books.

—(2007), 'Religion is natural', *Developmental Science, 10,* 147–51.

Boyer, P. (2001), *Religion Explained: The Evolutionary Origins of Religious Thought.* New York, NY: Basic Books.

Caws, P. (1974), 'Operational, representational, and explanatory models'. *American Anthropologist, New Series 76,* 1–10.

Cooper, J. M. (ed.), *Plato: The Complete Works.* Indianapolis, IN: Hackett Publishing.

Cox, M., E. Garrett and J. A. Graham (2005), 'Death in Disney films: implications for children's understanding of death'. *Omega, 50,* 267–80.

Culotta, E. (2009), 'On the origin of religion'. *Science, 326,* 784–7.

Dalley, S. (2000), *Myths from Mesopotamia: Creation, the Flood, Gilgamesh, and Others.* Oxford: Oxford University Press.

Dennett, D. (1990a), 'Three kinds of intentional psychology'. In J. L. Garfield (ed.), *Foundations of Cognitive Science: The Essential Readings.* New York, NY: Paragon Housem oo, 88–110.

—(1990b), 'the interpretation of texts, people and other artifacts'. *Philosophy and Phenomenological Research, 50,* 177–94.

—(1996), *Kinds of Minds: Towards an Understanding of Consciousness.* New York, NY: Basic Books.

—(2006), *Breaking the Spell: Religion as a Natural Phenomenon.* New York, NY: Viking Penguin.

—(2007), 'Philosophy as naive anthropology: a comment on Bennett and Hacker'. In M. Bennett, D. Dennett, P. Hacker and J. Searle (eds), *Neuroscience & Philosophy: Brain, Mind, & Language.* New York, NY: Columbia University, Press pp. 74–95.

Gendler, T. S. (2008a), 'Alief and belief'. *Journal of Philosophy, 105,* 634–63.

—(2008b), 'Alief in action (and reaction)'. *Mind and Language, 23,* 552–85.

Gentner, D. and D. R. Gentner (1983), 'Flowing waters or teeming crowds: mental models of electricity'. In D. Gentner and A. L. Stevens (eds), *Mental Models.* Hillsdale, NJ: Lawrence Erlbaum, pp. 99–129.

Gentner, D. and A. B. Markman (1997), 'Structure mapping in analogy and similarity'. *American Psychologist, 52,* 45–56.

Griffin, R. and S. Baron-Cohen (2002), 'The intentional stance: developmental and neurocognitive perspectives'. In A. Brook and D. Ross (eds), *Daniel Dennett: Contemporary Philosophy in Focus.* Cambridge: Cambridge University Press, pp. 83–116.

Harris, P. L. and M. Gimenéz (2005), 'Children's acceptance of conflicting testimony: the case of death'. *Journal of Cognition and Culture, 5,* 143–64.

Hodge, K. M. (2008), 'Descartes mistake: how afterlife beliefs challenge the assumption that humans are intuitive cartesian substance dualists'. *Journal of Cognition and Culture, 8,* 387–415.

—(2011a), 'On imagining the afterlife'. *Journal of Cognition and Culture, 11* (3–4): 367–389. doi:10.1163/156853711X591305

—(2011b), 'Why immortality alone will not get me to the afterlife'. *Philosophical Psychology, 24* (3): 395–410. doi:10.1080/09515089.2011.559620

Horst, S. (2010), 'Whose intuitions? Whose dualism?'. Unpublished manuscript *ESSSAT XIIIth Annual Conference 2010.* Edinburgh, UK.

Kim, J. (2001), 'Lonely souls: causality and substance dualism'. In K. Corcoran (ed.), *Soul, Body, and Survival: Essays on the Metaphysics of Human Persons.* Ithaca, NY: Cornell University Press.

Knobe, J. and J. Prinz (2008), 'Intuitions about consciousness: experimental studies'. *Phenomenology and Cognitive Science, 7,* 67–83.

Lakoff, G. and M. Johnson (1999), *Philosophy in the Flesh: The Embodied Mind and its Challenge to Western Thought.* New York, NY: Basic Books.

Lawson, E. T. (2007), 'Cognitive constraints on imagining other worlds'. In M. Grebowicz (ed.), *SciFi in the Mind's Eye: Reading Science through Science Fiction.* Chicago, IL: Open Court.

Mahalingam, R. and J. Rodriguez (2006), 'Culture, brain transplants and implicit theories of identity'. *Journal of Cognition and Culture, 6,* 453–62.

Meltzoff, A. N. and M. K. Moore (1995), 'Infant's understanding of people and things: from body imitation to folk psychology'. In J. L. Bermudez, A. Marcel and N. Eilan (eds), *The Body and the Self.* Cambridge, MA: MIT Press, pp. 43–69.

Nichols, S. (2007), 'Imagination and immortality: thinking of me'. *Synthese, 159,* 215–33.

Norris-Shortle, C., P. A. Young and M. A. Williams (1993), 'Understanding death and grief for children three and younger'. *Social Work, 38,* 736–41.

Northern Arizona Healthcare (2010), *10 Stages of Grief.* Flagstaff, AZ: Northern Arizona Healthcare. Available from http://www.nahealth.com/OurServices/NorthernArizonaHospice/EmotionalandSpiritualSupport/10_Stages_of_grief

Palgi, P. and H. Abramovitch (1984), 'Death: a cross-cultural perspective'. *Annual Review of Anthropology, 13,* 385–417.

Richert, R. A. and P. L. Harris (2006), 'The ghost in my body: children's developing concept of the soul'. *Journal of Cognition and Culture, 6,* 409–27.

—(2008), 'Dualism revisited: body vs. mind vs. soul'. *Journal of Cognition and Culture, 8*, 99–115.

Rose, H. J. (1995), *Ancient Greek and Roman Religion: Two Volumes in One*. New York, NY: Barnes and Noble.

Schmidt, B. (2000), 'Memory as immortality'. *Near Eastern Archaeology, 63*, 236–9.

Speece, M. W. and B. B. Sandor (1984), 'Children's understanding of death: a review of three components of a death concept'. *Child Development, 55*, 1671–86.

Sytsma, J. M. and E. Machery (2009), 'How to study folk intuitions about phenomenal consciousness'. *Philosophical Psychology, 22*, 21–35.

Wilkin, C. S. and J. Powell (1996), *Learning to Live through Loss: Helping Children Understand Death*. Manhattan, KS: National Network for Childcare/Kansas State University Cooperative Extension Service. Available from http://www.nncc.org/Guidance/understand.death.html

Zeitlin, F. I. (ed.) (1991), *Mortals and Immortals: Collected Essays: Jean-Pierre Vernant* Princeton, NJ: Princeton University Press.

Part II

Religion – Naturally?
Philosophical Reflections

5 Religion – Naturally: Religion, Theology and Science

Ilkka Pyysiäinen

I. Three meanings of 'natural'

The claim that religion is natural has been defended by representatives of the cognitive science of religion (e.g. Boyer 1994; McCauley 2000). Although at first blush the claim may seem too obvious to be interesting, I try to show that it leads us to reconsider some of the methodological claims within religious studies as well as the various arguments concerning the compatibility of religion and science. I focus on the cognitive science of religion and its critics in particular, although the debate concerning naturalism and religion is, of course, a much wider issue.

From the cognitive scientific perspective, religion is natural because it is something humans do, think and feel; as such it can be studied apart from ontological commitments to religious truth claims. The question of the naturalness of religion is different from the question of whether God exists. An illuminating way to approach the presuppositions and implications of the naturalist claim is to ask what kind of counterfactual the cognitive scientists of religion have in mind: 'religion is natural {rather than X}' (see Garfinkel 1981; Ylikoski 2006). There are at least three options:

1   Religion is natural {rather than supernatural}.
2   Religion is natural {rather than unnatural}.
3   Religion is natural {rather than cultural}.

Contrast (1) is implied in such claims as, for example, 'The differences between everyday action and religious ritual action turn out to be fairly minor from the standpoint of their cognitive representation' (McCauley and Lawson 2002: 8). Religious thought and behaviour are mediated by the same cognitive mechanisms as any thought and behaviour. As Pascal Boyer (1994) points out, even if a god revealed himself to humans, information about his revelation could only be spread through human communication.

This point might be regarded as almost trivial, as the contrasting claim that religion is supernatural comes close to being eccentric. Religion is natural, although God might be supernatural (God does not practice religion). What could be claimed (and often is), however, is that religion is human communication with some supernatural entities. This is suggested in, for instance, the title of Stark and Finke's (2000) book, *Acts of faith: Explaining the Human Side of Religion*. To the extent that there is a human side of religion there must also be a superhuman side; otherwise there would be no point in emphasizing the human side. Only a contrast gives this claim a meaning. Likewise, Patrick McNamara (2009: ix) writes that religion 'is, *at least partly*, created by human beings' (emphasis added).

This brings us to consider the question of the proper way to study religion. The cognitive naturalists claim that even if supernatural agents existed, religion should still be studied in a naturalistic fashion, because supernatural concepts do not have any explanatory role in modern science (see Edis 2008). Most cognitive naturalists only want to disentangle the study of religion from the ontological question about the existence of supernatural agents. Scholars only studying human behaviour need not worry about such metaphysical issues which are best 'left to theologians or retired scientists' (Boyer 2001: 48).

In the standard model of the cognitive science of religion (Boyer 2005), representations of supernatural agents are formed by combining intuitively human properties, such as memory, and one violation of intuitive expectations concerning agents, such as being invisible (see Pyysiäinen 2009). God concepts are natural {rather than unnatural} in the sense that to acquire, recall and pass them on to others does not take much time or effort, not to mention explicit instruction. They are cognitively 'cheap' because they correspond to pre-existing 'slots' in our mental architecture. An important part of this architecture is formed by cognitive mechanisms for representing agency. These mechanisms are triggered by minimal cues from the environment; a vague feeling of presence can, then, continue even when no agent is perceived (Guthrie 1993; Lawson and McCauley 1990; Atran 2002; Barrett 2004; Boyer 1994, 2001; Pyysiäinen 2009).

Their intuitive elements notwithstanding, supernatural agents are not represented as totally natural. The violations of intuitive expectations make them counterintuitive. However, counterintuitiveness does not mean that religious concepts were 'strange, inexplicable, funny' and so forth (Boyer 2001: 65). 'Counterintuitive' is not the same as 'unreal' (Boyer 1998: 881). Thus, Lawson and McCauley (1990) write in the dedication to their book that religion is 'neither a force to be feared nor a dogma to be embraced but simply a way of life'. Religion is natural [rather than unnatural] in the sense that it is not merely an accidental error or something forced on people from outside.

The naturalness of religion springs from the naturalness of an early developing intuitive ontology, a tendency to assign entities to general categories such as objects, plants and animals, events, substances, and personal agents (Boyer 1994, 2001; Barrett 2004; Bloom 2004). Religious concepts are construed either by adding to an entity one property picked from another category or by deleting one such property that would have been intuitively expected in the category in question.

Minimal counterintuitiveness makes a concept or belief at once salient and memorable, while its intuitive aspects make it easy to process mentally. Such *cognitively optimal* representations are good candidates for becoming widespread within and across cultures (Boyer 2001: 85–7; Barrett and Nyhof 2001; Boyer and Ramble 2001). The idea of a statue that hears prayers, for example, violates the tacit and intuitive expectation that artifacts do not have mentality. A statue that hears prayers *from afar* involves two violations and thus is cognitively more costly; therefore it may not be passed on to others without being simplified (Boyer 2001: 85–7).

Counterintuitiveness also does not mean that the believers in question would feel their beliefs to be unnatural. Quite the contrary; they are felt to be natural and self-evident because people have become routinized in using them as premises in reasoning. The beliefs of other traditions, however, are often regarded as weird, funny and even wicked. That cognitively optimal representations are recalled better in a laboratory context is a robust finding but it comes from studies using fictional examples. There is no experimental evidence to support the assumption that people's actual supernatural agent concepts also fit this model (Shtulman 2008: 1123). In Shtulman's study, subjects rated the likelihood with which nine human properties could be coherently attributed to fictional and religious supernatural agents. Fictional agents were anthropomorphized more than religious agents, and both were anthropomorphized more in the domain of psychological properties as compared to biological and physical. Shtulman argues that there is little evidence that people actually represent supernatural agents as human agents plus or minus one counterintuitive property. Instead, there seems to be more variation in what kinds of properties are included or blocked in each case (Shtulman 2008). Also, Day (2007: 60) argues that in reality religious concepts are hardly confined to cognitively optimal ones only. So far the cognitive optimum theory is supported mostly by anecdotal evidence (but see Barrett et al. 2009).

That religion is natural {rather than cultural} means that religious ideas and behaviours are not merely learned from culture ('whatever is in the air') but are widespread because there is something in human nature that immediately makes some ideas more plausible and easier to acquire than some others. Human mental structures with a biological basis canalize the spread of cultural traditions. Not only are religious ideas more 'contagious' than nonreligious ideas; also some religious ideas are more contagious than some other religious ideas (Boyer 1994; Atran 2002).

Counterintuitive representations with more than one violation are difficult to recall and to use as premises in reasoning, whereas purely intuitive representations are not salient enough to be remembered and effectively propagated. Boyer's advice for religious proselytization thus is to 'avoid bombarding people with cogent and coherent arguments for particular metaphysical claims and to provide them instead with many occasions where the claims in question can be used to produce relevant interpretations of particular situations' (Boyer 2001: 317). 'Metaphysical "religions" that will not dirty their hands with such human purposes and concerns are as marketable as a car without an engine' (Boyer 2001: 321). Theological doctrines are cognitively costly and cognitively costly representations are at a disadvantage in cultural selection; they are either ignored or will be transformed into simpler forms

(Sperber 1996; Pyysiäinen 2010). Sperber and Wilson's (1986) relevance theory thus yields the following predictions:

(a) When the processing costs of two interpretations are equivalent, an inferentially richer interpretation is favoured.
(b) When the inferential potential is the same, the less costly interpretation is favoured (Boyer 2003: 352).

II. Some critiques of naturalism

The cognitive science of religion has repeatedly been challenged by those who argue that religion can only be properly studied when supernatural claims are taken seriously. As Michael Ruse (2006) puts it, '[…] a degree of empathy is needed, and it is this that is missing [in Daniel Dennett's book]. Unless you have some sense of what fires people up, you are never going to reach them or have any hope of shifting their beliefs' (as if cognitive scientists would like to change people's beliefs; but cf. Ruse 2010).

Paul J. Griffiths (2002), for his part, criticizes Boyer's book on the grounds that Boyer has explained religion 'away'. Griffiths obviously – and quite incorrectly – assumes that Boyer's evolutionary explanation of religious behaviour is (only) meant as a tool for criticizing religion. After such misconstrual of Boyer's position, Griffiths rushes to point out that from explaining the unconscious motives underlying human action 'it by no means follows that the reasons that Catholics give for why they go to the Mass are automatically false' (p. 54). Yet, in Griffiths's opinion, these two explanations for Mass-going are 'not obviously contradictory' (p. 56). As the fact that some ideas are the (by-)products of evolution does not in itself make these ideas false, Boyer 'fails to establish the unacceptability of religious people's explanations of their religion …' (p. 56).

Yet Boyer never says that he aims to 'establish the unacceptability of religious people's explanations'. All he tries to show is that in many cases the reasons people give for their choices, decisions and actions are *post hoc* rationalizations and that our behaviour is by and large driven by unconscious intuitions. As any psychologist knows, this is true of all forms of human behaviour, not only religion (see Pyysiäinen 2009: 189–92). Accepting this need not involve any attempt to change people's reflective beliefs. It is a purely scientific observation about human cognition and behaviour.

Thus, to say that one's religious behaviour is made possible by mental mechanisms beyond conscious access is not a metaphysical statement about religious truth. However, Griffiths himself does think that 'it may be that God's act and our response to it suffices to establish Mass-going as an enduring social practice' (p. 56). This could only be proven wrong by showing it to be wrong 'in its own terms', not merely by providing an alternative explanation (p. 56).

But Boyer's aim never was to show the unacceptability of religious claims; his sole aim is to provide neuroscientific and cognitive scientific explanations of human behaviour. It is therefore irrelevant to claim that there might be an alternative, nonscientific explanation. Yet Griffiths is actually saying that religion (and not only God) should be supernaturally explained. This is the kind of position I called eccentric: religious behaviour is scientifically explained by referring to God as a cause. It is and will not be possible to do any kind of behavioural science along such lines.

If, however, Griffiths only wants to say that neuroscientific explanations of human behaviour cannot establish the non-existence of God, there is no disagreement between him and Boyer. Boyer explicitly says that he is not arguing about the existence of God. Griffiths, however, does not make it clear which way he wants to have it, that scientific and religious explanations can coexist, or that they compete. In another review, he does say that a scientific discourse on religion that makes no explicit or implicit claims about the existence of supernatural agents is an illusion, though. Therefore, 'everything is theology' (Griffiths 1998: 48).

III. Religion and science

It is not possible to refute or even criticize Griffiths's last thesis because everything the critic says can immediately be used against him or her, and thus to apparently reaffirm Griffiths's position, much as is the case with psychoanalytical theory. A milder and more common form of apology only aims at a peaceful coexistence of the two 'nonoverlapping magisteria' religion and science (Gould 1997). This may seem like a relatively easy task as long as we talk about science and religion as object-like abstract entities, without going into the details (Boyer 2001: 320). Geneticist Francis Collins (2007: 6), for instance, writes that there still is 'the possibility of a richly satisfying harmony between the scientific and spiritual worldviews'. In his view, there is 'no conflict in being a rigorous scientist and a person who believes in a God who takes a personal interest in each one of us'. This is because the domain of science is to explore nature, while 'God's domain is in the spiritual world, a realm not possible to explore with the tools and language of science'.

I agree that there may not be any 'conflict in being a rigorous scientist and a person who believes in a God', but this is not the issue; the debate rather is about science and religion as ways of knowing. Yet, and without pushing the argument too far, being scientific is a property of theories and methods, whereas religiousness is a property of persons. A scientist can be religious but the theories and methods he or she uses are scientific. They cannot be religious, although a religious person may view them in the context of religion. This makes the question of whether science and religion are compatible rather opaque.

Thus, when we want to explore whether science and religion are compatible or not, the proper way of proceeding is to focus on specific claims that might involve a conflict between science and religion, not on the personalities of scientists. Also, arguing about 'religion' and 'science' as abstractions hardly leads to more than what was known (or believed) from the beginning. To avoid this, one should rather ask *what* religion and *which* science, and to focus on specific beliefs and facts or hypotheses. However, I am afraid that we can only go as far as to show that there are scientific and religious claims that contradict each other and other scientific and religious claims that, perhaps, do not. Thus, the claim that 'science' and 'religion' are or are not compatible can make us blind to variation within these two categories.

Science has thus far described the natural world better than religion has done. As Boyer (2001: 320) puts it, 'In every instance where the Church has tried to offer its own description of what happens in the world *and* there was some scientific alternative on the very same topic, the latter has proved better. Every battle has been lost and conclusively so.' Moreover, many religious beliefs concerning God have also become problematic with the advance of science. Yet it still is possible to argue that God is somehow 'behind' everything, but then all causal links between God and the natural world seem to disappear.

In the background is the obvious fact that before the rise of natural science there was no real alternative for myth and religion (Young and Strode 2009: 33–4). Now that science has shown its promise, religious beliefs have an alternative, and conflict with religion has become inevitable (see Pyysiäinen 2009: 107–12). We now know, for example, that the universe is not 6,000 years old; it was not created in 6 days; the sun does not move around the earth; humans descend from earlier forms of life; and so forth. That our own galaxy is only one among over 100 billion others was realized only a hundred years ago.

Yet millions of laypeople and theologians still think that in many questions religion and science compete with each other and that science is a threat to religion (see Edis 2008). Physicist Stephen Unwin has even calculated that God exists with the probability of .67. He assumes that the a priori probability of God's existence is .50, assigns probabilities to various pieces of evidence for God's existence, and then uses the Bayesian theorem to count the probability of God's existence in the light of the evidence (Unwin 2003).

However, the doctrine of two magisteria says that science is not any kind of threat to religion because scientific arguments and evidence can say nothing about the realm of values and meaning. Yet it may not always be easy to see whether this is an empirical observation or a conceptual necessity. Perhaps the most uncompromising formulation of this doctrine is *fideism* inspired by Wittgenstein's later philosophy, especially his ideas of 'forms of life' and of the inaccessibility of semantics. In this view, religious language is autonomous in relation to science (but not necessarily in relation to other non-religious domains) and it does not presuppose any specific non-religious ontology. Religious concepts and beliefs do not refer beyond themselves; to know how to use the word 'God' is to know God (Phillips 1995a, 1995b, 2000).

This is only one view among many in the philosophy of religion, but it and its parallels have had an influence beyond the Academy (see Taliaferro and Griffiths 2003; Stump and Murray 1999; Yandell 1999). Many liberal-minded theologians without any explicit commitment to philosophical theories are prone to defend religion with arguments that come more or less close to fideism (see Pyysiäinen 2009: 114–36).

Although the advancement of the natural sciences has prompted the reinterpretation of religious beliefs, non-literal interpretation of Scripture is not a completely new phenomenon. The allegorical method of interpreting the Bible was born in Antiquity and the theory of two truths was further developed in Arabian Aristotelianism, for example (see Wolfson 1961; Gauthier 1948). Clement of Alexandria (c.150–c.215) argued that the 'faith of the simple' (*fides simpliciorum*) differed from that of the wise. According to him, literalism arose from intellectual deficiency and spiritual laziness. Without the guiding hand of the spiritually more advanced, literalists might easily have brought the whole of Christianity into peril. As God naturally foresaw this, he hid the allegorical sense from the multitude and gave them the literal sense of the Scripture instead, reserving the allegorical interpretation for the spiritually more advanced only (af Hällström 1984; see Charlesworth 1972).

Medieval scholasticism brought along new subtle debates on whether God can be described in human language literally, only through analogies, or only negatively (see Pyysiäinen 2009: 107–12). In modern discussion, we can distinguish the following alternatives:

1   Religious language describes God directly and in a literal sense.
2   Religious language is analogical but yet literally refers to God.
3   Religious language is non-referential and God only exists in this language.
4   Religious language is only metaphorical
5   Religious language is meaningless nonsense.

The first option immediately leads to a conflict with science, while (2)–(4) are attempts at solving the conflict, and (5) is a counter-reaction to (1). (3) represents fideism which differs from (4) in that in fideism religious language need not be metaphorical as it does not refer to anything outside of itself. Metaphors, for their part, are based on comparison: something is likened to something else.

In its strongest form, (4) claims that we can *only* talk about God metaphorically and that all claims about God are metaphorical (see McFague 1982). Metaphorical views of religious language often lack a theory that indicates how these metaphors should be understood. To the extent that God cannot be literally described there is no way of fixing the reference of the metaphors describing 'God'. The idea of a word that can only be used metaphorically means that 'anything goes': consequently, we have no idea what we are talking about when we talk about God. Although metaphorical theories were introduced to avoid anthropomorphism, they may actually reaffirm it in seeking to describe God only by drawing from human experience. God is the King much as human kings are kings, although in some more 'purified' (metaphorical) sense of the concept. But it is also possible to argue that 'God is the King' in a quite literal sense, and that the word 'king' is a metaphor only when applied to human kings. This was the view of Thomas Aquinas and Karl Barth, for example (White 2010: 3, 183–5).

(2) is an attempt at solving this problem. It introduces a way of using human language to speak about God and to make claims that are literally true of God, while yet respecting the fundamental difference between God and humans (White 2010: 183). This view is based on Aristotle's concept of analogical relationships which he introduced to make it possible to compare entities that belong to different

categories and are incapable of being directly compared. One situation could then be used as a model for another. By analogy is here meant a relationship in which A is to B as C is to D. Within mathematics, this formula requires that A and B are of the same kind, whereas in non-mathematical applications it is typically only A and C that are required to be of the same kind (White 2010: 8, 19, 25, 48).

According to Aristotle, there are two ways of comparing things: in a direct comparison, one notes common properties of two things, whereas in indirect comparison one introduces a third and fourth term, irrespective of whether the two things have significant common properties. Only indirect comparison can yield genuinely new insights. Analogies are important because they allow us to compare things that are too remote for direct comparison to be possible. We can compare things that are different in kind, without violating the fact that they are different. Thus, analogy seems to offer a way of comparing God and humans without violating the huge difference between them. Note also that, for Aristotle, analogies and metaphors are not the same thing; instead, successful metaphors are based on analogies (White 2010: 51–2, 69).

To avoid anthropomorphism, one does not need to get rid of a certain vocabulary but only to be careful in how one interprets and understands this vocabulary. Roger White sympathizes with Aquinas and Barth, who argued that we can only compare humans to God, not God to humans, and that the primary and proper meanings of the words we use in religious language is in their application to God. The meaningfulness of religious language is thereby guaranteed, but with the price that the users of that language seem to be incapable of knowing what the meaning is (White 2010: 186–8).

Philosophical reasoning and taking science seriously have forced theologians to retreat into this kind of position. In accepting the inevitable, they have made the necessary into a virtue: although science has pushed God farther and farther away from empirical reality, this is not merely an inconvenient side-effect of scientific progress but actually the greatest theological achievement ever. Only now do we realize how great God truly is (e.g. Dowd 2009). Science has actually done a favour to religion. Big bang cosmology and evolutionary theory show us how marvellous God's creation really is. He is still behind everything that happens. When evolutionary theory explains how life has developed, this is only an explication of how God's creation works. Some call this 'theistic evolution' (Collins 2007: 199–211; cf. Edis 2008: 84–8).

Theistic evolution differs from creationism in that it accepts evolution as a fact but places God somehow behind it. How exactly God is supposed to work behind the scenes is left totally unexplained. Creationism, for its part, denies evolution and describes God's work as a direct creation of the different species. Yet also in this case it is left unexplained how and by what mechanism such creation has actually happened. No mechanism whatsoever is described. The difference between theistic evolution and creationism is not so much in how God is understood as in what role is left for evolutionary theory.

Interestingly, when Collins dispels God from the immediate mechanisms of evolution, he yet reserves a place for creationism in the field of physics. He, for example, argues that '(o)nce evolution got under way, no special supernatural intervention was required'. But, as the properties of the universe 'appear to have been precisely tuned for life', it seems that the origin of life can only be explained by postulating God (Collins 2007: 200–1). But, in what sense does postulating God *explain* the origin of the universe and life? Surely creation is not a scientific explanation as it does not describe any mechanism through which the supposed creation would have taken place. This is rather a question of a religiously educated person being amazed about the wonderful phenomenon of intelligent life, and then linking this amazement with prior beliefs about God. God as creator is not a mechanical explanation but an 'existential truth' (cf. Bering 2003).

From the scientific point of view, there is no necessary relationship between God and cosmology. First, even if the universe were 'fine-tuned' for life to appear (and not the other way around), there is no reason why this should be the work of the Judeo-Christian God, or a god of any sort. Second, arguments for fine-tuning itself fail in the way the underlying physics is understood and probabilistic reasoning used (Ikeda and Jefferys 2006; Stenger 2009: 94–7, 2011; see Edis 2008: 55–88; Sober 2002). Carbon-based life as we know it is only one possibility, for example (Stenger 2007: 149–51). It is not the case that all the six physical 'constants' necessary for life (Rees 2000) are independent of each other; any variation in one of them would also mean variation in others. Only four parameters are needed to specify the broad features of life *as it exists today on Earth*: the masses of the electron and proton and the current strengths of the electromagnetic and strong interactions (Stenger 2007: 148). Yet, Collins argues that God 'created the universe and established natural laws that govern it'. He 'chose the elegant mechanism of evolution' to create life. 'This view is entirely compatible with everything that science teaches us about the natural world.' Yes, because it is empty of all factual meaning.

Such compatibility thus comes only at the price of cognitive relevance: a God who is compatible with scientific cosmology and so forth is so abstract that it is no longer possible to make relevant inferences from this concept in everyday life. First, God cannot be said to have existed before the big bang because in none of the various views in physical cosmology today is the big bang a special point lying ready, as it were, for the attachment of a supernatural cause. Either time emerged together with the universe, or it extends backwards infinitely (see Edis 2002; Stenger 2006, 2009). Thus, Collins's view is not, after all, 'entirely plausible, intellectually satisfying, and logically consistent' (Collins 2007: 200), unless it can be shown how creation actually happened: that is, what it was that God did, how he did it and how exactly this kind of religious argument completes a purely physical description.

Our universe emerged some 13.7 billion years ago. There was an expansion for a very short period of time, that is, the so-called Planck epoch that lasted for 0–10^{-43} seconds. The big bang started at the time of 10^{-43} and lasted to 10^{-32} seconds. Yet we know precious little about anything before the Planck time. But, during the first moments, complete entropy prevailed, although the amount of entropy was still small. Then, at about 10^{-6} seconds, quarks and gluons combined to form baryons such as protons and neutrons.

After this, the total entropy of the universe has grown, according to the laws of thermodynamics. On Earth, there is temporary order because of the energy provided by the sun. Yet the total entropy of the system formed by sun and Earth keeps growing. There is now larger entropy in the universe than in the beginning, because the amount of greatest possible entropy has grown. Contrary to some creationist opinions, the second law of thermodynamics does not make evolution impossible, because order is only temporary (Edis 2002: 67–9, 87–90). When evolving organisms get better and better adapted to their environment this actually increases entropy (Kaila and Annila 2008). Evolution thus works in accordance with the second law of thermodynamics, which says that the entropy of an isolated macroscopic system never decreases.

Thus, Collins's argument is not entirely intellectually satisfying. It may have existential meaning, but it lacks cognitive content that would be both informative and compatible with science. Scientific descriptions of reality, for their part, are intellectually satisfying and complete without God: adding a few religious concepts here and there leaves everything as it was. As physicist Taner Edis (2002: 74) puts it, 'when divine actions become indistinguishable from chance, theology becomes content-free verbal fog'. What religion can add here is an emotionally more satisfying view of the world, to the extent that one is religious from the beginning.

Another problem is that, although the idea of God could be made completely immune against all scientific criticism, it would then be so abstract that no practical inferences can be made from it. The price of getting rid of anthropomorphism is the lost relevance of religious concepts and beliefs: a completely un-humanlike god is either incomprehensible or lacks precisely those elements that make religion important (see Ferré 1984; Barrett and Keil 1996; Barrett 1998).

IV. Conclusion

Religion is natural in at least three different senses: it is not supernatural, unnatural or merely 'cultural'. The first contrast is absolute: religion is not at all supernatural. The latter two are relative in the sense that religion is partly unnatural and partly cultural. Cognitively costly forms of religion are unnatural in the sense that they cannot emerge through spontaneous triggering alone but rather require time, effort and various kinds of external memory stores (books, etc.). They are in constant danger of being transformed back into natural religion. This is because of the relevance principle, according to which people prefer an inferentially richer interpretation when two interpretations have the same cognitive cost. Conversely, when the inferential potential of two interpretations is the same, people will prefer the less costly interpretation. Religion is partly cultural and partly natural in the sense that input coming from cultural environment shapes one's religiosity while at the same time human mental architecture shapes how this input is selected and processed.

An important part of how the mind works is how we assign entities into ontological categories. Boyer's idea of intuitive ontology and its counterintuitive violations resembles Aristotle's view of categories and analogies as a way to generalize across categories, although Aristotle's ten categories are different from Boyer's ontological categories. Aristotle may be said to have systematized and elaborated folk intuitions concerning categories through philosophical reflection, whereas Boyer leans on experimental evidence concerning how humans reason in the domains of naïve physics, folk biology, and folk psychology as well as sociology.

Boyer adopted the adjective 'counterintuitive' to describe any attribute that is either borrowed from an alien category or is denied to an entity that is intuitively expected to have it. Entities in different categories do have some common attributes in the sense that, for example, personal agents are also living kinds and solid objects (but not vice versa). As an experimental cognitive scientist, Boyer is interested in explaining how humans reason, not in the metaphysical correctness of this reasoning. The opposite is true of Aristotle, who thought that it was analogies that made it possible to validly generalize across categories.

Boyer's model has raised some questions related to this. Bradley Franks (2003), for example, argues that 'God' is not necessarily represented as a (super)human minus a physical body. It might as well be that 'God' forms a category of its own. Second, Boyer's model requires that religious concepts are not metaphors or similes; they are understood literally. In practice it is not always clear whether we are dealing with literally understood beliefs or with metaphors. Counterintuitiveness is a property of concepts or representations of real entities.

From Aristotle's philosophical point of view, the question is whether counterintuitive representations depict reality correctly or incorrectly. Cognitive scientists of religion have not been interested in this issue; as behavioural and cognitive scientists they have not been concerned about such metaphysical questions. However, a theologian or a philosopher of religion asks whether counterintuitive representations refer to a real God (see White 2010). If they do not literally refer, they could still be analogies.

When such scholars as Boyer, and Stewart Guthrie (1993) argue that God is mentally represented as a human plus or minus something, they follow a very old tradition of interpreting religion as based on anthropomorphizing (see Guthrie 1980). Human agency is the starting point; nonhuman agency is then understood as more or less humanlike by projecting human features and properties to it (see Ferré 1984). Theologians such as Aquinas and Barth took the opposite view and theomorphized humanity (see White 2010: 73–103, 137–71). In religious language, the primary or proper meanings of words are in their application to God; the fact that God seems to have human properties results from the fact that we are accustomed to apply divine characteristics to humans metaphorically.

It is also possible to try to approach the issue empirically, as Justin Barrett and colleagues have done in numerous publications. They draw the clear conclusion: 'The human agency hypothesis is false' (Barrett et al. 2001: 60), that is, God is not represented as a (super)human minus a physical body. Drawing from empirical experiments and literature in developmental psychology, Barrett argues that the Piagetian idea of the child's anthropomorphic God becoming more and more abstract with the child's cognitive development is misguided. How God is represented depends on the situation; on the one hand children actually seem to be capable of understanding God in quite abstract terms; on the other hand, adults often anthropomorphize God under certain circumstance (Barrett 2001, 1998: 617; Barrett et al. 2001).

We know from developmental psychology that for children under four or five the mind is like a copy machine: whatever is the case in external reality is directly reflected in mind. From the child's point of view, all knowledge is interpersonal; the child assumes that whatever he or she knows is also known by all others. In a typical experiment, a child is shown a cracker box and asked what is in the closed box. The child then says: 'Crackers'. The experimenter now opens the box and shows that there are rocks inside. When the experimenter then asks what the child first thought was in the box, children under four or five say, 'Rocks'. They cannot understand that there was a moment when they did not know what they now know. When at this point asked what mother would believe is in the box, the child's answer is 'rocks'. As the approximately three year old child now knows that there are rocks in the closed box, he or she thinks that everybody knows what he or she now knows, including himself or herself a moment ago. This is all because children under five do not understand that the mind is a representational device and that people may act on the basis of false beliefs (Perner 1993; Bloom and German 2000; see Pyysiäinen 2009: 14–16).

This inability derives from the fact that children under five are incapable of understanding metarepresentation (Stone 2005). By metarepresentation is meant the representation of representations or beliefs about beliefs. In order to understand that somebody acts on the basis of false beliefs one has to metarepresent this person's beliefs by embedding them in one's own beliefs, as in 'I believe that "she believes that there are crackers in the box"'. 'She believes' here differentiates another's belief from one's own. I can have the belief 'there are crackers in the box' in my mind without it necessarily being my belief, because as a metarepresentation it is 'insulated' from my own beliefs. If the capacity of metarepresentation is lost, as in schizophrenia, one is no longer capable of distinguishing between one's own and others' beliefs (Corcoran et al. 1995; Sperber 2000; Pyysiäinen 2004: 72–7; see Coltheart et al. 2007).

Barrett and colleagues have constructed several experiments on the basis of this kind of knowledge to explore how children from Christian families understand God. When asked what God, mother, best friend and so forth would think is in the closed box, children under five assumed that God would know there were rocks in the box (because they themselves knew that there were rocks in the box). Around the fourth year, they begin to understand that mother, other humans and even some animals would be fooled by the appearance of the box and thus believe that there were crackers inside. God, however, would know better. In another experiment children had to say whether different sorts of agents would know that there is a red block in a dark box. The result was the same: God, and only God, is omniscient (Barrett et al. 2001; Knight et al. 2004; Richert and Barrett 2005).

On the basis of these studies, Barrett draws the conclusion that children under five are by no means anthropomorphists; instead, they are capable of representing

God as an omniscient being. The developing child's first concept of mind is universal and undifferentiated, and is only gradually split into many different minds that are insulated from each other. Here Barrett comes close to Aquinas's and Barth's theomorphism. As young children cannot understand the role of false beliefs in driving behaviour, they *seem* to have grasped the theological idea of omniscience (Barrett et al. [2001: 58] tellingly write that children reason about God 'more accurately'). Yet they simply attribute to God all knowledge they themselves have. A more parsimonious interpretation of this is that the children are not yet capable of metarepresentation and do not understand that false beliefs can motivate action.

Barrett, however, seems to think that three to five year old children hit upon the 'correct' interpretation, after all; it does not matter that the cause of their belief is their incapacity to understand false belief. The child's first concept of God is more or less theologically correct, but may be lost or radically modified later on (cf. Barrett and Keil 1996). The children's God is not a (super)human minus physical body; on the contrary, he is a unique kind of mind, something primary, a category of his own and children reason about him differently from other agents (Barrett et al. 2001). However, this result is somewhat at odds with Barrett and Keil's (1996) studies showing that in fast online cognition adults tend to make inferences from a more anthropomorphic concept of God than that which they explicit say they believe in.

A more abstract concept of God has been reinforced by advances in scientific cosmology, evolutionary theory and so forth. In saying that the proof of deism is 'largely a problem in astrophysics', Edward Wilson (1998: 241) gives expression to the scientific challenge to religion. Attempts to understand God so that conflict with science can be avoided has led to a situation where theologians and ministers preach one kind of God and defend against scientific criticism quite another kind of God. This is understandable because the science-inspired concept of God who is forever 'behind' everything is about as useful as a car without an engine, as Boyer put it. Such a God is difficult to understand and is cognitively costly; therefore people rather think of God as, for example, 'our father in heaven', which allows for relevant inferences in everyday contexts.

Where science drives liberal theology, folk psychology drives religion. This process draws theology and lived religion ever more apart from each other. It also is possible for a defender of faith to 'punish' non-believers by counter-criticism and also to punish those who refuse to punish, without necessarily being genuinely committed oneself (Pyysiäinen 2010; see Henrich and Henrich 2007: 64–7). The situation is somewhat different among such groups as North American evangel-icals, however. It has been argued that 'at a deeper level' more fundamentalist believers can be more positive toward science than liberals. They respect science too much to be willing to confine it only to religiously harmless domains. Debates between them and nonbelievers tend to focus on claims of fact, whereas debates between liberal believers and their critics focus on meaning. From the liberals' point of view, both fundamentalists and nonbelievers have a superficial conception of spirituality (Edis 2008: 92).

Let me finally put on my fortuneteller's hat and make a prediction. It is loosely based on the principle that when people are given equal opportunities, the winners will be those who are inherently stronger, more intelligent, more creative and so forth. Thus, when we join the liberals and try to maintain a neat division of labour between religion and science, and to give each equal opportunities, science tends to win and religion to lose. As Boyer pointed out, religion has 'lost every battle' when it comes to accurately describing, not to mention explaining, natural phenomena. Such is the power of science.

Believers of a more fundamentalist stripe do not want to accept this and try to bring religion and science back together. In this case, science is in danger of losing its autonomy with faith providing constraints on what is acceptable in science (see Stenger 2009: 52, 56, 74, 98–9). Time will tell whether the inherent potential of science is strong enough to ensure its autonomy in the future. This does not necessarily have to mean that religion automatically loses, however. Yet open and critical debate is the only way forward. I have tried to show how the cognitive science of religion can offer theoretical concepts and a model that can be used in evaluating the mutual compatibility of religion and science, although the cognitive science of religion as such is not normative.

Acknowledgements

I would like to thank Taner Edis and Gereon Wolters for comments on an earlier draft, as well as the numerous participants of the ESSSAT conference in Edinburgh, for their comments on my talk on which this completely rewritten chapter is based. Thanks also to Victor Stenger for letting me read his forthcoming book in manuscript

References

Atran, S. (2002), *In Gods we Trust: The Evolutionary Landscape of Religion.* New York, NY: Oxford University Press.
Barrett, J. L. 1998, 'Cognitive constraints on Hindu concepts of the divine'. *Journal for the Scientific Study of Religion, 37*, 608–19.
—(2001), 'Do children experience God as adults do?' In J. Andresen (ed.), *Religion in Mind* Cambridge: Cambridge University Press, pp. 173–90.
—(2004), *Why Would Anyone Believe in God?* Walnut Creek, CA: AltaMira Press.
Barrett, J. L., E. R. Burdett and T. J. Porter (2009), 'Counterintuitiveness in folktales: finding the cognitive optimum'. *Journal of Cognition and Culture, 9* (3–4), 271–87.
Barrett, J. L. and F. Keil (1996), 'Conceptualizing a nonnatural entity: anthropomorphism in God concepts'. *Cognitive Psychology, 31*, 219–47.
Barrett, J. L. and M. A. Nyhof (2001), 'Spreading non-natural concepts: the role of intuitive conceptual structures in memory and transmission of cultural materials'. *Journal of Cognition and Culture, 1* (1), 69–100.

Barrett, J. L., R. A. Richert and A. Driesenga (2001), 'God's beliefs versus mother's: the development of nonhuman agent concepts'. *Child Development, 72* (1), 50–65.

Bering, J. M. (2003), 'Towards a cognitive theory of existential meaning'. *New Ideas in Psychology, 21,* 101–20.

Bloom, P. (2004), *Descartes' Baby: How the Science of Child Development Explains What Makes us Human.* New York, NY: Basic Books.

Bloom, P. and T. P. German (2000), 'Two reasons to abandon the false belief task as a test of theory of mind'. *Cognition, 77,* B25–B31.

Boyer, P. (1994), *The Naturalness of Religious Ideas: A Cognitive Theory of Religion.* Berkeley, CA: University of California Press.

—(1998), 'Cognitive tracks of cultural inheritance: how evolved intuitive ontology governs cultural transmission'. *American Anthropologist, 100* (4), 876–89.

—(2001), *Religion Explained: The Evolutionary Origins of Religious Thought.* New York, NY: Basic Books.

—(2003), 'Science, erudition and relevant connections'. *Journal of Cognition and Culture, 3* (4), 344–58.

—(2005), 'A reductionistic model of distinct modes of religious transmission'. In H. Whitehouse and R. N. McCauley (eds), *Mind and Religion: Psychological and Cognitive Foundations of Religiosity.* Walnut Creek, CA: AltaMira Press, pp. 3–29.

Boyer, P. and C. Ramble (2001), 'Cognitive templates for religious concepts: cross-cultural evidence for recall of counterintuitive representations'. *Cognitive Science, 25* (4), 535–64.

Charlesworth, M. J. (1972), *Philosophy of Religion: The Historic Approaches.* London: Macmillan.

Collins, F. S. (2007), *The Language of God: A Scientist Presents Evidence for Belief.* London: Pocket Books.

Coltheart, M., R. Langdon and R. McKay (2007), 'Schizophrenia and mono-thematic delusions'. *Schizophrenia Bulletin, 33* (3), 642–7.

Corcoran, R., G. Merver and C. D. Frith (1995), 'Schizophrenia, symptomatology and social inference: investigating "theory of mind" in people with schizophrenia'. *Schizophrenia Research, 17,* 5–13.

Day, M. (2007), 'Let's be realistic: evolutionary complexity, epistemic probabilism, and the cognitive science of religion'. *Harvard Theological Review, 100* (1), 47–64.

Dowd, M. (2009), *Thank God for Evolution: How the Marriage of Science and Religion will Transform your Life and our World.* New York, NY: Plume.

Edis, T. (2002), *The Ghost in the Universe: God in Light of Modern Science.* Amherst, NY: Prometheus Books.

—(2008 [2006]), *Science and Nonbelief.* Amherst, NY: Prometheus Books.

Ferré, F. (1984), 'In praise of anthropomorphism'. *International Journal for the Philosophy of Religion, 16,* 203–12.

Franks, B. (2003), 'The nature of unnaturalness in religious representations: negation and concept combination'. *Journal of Cognition and Culture, 3* (1), 41–68.

Garfinkel, A. (1981), *Forms of Explanation.* New Haven, CT: Yale University Press.

Gauthier, L. (1948), *Ibn Rochd (Avërroes).* Paris: unknown publisher.

Gould, S. J. (1997), 'Nonoverlapping magisteria'. *Natural History, 106*, 16–22.

Griffiths, P. J. (1998), 'Tu quoque. Review of *Manufacturing religion* by Russell T. McCutcheon'. *First Things, 81*, 44–8.

—(2002), 'Faith seeking explanation. Review of *Religion Explained* by Pascal Boyer'. *First Things, 119*, 53–7.

Guthrie, S. E. (1980), 'A cognitive theory of religion'. *Current Anthropology, 21* (2), 181–203.

—(1993), *Faces in the Clouds.* New York, NY: Oxford University Press.

af Hällström, G. (1984), *Fides Simpliciorum According to Origen of Alexandria.* (*Commentationes Humanarum Litterarum*, 76.) Helsinki: Societas Scientiarum Fennica.

Henrich, N. and J. Henrich (2007), *Why Humans Cooperate: A Cultural and Evolutionary Explanation.* Oxford: Oxford University Press.

Ikeda, M. and B. Jefferys (2006), 'The anthropic principle does not support supernaturalism' In M. Martin and R. Monnier (eds), *The Improbability of God.* Amherst, NY: Prometheus Books, pp. 150–66. Available from http://www.talkreason.org/articles/super.cfm

Kaila, V. R. I. and A. Annila (2008), 'Natural selection for least action'. *Proceedings of the Royal Society A.* doi:10.1098/rspa.2008.0178.

Knight, N., P. Sousa, J. L. Barrett and S. Atran (2004), 'Children's attributions of beliefs to humans and God: cross-cultural evidence'. *Cognitive Science, 28*, 117–26.

Lawson, E. T. and R. N. McCauley (1990), *Rethinking Religion: Connecting Cognition and Culture.* Cambridge: Cambridge University Press.

McCauley, R. N. (2000), 'The naturalness of religion and the unnaturalness of science'. In F. C. Keil and R. A. Wilson (eds), *Explanation and Cognition.* Cambridge, MA: MIT Press, pp. 61–85.

McCauley, R. N. and E. T. Lawson, *Bringing Ritual to Mind: Psychological Foundations of Cultural Forms.* Cambridge: Cambridge University Press.

McFague, S. (1982), *Metaphorical Theology: Models of God in Religious Language.* London: SCM Press.

McNamara, P. (2009), *The Neuroscience of Religious Experience.* Cambridge: Cambridge University Press.

Perner, J. (1993 [1991]), *Understanding the Representational Mind.* Cambridge, MA: MIT Press.

Phillips, D. Z. (1995 [1965]), *The Concept of Prayer.* London: Routledge.

—(1995 [1988]), *Faith after Foundationalism.* Boulder, CO: Westview Press.

—(2000), *Recovering Religious Concepts: Closing Epistemic Divides.* London: Macmillan.

Pyysiäinen, I. (2004), *Magic, Miracles, and Religion.* Walnut Creek, CA: AltaMira Press.

—(2009), *Supernatural Agents: Why We Believe in Souls, Gods and Buddhas.* New York, NY: Oxford University Press.

—(2010), 'How religion resists the challenge of science'. *Skeptical Inquirer, 34* (3), 39–41.

Rees, M. J. (2000), *Just Six Numbers: The Deep Forces that Shape the Universe*. New York, NY: Basic Books.

Richert, R. A. and J. L. Barrett (2005), 'Do you see what I see? Young children's assumptions about God's perceptual abilities'. *International Journal for the Psychology of Religion, 15* (4), 283–95.

Ruse, M. (2006), 'A natural history of religion: a Darwinian philosopher turns his attention to the strength of religion in the United States. Review of *Breaking the Spell: Religion as a Natural Phenomenon* by Daniel C. Dennett'. *Nature, 439,* 535. doi:10.1038/439535a.

—(2010), 'The Catholic Church: Why Richard Dawkins was right and I was wrong'. *Huffington Post*, April 10. Available from http://www.huffingtonpost.com/michael-ruse/the-catholic-church-why-r_b_532987.html

Shtulman, A. (2008), 'Variation in the anthropomophization of supernatural beings and its implications for cognitive theories of religion'. *Journal of Experimental Psychology, 34* (5), 1123–38.

Sober, E. (2002), 'Intelligent design and probability reasoning'. *International Journal for the Philosophy of Religion, 52,* 65–80.

Sperber, D. (1996), *Explaining Culture: A Naturalistic Approach*. Oxford: Blackwell.

—(ed.) (2000), *Metarepresentations: A Multidisciplinary Perspective*. Oxford: Oxford University Press.

Sperber, D. and D. Wilson, (1986) *Relevance: Communication and Cognition*. Cambridge, MA: Harvard University Press.

Stark, R. and R. Finke (2000), *Acts of Faith: Explaining the Human Side of Religion*. Berkeley, CA: University of California Press.

Stenger, V. J. (2006), 'A scenario for a natural origin of our universe using a mathematical model based on established physics and cosmology'. *Philo, 92,* 93–102.

—(2007), *God: The Failed Hypothesis*. Amherst, NY: Prometheus Books.

—(2009), *The New Atheism: Taking a Stand for Science and Reason*. Amherst, NY: Prometheus Books.

—(2011), *The Fallacy of Fine-Tuning: How the Universe is Not Designed for Us*. Amherst, NY: Prometheus Books.

Stone, V. (2005), 'Theory of mind and the evolution of social intelligence'. In J. T. Cacioppo, P. S. Visser and C. L. Pickett (eds), *Social Neuroscience: People Thinking About People*. Cambridge, MA: MIT Press.

Stump, E. and M. J. Murray (1999), *Philosophy of Religion: The Big Questions*. Malden, MA: Macmillan.

Taliaferro, Ch. and P. J. Griffiths (2003), *Philosophy Of Religion: An Anthology*. Malden, MA: Blackwell.

Unwin, S. D. (2003), *The Probability of God: A Simple Calculation that Proves the Ultimate Truth*. New York, NY: Crown Forum.

White, R. M. (2010), *Talking about God: The Concept of Analogy and the Problem of Religious Language*. Farnham: Ashgate.

Wilson, E. O. (1998), *Consilience: The Unity of Knowledge*. New York, NY: Knopf.

Wolfson, H. A. (1961), *Religious Philosophy*. Cambridge, MA: Harvard University Press.

Ylikoski, P. (2006), 'The idea of contrastive *explanandum*'. In J. Persson and P. Ylikoski (eds), *Rethinking Explanation*, (*Boston Studies in the Philosophy of Science*, 252.) Dordrecht: Springer, pp. 27–42.

Yandell, K. E. (1999), *Philosophy of Religion: A Contemporary Introduction.* London: Routlege.

Young, M. and P. K. Strode (2009), *Why Evolution Works (and Creationism Fails).* New Brunswick, NJ: Rutgers University Press.

6 Do We Need to Naturalize Religion?

Lluis Oviedo

The most logical and immediate answer to this emphatic question could be: it depends on what we mean by 'naturalizing' and it depends 'for whom'.

Put simply, to 'naturalize' means to give a natural explanation of a phenomenon or an experience, i.e. without resorting to supernatural or mystical events or entities. The claim that religion belongs to the 'natural realm' simply states that living religious experiences have no extraordinary and out-of-this-world characteristics. Religion is in line with many other 'natural' realities or events: falling in love, getting excited about a work of art, wondering about an elegant theory or enjoying the intimacy of friendship.

For many, this is not enough as an explanation; it is like saying: it just happens. On the theological side, the programme in question probably points to the traditional idea of the 'natural capacity for humans to long for God or to be able to receive and understand his revelation'. Such an idea goes back at least to S. Augustine, and has been repeatedly stated in several versions since the Middle Ages. Now, it belongs to what could be called an 'elemental axiom' of fundamental theology: every person is made in such a way that she can understand the basics of the idea of God and all that concerns his revelation.

However, the current naturalistic scientific programmes of explaining religion and showing its structure imply a rather different agenda: since we can explain all aspects of religious behaviour and thinking, we are inclined to reduce it to the mere natural level, and, after showing its hidden mechanisms, we are in a position to control its dynamics and to unveil every mysterious or supernatural aspect of such behaviour or beliefs.

It is useful to pose the question as to whether the current state of research in the different fields trying to explain religion has managed to reach its goal. To put it differently to what extent can a quite satisfactory theory or a set of theories clarify the nature, the structure and the functions of religious experience? Going on, we could further ask in what sense the available knowledge might mean an effective overcoming of religious beliefs and behaviours, or their complete 'naturalization' or 'reduction'. In other words: What is left when science manages to explain in a naturalistic way religious ideas, feelings or behaviours?

Let me first introduce some critical remarks on the current programme of 'explaining religion'. Only when a more nuanced view of the new approaches to religion is attained, will we be able to give further steps in a more constructive endeavour. These will include the broadening of the current scientific programme, in order to avoid forms of un-scientific reductionism; and an openness to interdisciplinary work, especially with the hermeneutical traditions dealing with religion and faith. Only when such an endeavour has been achieved will the scientific study of religion be able to overcome the flaws threatening this important and salutary project. These flaws are often the result of isolation, and hence collaboration and linking to a broader network of social knowledge are the required answers.

I. Who needs religion to be explained?

In recent years, newspapers and weekly journals have paid a significant amount of attention to several research projects aimed at 'explaining religion'. These projects are well-funded, backed both by private and public institutions, and are proposed as means to observe religious experiences better ('under the microscope', explains one informed voice). Their aim is to understand better what is going on, to uncover the 'mystery' of religious belief and practice, to assess their benefits and dangers, and to assign them their most convenient place within the social fabric and within individual minds.

Not everybody seems to be happy about such an enlightened initiative, and not everybody agrees about its convenience and beneficial effects. After all, religious people usually do not need somebody to explain to them what religion is – that is, what and why they believe, and what the social or psychological value of their belief is. To understand this situation better, an analogy could be considered. Suppose that someone tried to describe the meaning of love or aesthetic experience in similar terms. If we limit such studies to those inside well-defined disciplinary boundaries (biology, cognitive science, sociology), it is possible to meaningfully describe the key aspects of how such experiences work in a human mind – their general dynamic of cause and effect, on the given level. But probably there are many reasonable, healthy lovers who would emphatically reject the idea that such studies really grasp the key point of the human realities that scientists partially describe. Neither art nor romance can be entirely understood in terms of iron-clad, material cause-and-effect, and so the scientific approach meets an intrinsically limited application.

Of course, religionists rely on a long-living theological tradition, but that tradition – to my knowledge – has never aimed at 'explaining religion', but rather at improving religious practice and knowledge – for example, correcting wrong moral and spiritual paths, further illuminating the mystery of the believed God, or teaching the believer to love Him more, and better appreciate His works and deeds. Religion did not need to be explained, but awakened, guided and nourished.

Things are quite different now. Well, in reality things started to change some time ago, at least two centuries ago, with the Enlightenment and its many attempts to come to terms with religion, to rationalize it, to render a comprehensive account of its development, its risks and possible benefits. When that history is recalled, a certain feeling of déjà vu comes to mind.

II. Still struggling with religion

It is relatively easy to compose a history of the different waves crashing in modern times against the shores of religious consciousness and its social forms. Reconstructing them could help to understand the possible relationships between cultural and social developments, on the one hand, and philosophical and scientific endeavours, on the other. What makes a given generation of thinkers especially aware of the importance of religion and leads them to focus on researching it? The reasons may be quite clear: since the middle of the eighteenth century the intellectual elite has been engaged in a sort of 'culture war' with religious-backed 'ideologies' and powers. Such kinds of hostilities become less clear in successive times, when Christendom was clearly declining and losing much political and intellectual sway. It is not clear whether the theoretical and 'external' study of religion has been promoted – after the time of the epic culture wars – more by the apparent tendency of religion to 'fade away' and so being threatened with extinction, or more by sudden episodes of religious revival in the modern world. Or is there anything else that could clarify why sometimes the need to know and 'explain' religion better is felt with particular intensity?

Who needs religion to be explained, if religionists are already happy with their theology and spiritual texts? And why should religion be better explained now than, say, 20 years ago? Some explanations may be given to make sense of such enterprises and of the amount of money devoted to that research. First, and perhaps most obviously, the practical discreet claim – because an explicit statement would be politically incorrect – is that religion needs to be tamed. Whether it is the dominant form of Christianity in a given country or a 'new import' from abroad, religion has become a little too wild in recent years, and it is time to ensure that religion will not prompt more troubles. By the same token, we can get the best of religion for civil societies, without risking too much the worst of it, if we are able to control it: to take what is positive, and to discard what is negative. Indeed, this was already a classic ideal of the Enlightenment: religion was linked to wars and destruction, and it needed to be rationalized and tamed. Taking Kant's *Religion Within the Boundaries of Mere Reason* and his *Perpetual Peace* may furnish a glimpse of this not-too-original idea (Kant 1998, 1992). Already in his rational treatment of religion, this prince of the Enlightened Philosophers expected faith mainly to serve moral and social interests. The same story can be attributed to many other philosophers, theologians and social thinkers throughout the nineteenth century, and it has retained great influence up to the present day. So it is not surprising that new attempts will be made to tame religion now, when we can resort to much better and richer means, provided by the development of social and behavioural sciences, in order to explain what religion is and how it works.

The second task of the programmes aimed at 'explaining' and 'naturalizing' religion appears to be to finally uncover its hidden side, to show its shadowy aspects, to reveal its unconscious dimensions, its secret mechanisms. Why is this of interest? Because in this way we can unveil the true nature of religion and, with a better explanation of what seems natural or traditional for human religion, we can finally get rid of alienations or 'false consciousness' and even at last discard some of religion's less healthy structures. Scientific reason can provide an enlightened view of the otherwise most dark and mysterious experiences, covered by human ignorance. Here the references to eighteenth- and nineteenth-century philosophers are so obvious that they do not require further explanation.

The third reason is a modern one, too; it has to do with current efforts to classify, control, order, and test every kind of human and social experience or dimension. This effort has been a modern obsession that has more recently been thoroughly mocked by such critics as Michel Foucault. Modern reason claims to dominate everything; by nature, it is not able to leave religion alone, just as it could not abstain from trying to analyse away sex and madness. It seems that such an aggressive approach to reason cannot help but resent – then and now – any aspect of reality striving to stay outside its reach. From this point of view, 'explaining religion' belongs to the same genre of rational imperialism as every other enterprise of modern reason dealing with 'strange subjects'. The 'will to analyse', as a version of modern 'will to power', or the will to dominate and subdue, emerges patently in the case of religion (Foucault 1970). Indeed, perhaps this is the ultimate, the 'last frontier' to be conquered; but then again, it is not alone; consciousness, for one, certainly remains on the waiting list.

The age of science has extolled and intensified the ideal of 'dominating knowledge'. The perceived power of science thus becomes the pretext for a new wave of efforts aimed at resuming various projects started in the late eighteenth century, and then left unfinished because of lack of means. Now, endowed with better technical tools and better funding, religion and all its strange worlds of transcendence are within our reach, and they can be submitted to a totalizing scientific reason. Even if philosophy – particularly phenomenology – and some human and social sciences have already tried to do the job, now, with the advancement of the 'hard' sciences, things can go much more smoothly, and shed more light on what has been otherwise too 'special' or heterogeneous (Taves 2009).

The fourth way in which to understand this project of naturalizing religion is more subtle. For some refined minds, 'explaining religion' and framing it in a naturalistic pattern is not at all concerned with the weird beliefs some strange people still entertain, but has to do with our need to 'explain ourselves', our consciousness, our social being, our last expectations – and their meaning. We have to do with the most reflexive issues, the ultimate meaning of reality and ourselves, and we are not dealing so much with rituals and codes of transcendence, but with our need to explain everything, to become aware of our possibilities and limita- tions. We are dealing with ultimate reasons for our being here and struggling to keep social bonds and moral codes. Anyone who knows the history of the modern philosophy of religion identifies what lies behind such a reflexive programme. That history unfolds repeatedly as a self-referential exercise seeking to offer ultimate justifications, to give new moral foundations, and to reflect on the cyclic crises of modernity. Religion becomes an excuse, a pretext to launch a radical reflexivity, aimed precisely at accomplishing the modern project of 'secularizing' religion (which is clearly another name for 'explaining' it). However, things often go against the goals of the agents – in another version of 'unintended consequences' – and the reflection aimed at secularizing ends up at recovering or re-instantiating religion, if only as an insurmountable question (Olivetti 1995).

Who needs – again – religion to be explained? Not the believers, of course. You could never pretend that a deaf person could explain to a virtuoso musician the meaning of a symphony, or what music is about. The impaired person cannot teach how things work on that level to the normal perceiver. The conflict between first- and third-person perspectives arises immediately. We cannot get both without some epistemic manoeuvring or integration, some attempt to link one dimension to the other.

Following this path, I consider it important to obtain the best information possible about religion through scientific approaches. Nevertheless, it is convenient to remain aware that such attempts at explaining religion will always be short-sighted if they are not able to connect with more comprehensive or hermeneutical approaches, by which I mean those dealing with the subjective dimension, and those aimed at better understanding the object of religious faith – that is, its theological dimension.

The contrast and tension between scientific and hermeneutic views emerges in a paradoxical way in several new scientific approaches to religion, e.g. the so called 'adaptationist' approach (Sosis and Alcorta 2003; Norenzayan and Shariff 2008). Religion has evolved and expanded because it has served the survival and reproductive interests of old and new human populations. The self-undermining paradox consists in stating the utility of religion, but at the same time refusing to adopt it, or to advise it to be adopted as a positive experience. Some scholars escape the paradox by pointing at the anachronistic character of religious beliefs and practices: they were useful in the past, no longer at the present. Other ways of escape consist in distinguishing social convenience and personal freedom. Everybody should decide whether it is more or less appropriate for him or her to be religious, after each person calculates the balance between the advantages and disadvantages of religion for him or her. But it is obvious that this is not a real escape, as it maintains some level of incoherence between personal perception and social needs, a contrast that a scientist should not tolerate.

Furthermore, some concerns arise about the adequacy of the category 'religion' for the assumed programme of 'explaining religion'. Even if such a modern concept is of any heuristic value (Beyer 2006), it is very unlikely that we could disclose the meaning of 'religion' in general terms, without grappling directly with real, historical religions. After all, the meticulous historical research of Ernst Feil has evidenced the flaws of such a modern construction, aimed rather at keeping religion under control (Feil 2001). Perhaps the time of deism and artificially constructed religion is not yet gone, as new attempts try again to build some kind of 'religion'. It almost seems that a new kind of 'religion' is being created in order for 'religion' to be explained. The negative experiences of some historical efforts at 'constructing religion' *ad hoc* for a time of reason and science – for example, the 'positivist religion' of August Comte – should discourage us from constructing new versions. If anybody wants to 'explain religion' he or she should rather try to explain 'Christianity', 'Islam', 'Buddhism' or 'Hinduism', and even animism and shamanism (Appiah 2009). Otherwise the new programme will end up explaining something that only exists in the minds of scientists, a kind of 'scientific construction' or 'ideal model', but nothing else.

Only by taking into account real religions would it be possible to identify 'common grounds' or 'broadly shared patterns' that might reflect the universal character of religiosity as a human predicament. But, obviously, this is a different story, one more concerned with religion as a specific human trait, and less with religion as a common misrepresentation or a cognitive flaw. As may have already become apparent, considering 'religion' as a 'genus' of the human mind and social constitution, we risk missing the point of real religion and its multiple forms. But to look for universal religious patterns or shared structures may help to stress religion's very human character, deeply rooted in our personal constitution. Similar attempts have been made in cases of language, morality, art and social communication, and all these provide a new universalistic account of the human nature, overcoming the poverty of more relativistic views (Gazzaniga 2005; Hauser 2006; Turner 2006).

By the same token, the scientific study of religion should take into account its most standard forms rather than its weirdest; its most evolved rather than its most primitive; its more balanced, rather than its radical tendencies (Stark and Finke 2000: 1–25). From a methodological point of view, and taking into account the anthropological method of research, we can gain more of a grasp on a cultural phenomenon only when we move to study the extreme forms, or the simplest social structures. This can constitute a starting point, but it should never be taken as a general explanation to be applied to more complex religious realities. The problem is that, with this kind of reduction, part of the explanatory power gets lost. To understand contemporary religious trends, much more than the reductivist method is required.

Taking into account all of these obstacles, I suggest an alternative path, since religion in any case deserves more study and clearer understanding in order to better deal with its challenges and better acknowledge its virtues. This path should try to integrate the more objective-scientific dimension with the more first-person and theological aspects, in order to avoid half-way results, unable to understand religion adequately. I prefer to devote a paragraph to the hermeneutic dimension of the study of religion, and how it should be assumed into a broader vision.

First, the scientific side: the scientific approach should take into account several variables or factors involved in the origin and development of religion. Many of them are identified below; however some are systematically neglected in the current scientific study of religion (the traditional sociological and psychological approaches are presupposed):

- The conscious religious mind and how conscious processes influence religious perception and behaviour; religion as a means of 'awakening' or 'awareness'.
- The developmental dimension, as a religion goes through a process of ontogenetic growth, maturation and/or decline.
- The rational dimension, as religion is influenced by, and exerts influence upon, contemporary standards of rationality.
- The distinct levels of religiosity and religious perception and involvement; the distinct 'religious forms': mystical, ascetic and fraternal (James 1985; Weber 1993).
- The greater or lower involvement of emotions and feelings in different kinds of religious experiences.
- The centrality of language and symbols, not only in ritual and myth, but in the constitution of every religious form.
- The role played by 'external processors': community and social networks, distributed cognition, and shared patterns.
- The systemic character of religion, its function as a way to process information or to solve in an efficient way particular issues of social representation and management (Luhmann 2000).
- The questions related to a possible 'universal religious grammar', such as a shared sense for transcendence and a specific human claim for eternity or wholeness, and how this template is related to the historical religions, in the tradition of the 'comparative study of religion'.
- And, last but not least, the consequences of being religious, as it has been shown that religion makes a difference in the lives of many people.

Religion should be considered as more than just an epiphenomenon, resulting from the hyperactive function of some modules in the human mind (Boyer 2001); or as a way to deal with some survival and reproductive constraints. Religion – if we still want to explain it and not to 'explain it away' – is a much more complex phenomenon, from an objective and scientific point of view, and not only when it appears as a question 'in the first person'. Neglecting the aforementioned factors would result in a poor and biased outcome.

III. Why we cannot get rid of the hermeneutical approach to religion

It is absolutely legitimate to study religion inside an exclusive scientific framework, just as for aesthetic perceptions, feelings of love and other characteristics of human experience, such as consciousness. The question is not whether or how legitimate it is, but how much utility and how much explanatory power can we wield when we apply scientifically oriented methods alone, by which I mean those methods relying on empirical observation, testing processes, explanation of the outcomes inside of a broad accepted theoretical framework and successive processes of verification or falsification. This method requires from its inception a consequent reduction of variables involved in the experience, and has to translate subjective or first-person experiences into specific and clear objective data, corresponding to inter-subjective observations. Its scope is unavoidably very limited, and at most will be able to explain some minor aspects or dimensions of religious experience.

My point is that we can hardly avoid the 'hermeneutic approach' to religion, if we want to understand this kind of experience. Such an approach has to include: traditional theology, the philosophy of religion, and the twentieth-century tradition of anthropology and phenomenology of religion.

There are at least six main objections to the reductive programme. The first is a general one, and concerns the recent criticism levelled against reductionist programmes applied to a related issue: the functioning of the mind. The second problem has to do with the very subjective nature of religious experience, and the harshness of any attempt to translate it into more objective terms. The third problem is related to the high level of complexity of such a process, which involves many variables, and challenges every attempt to account for them all in terms of one coherent model. The fourth problem is the conscious nature of most religious phenomena; they involve processes of language and social exchange, the use of symbols and a high degree of communication, which render unavoidable an extension of the range of observation beyond sheer individual elaboration. The fifth problem concerns the very historical nature of religious ideas and views; they are hardly static, they evolve in time following intricate patterns which challenge the usual simplifications. The last issue recalls the probabilistic status of the so-called 'special sciences', and therefore points to a greater hermeneutic engagement. Each one of these issues deserves a more detailed examination.

1   The entire programme of reductionism has suffered severe damage at the hands of its critics in the field of philosophy of science. Steven Horst (2007) has recently shown how misleading such a programme becomes when applied to attempts to explaining mental processes. He reminds us that the standard philosophy of science has abandoned this programme in recent decades, as scientists and philosophers have become more aware of the so-called 'explanatory gaps' arising in the passages between different levels of reality. Horst states that the reductionist programme still survives in the area of philosophy of mind, unaware of the changes being enacted in other scientific areas. There are many sources of criticism to be conveyed. Davidson's (1970, 1984) philosophy, for example, claims that mental states cannot be reduced to physical or brain states, and that the former require an 'intentional stance' in order to interpret them (the so called 'principle of charity'): 'the mind is unique in its irreducibility', and so it 'requires rational interpretation' (Horst 2007: 97). Horst contends that the realm of the mind is not the only one where monistic reductionism does not apply; the chemical and biological realms are affected by similar limitations. At the same time, social scientists complain about the narrowness of the reductionist programme, and demand approaches able to take into account both the individual and the structural dimension (Sawyer 2005: 230). Of particular interest is the criticism of Horst regarding the application of Ockham's razor to settle questions of

reductionism. The razor theory states that when we can provide a simple explanation of a given phenomenon, we do not need a more complex one. The problem is that we do not have such 'simple explanations' of mental processes in physical terms. At most, we just have hypotheses about how neurological dynamics correlate to mental processes, but not explanations in the true sense. If this is the case, 'scientific explanations' of subjective phenomena should be taken with extreme caution, as their explanatory power is usually very weak. The same criticism applies to the re-introduction of 'naturalistic theories', which is just another name for the reductionist programme. Recent book titles exhibit the discussion between the advocates and critics of the naturalistic approach, a reminder of its much disputed nature (De Caro and Macarthur 2004; Gasser 2007). 'Naturalists claim that natural science provides a complete account of all forms of existence', states the back cover of Gasser's collection; and stated in this way the claim seems somewhat extreme and even arrogant. Some authors have tried to soften such pretensions and sell more 'consumer-friendly' forms of naturalism (Flanagan 2007). Nevertheless, many critics point to the limits of this programme and remind us of the existence of areas, like those belonging to the subjective realm, where this attempt simply does not bear fruit. The critics usually advocate a model of 'conceptual' or 'cognitive pluralism' instead, where the coexistence of various methods and approaches to different levels of reality may be pacifically accepted (Putnam 2004). Of course the issue reaches the core of religious thinking, i.e. the existence of supernatural agents and causes, but the key question is deeper, as it deals with the possibility of extending such an explanatory model beyond the material realm. The 'pluralism' advocated by the critics, as a consequence of some 'disunity of science' (Horst 2007: 127ss), applies clearly to the study of religion, which requires methods and approaches appropriate for its peculiar object, and distinct from other methods used in other realms. If the reductionistic and naturalistic method has to be subject to deep revisions for good reasons, then the scientific programme aimed at explaining religion is particularly misleading, at least so long as it does not take into account other sources of knowledge able to overcome the outlined limits.

2   The nature of religious experience is personal, even if it manifests itself in a broad range of external forms: behaviours, texts, rituals, institutions … Different sciences can deal with some of these external (or more 'objective') aspects: sociology, psychology, anthropology and even economics – but there will be a 'core' which can be accessed only by a certain kind of theory, so long as the subjective or first person experience is not available for objective inspection and measurement. Furthermore, philosophers of religion, like the late Marco Olivetti, have emphasized the circularity involved in any study of religion which has to take into account the subjective dimension, or the experience of believing and trusting in God, on one hand, and the objective dimension, or the doctrinal contents and the external reference to a deity or a supernatural world, on the other (Olivetti 1995). Such a state of affairs shows an intrinsic limit to any attempt to rationalize the religious

dimension which resists this manoeuvring. Furthermore, such a programme risks becoming entrapped within Olivetti's circularity, since understanding the inner experience will require reference to its external contents; and, at the same time, the latter would be unassailable without resorting to the faith experience of the person and how he or she understands or lives such beliefs (Oviedo 2006). Only theories able to take account of both sides, and to share in the axioms of the believer's mind, would be able to account for what is going on, and then to deliver some normative conclusions.

3   The third issue concerns the high level of complexity which is character-istic of religious experience. This objection goes in line with the first one – the limits of the reductionist programme – and also involves other issues. Complexity means taking into account both the subjective and the objective dimensions, the role played by conscious processes linked to external means and the temporal dimension. Tackling complexity is becoming one of the hardest endeavours of current science. New paradigms are arising: the appli-cation of a broad range of thermodynamic concepts, the study of complex networks, the emergence of systems, both in life and social sciences, and a set of interdisciplinary theories trying to account for the exciting processes which turn chaos to order in many settings (cosmology, life, mind …). The scientific study of religion risks missing the point by isolating just a few of the intervening variables, and pretending that their dynamic explains the lion's share of religious experience. Complexity means awareness of the difficulty of providing a complete picture of a reality, which cannot be reduced to a few variables. Take, for instance, the case of the attempt to provide explanations of social phenomena that are able to account for individual and collective levels of action and influence. A similar attempt is the effort to understand religious processes which, by their own nature, include both the individual and social dimensions; and this is just one aspect of their complexity. At most we can get to some of the underlying rules governing the process, but not to the whole process. Complex realities are better approached with the help of hermeneutic theories, bringing in an amount of historical experience and learning and cultivated human wisdom. Meanwhile, there is an absolute affinity between religious understanding and the quest for order, or the overcoming of chaos. It would be naïve to ignore such a deep link that becomes apparent in most of the elaborated religious traditions. Religious experience may be examined from different points of view as a phenomenon that provides individuals and communities with a strong source of order or, in other words, an ability to see order and discipline in a chaotic mind or social aggregate. Of course, science tries to play a similar role, as when it provides an ordered view of reality, or when it aims at building models to better understand the real world. Religion and science compete in some ways when they both try to organize reality exhaustively or to diminish the inevitable effects of chaos and noise; each may be seen as a kind of 'super-theory' dealing with these issues. Perhaps theistic religion survives this conflict because it can deal with the kind of 'noise' that scientific insights seem unable to reduce. It would be better to deepen such

aspects with the help of good philosophy of religion, instead of taking the short cut and trying to make religion just another 'source of noise' that needs to be neutralized by systematically placing it within a 'super-theory'.

4 The fourth reason for scepticism concerning the scientific programme points to the involvement of conscious processes and intersubjective communication in religion. It is hard to decide what a 'science of consciousness' should look like. Many might pretend that it would constitute the ultimate science, the theory of everything or the 'mother of all theories', since consciousness is the setting of mental processes dealing with almost everything. Because such a view elicits suspicions of 'too broad a scope', conscious processes seem to be still unassailable and out of scientific reach. For some scholars eliminationism is the easy way out: if you declare that consciousness is only an illusion, a by-product, then everything is solved (Dennett 1991). Indeed the issue is simpler: offering a science of consciousness or conscious thinking is what traditional philosophy, psychology, even literature and other humanities, have tried to do. In other words, a 'science of conscious religious processes' is more or less inevitably a kind of hermeneutic mixed with phenomenology, or a theory trying to know what is going on inside the conscious human mind through introspection, communication and the accumulation of lived experience, which gives rise to classic works and broadly shared views on human nature and life. Furthermore, any talk of consciousness should be aware of its position within a network of relations and exchanges which provides, through symbols and language, shared categories or ideas which constitute the bricks of any conscious elaboration. This is especially true in the case of the religious mind, which even if based in universally shared 'principles' (resorting analogically to Chomsky's terminology), is activated through interaction with a mature community skilled in the use of such symbols and language. To some extent, once again, approaching this dynamic clearly requires a kind of broader knowledge than is habitual in the scientific method.

5 The fifth cause of concern is linked to the historical nature of religious perception and codification. The synchronic study of religion is of great value but incomplete, since current religions are the result of a long process of selections and adaptations (if we are allowed to use the evolutionary jargon), or changes which challenge too-simple views. Indeed religious ideas seem to have evolved to cope with various human and social needs, and have struggled throughout history to incorporate the best solutions within their own 'programme' (if we accept that every religion develops a particular programme dealing with the code transcendence/immanence, as Luhmann (2000) stated. How to follow and understand these changes and this evolution is one of the greatest challenges of any theoretical approach to religion. Indeed, it is not easy to identify the factors which were the most important in that process. In my opinion, such processes could be 'internally guided' (or driven by specific human needs, decisions and experiences), rather than constrained by sheer survival and reproductive needs, as happens in purely

biological realms. Surely humans add more factors to the biological evolutionary process: when intelligence comes into play, the cards are changed and a new game begins. If we accept such a premise, even if we were to rule out *a priori* the possibility of spiritual and moral discoveries or metaphysical agents, the consequence is that we need a broader theory which accounts for these 'human factors' guiding the evolution of historical religions. Once again, such a theory will unavoidably have a hermeneutic character, since the hermeneutic tradition is better endowed to deal with the kind of factors that transcend the biological level.

6   Several studies outline the probabilistic status of a set of sciences dealing with phenomena whose levels of complexity do not allow for the simple, mechanistic and accurate approach of, for example, classical physics. There have been many claims according to which the so-called 'special sciences' (Fodor 1974) require a distinct method and their results have a probabilistic and proximate format (Oaksford and Chater 2008; Day 2007). This situation may be seen as a result of the complexity of their subject, which can be clearly appreciated in biology, and in the therapeutic and cognitive sciences, and, surely, even more when we try to develop human and social sciences. The point is that, in such contexts, science often advances through the management of statistical figures, without a clear and concise contour, without the exact characteristic of physical sciences. Therefore, when the results are less clear and concise, more hermeneutical intervention could be expected. When a scientist has to deal with a set of data that could be understood in different theoretical frameworks or provide support for more than one theory, interpretation becomes unavoidable. There is a correlation between probabilistic and approximate sciences, and increased hermeneutic involvement. All this is true when the object of study is religion. Any scientific access to this topic has to deal with not only the data, but with high interpretive elaboration of these data. Pretending to avoid this does not produce better science of religion, but rather very poor and useless knowledge.

IV. Deepening the study of religion

The scientific programme of naturalizing religion exhibits some unavoidable weaknesses. A preliminary question is whether the naturalistic approach can provide a 'complete' account of the phenomenon under scrutiny, and so be capable of reducing every aspect of it to a scientific, or at least rational, pattern. The presence of an 'irreducible remainder' would constitute a limit to that programme. This happens eventually with most realities related to the conscious mind and to human culture.

Furthermore, it might be that science cannot provide by itself a satisfying view or understanding of every aspect of the world. Even in broader terms, secular humanism – as stated by Charles Taylor – seems to be unable to give a reason for several aspects of human and social life; by the way, neither Christian theology nor philosophy manages to provide a global and satisfactory answer either. This observation points to a statute of limitation of both lines of thought and, as a consequence, to an objection to any attempt to eliminate or operate an *Aufhebung* of the religious sphere (Taylor 2007).

In a nutshell, religious experience is fundamentally a human experience, and so a meaningful one. If anybody expects to account for human phenomena, he or she should resort sooner or later to the disciplines that have dealt with the different aspects of human beings and how humans build structures of meaning, which in turn grasp at, should we dare to use the words, truth and ultimate realities. A holistic or 'human' approach does not mean that the new scientific methods will be of no use, but rather that such approaches should not ignore the corpus of hermeneutic wisdom, and phenomenological studies. Hermeneutical insights should be integrated into the corpus of new scientific theories, negotiating when necessary new insights that might subvert some inherited wisdom. But it is extremely misleading to pretend to substitute some forms of knowledge of religion (the hermeneutic and phenomenological) with another (the scientific), in the wrong conviction of possessing a superior system which renders redundant any other approach. Again, Ockham's razor does not apply in these very complex cases, especially when scientific theories of religion provide rather little explanatory power. Such theories apply to a small set of cases, leaving most of the real complex manifestations of more committed religious forms untouched, and the vast issue of the 'meaning' of religious experiences ignored.

Beside all this, the task of explaining religion requires us to take into account dimensions that are hard to reach through objective scientific methods alone. There is an amount of accumulated wisdom that has been growing in modern times, and which becomes very helpful, not just to 'explain', but also to go into the world of religious experience and faith to 'get in tune' with it. First of all, there is the theological tradition, which should never be excluded from such attempts. Theology gathers a huge quantity of interpretations and paths to share and communicate religion, and to provide a reasonable view of religious experiences at all times and in the main religious settings. Theology is here understood as a discipline which can be (and generally is) developed inside each main religious tradition, not just Christianity.

Second, there is a consistent modern tradition of philosophy of religion and 'philosophical theology'. Its contribution is crucial for all comprehensive views of religion. The debates and arguments about the possibility of theism, recorded throughout its history, form one of the best examples of modern reasoning and exchange on a problematic issue. For the philosophy of religion, engaging in such discussions has already been a *tour de force* between reason trying to clarify and prove, and faith trying to believe and hope. To dismiss this corpus of knowledge in the name of a supposedly better approach, which has so far delivered sometimes 'trivial results', seems at best a sign of ignorance (Kundt 2007).

The third dimension to be included in a more comprehensive view of the study of religion is the historical dimension. Nobody can grasp the complexity and richness of religion without a good deal of historical research and reconstruction.

This can be understood as an enterprise of universal human outreach, trying to unfold the evolution of historical religious forms or the particular narratives of each religion. After the huge amount of documented historical and philological studies concerning each main religion that has been done, it is a shame when some scholars, ignoring all this, try to create their own theoretical shortcut. The result is a poor version of a richer reality.

Some other dimensions should not be left aside: for example, the aesthetic approach to religion, which can be found in plastic, literary and musical art expressions. It may be claimed that artistic intuition provides better insights into the meaning of religion through the expert analysis of classical masterworks than through theoretical development, although, of course, sensitivity and caution are required.

The issue of legitimacy and, still more, of the need for a reductive programme in the study of religion has been a hotly debated topic for several years now (McCutcheon 1997; Slingerland 2008). It seems that the debate is not going to go away, and in my opinion it should be welcomed as a good opportunity to clarify the grounds and perhaps to distinguish clearly the various parties and the distinct schools and methods. But one thing is certain: it is hard to be impressed by the results of approaches applying the reductive stance, when compared with the existing hermeneutic, interpretive traditions of what the various religions are about. But, of course, scholarly popularity depends, as in every academic market, on the tastes and inclinations of readers and students. In our case, the choice is between the reductive stance, with its purported scientific certainty and the hermeneutic one. The traditional approach could appear less sound from that point of view, but richer and more suggestive.

In any case, the question of what constitutes a 'good science of religion' is far from being settled. According to Horst's 'cognitive pluralism' and his criticism of the reductionist programme, there are particular conditions for scientific study in all domains of reality: from the physical and biological to the mental. The qualities of 'good science' are relative to each particular scientific field. A universal pattern can hardly be pursued (Horst 2007: 58). Consequently, cognitive pluralism discloses a more open space for specific developments. It would be a mistake to try to constrain the study of religion to the model of physics or biology. Even if we take for granted that religious phenomena belong to the mental sphere, a reductive methodology – say in a neurophysiological vein – would still not constitute the best approach. What 'cognitive pluralism' claims is that every domain of reality requires a specific approach and particular methods which are suitable for the characteristics of that domain. Similarly, since we cannot understand mental processes by resorting to mechanistic theories, we cannot understand religious experiences by resorting to reductive systems. Instead we need appropriate tools and instruments of observation that necessarily include the hermeneutic and phenomenological dimensions.

An additional issue should be addressed when attempting to create the next wave of 'religious studies'. It concerns the practical features and consequences when fanaticism and other pathologies associated with religion are taken into account. A good point to be made is that the study of religion should discourage bigotry and its most fanatic and violent expressions. It is important to consider whether such extremes are rather physiological, in the sense of whether or not they belong to the proper nature of religion – and similarly, whether they are just pathologies, or forms gone wrong and derailed expressions of what is otherwise (and overwhelmingly) a positive and constructive experience, both for individuals and for societies. The same may be said of many other social forms, subject to the vagaries of the mind. The question is to what extent the new stance in the scientific study of religion helps to tame its most virulent expressions. We can also ask whether the dismissal of religion by explaining it away entirely is of any use in the new troubled international context. In my opinion, the strategies that end by denying religion do not contribute to the effort of pacification, since they just deny what is so important for many people. Such a tactic only ignores what is for many an essential need, and even represses human instinct. I am convinced, on the basis of rational observation distinguishable from my religious faith, that this line of thought leads to bad outcomes. A more congenial treatment of religion, not aimed at concealing it, but addressing and cultivating its best side, its wisdom and healing properties, could tackle the problem more appropriately. As everybody knows, repressing or denying human needs has very rarely worked in past history.

In conclusion, a programme aimed at 'naturalizing religion' can become misleading when it does not take into account some essential dimensions of religion. The problem is that the researcher will invade foreign territory, and create confusion rather than understanding, unless she can get in contact with its inhabitants, learn their language and participate in their cultural and symbolic forms. Understanding other people's practices requires sharing some common ground with them. Without this kind of participation, the 'research' will simply be a projection of the researcher's own categories into the world of the subjects. This interpretive (or hermeneutic) model does not aim to dismiss the scientific approach, or proclaim its self-sufficiency, but rather it is conscious of its limits, the need of mutual integration, and the utility of interdisciplinary cooperation. The new scientific approaches to religion can contribute a great deal by offering us a better understanding of some of the processes and dynamics of religion. The only condition is that such knowledge should be linked to the accounts given by the religious traditions themselves, in a common effort to help humanity to cope with its challenges.

It is noteworthy to recall that almost every intellectual generation since the Enlightenment has struggled to understand and rationalize religion. The relentless pursuit of new attempts to prolong and correct earlier accounts of religion is still unfinished after a couple of centuries. What does religion have, that requires explanation time and time again? Why is it that every attempt to explain religion leaves us with an unfinished and incomplete programme? After two centuries and numerous attempts, it still seems that religion has not yet been 'explained' in a satisfactory way. Will the new approaches operating inside a contemporary naturalistic framework accomplish what their predecessors were not able to achieve? I doubt it. In any case, it seems that naturalistically engaging religion is strongly appealing to modern reason. Such engagements as unaccomplished projects and deferred endeavours are characteristic of the identity of modern reason. Or perhaps they are one of the most exciting and challenging intellectual enterprises of modern reason. There seems to be an inherent value in trying again and enjoying the excitement of touching the limits of reason and reflexivity, and feeling dissatisfied with this state of things.

All in all, one of my main worries concerning the programme of scientific naturalism is that it could mean – at the very end – an attempt to reduce religion to a projection of human mind, desires and needs. This has already happened many times since the inception of modernity. The problem is that such manoeuvrings deepen the solipsistic tendency of the modern human condition and render any kind of external reference impossible, since every attempt at transcending ourselves would be damned to be a form of self-reference. Such a situation would render any ethical project, any true alterity, impossible once we recognize that every form of transcendence simply reflects our own agendas. Absorbing religious revelation and faith into naturally projective mechanisms may exhaust one of the few sources providing hope and motivating engagement for the good of all.

I would like to conclude with a final piece of unsolicited, though less abstractly epistemological, advice: we need to make sure that a proper balance of scholars in the scientific study of religion remains. What I mean is that religious believers and theologians should be more proportionately represented within that scholarly community, for promoting the fruitful coexistence of 'first-person' and 'third-person' understandings of religious life. Religious believers working in that field should not feel ashamed of having their own views about metaphysical, extra-scientific issues. To say the least, scientific views are not free of metaphysical values. The claim that religion is better known by outsiders is far from convincing. It is as unpersuasive as the claim that music is better known by unmusical people, or that love is better studied by people who have never fallen in love – or, and this is also very important, that a knowledge of the chemical and social dynamics involved in love requires one to give up on the importance or reality of love in the world or in one's own life. In my judgement, addressing this professional imbalance would genuinely help to re-establish a different balance: that between scientific and hermeneutic approaches aimed at understanding religion.

References

Appiah, K. A. (2009), 'Explaining religion: notes toward a research agenda'. In S. A. Levin (ed.), *Games, Groups, and the Global Good*. Berlin/Heidelberg: Springer Verlag, pp. 195–202.
Beyer, P. (2006), *Religions in Global Society*. Abingdon/New York, NY: Routledge.
—(2001), *Religion Explained: The Evolutionary Origins of Religious Thought*. New York, NY: Basic Books.
Davidson, D. (1970), 'Mental events'. In L. Foster and J. W. Swanson (eds), *Experience and Theory*. London: Duckworth, pp. 79–101.

—(1984), 'Thought and talk' In D. Davidson (ed.), *Truth and Interpretation*. Oxford: Clarendon Press.

Day, M. (2007), 'Let's be realistic: evolutionary complexity, epistemic probabilism, and the cognitive science of religion'. *Harvard Theological Review, 100*, 47–64.

De Caro, M. and Macarthur, D. (eds), *Naturalism in Question*. Cambridge, MA/ London: Harvard University Press.

Dennett, D. (1991), *Consciousness Explained*. Boston. MA/London: Little Brown.

Feil, E. (2001), *Religio III. Die Geschichte eines neuzeitlichen Grundbegriffs im 17. und 18. Jahrhundert*. Göttingen: Vandenhoeck & Ruprecht.

Flanagan, O. (2007), 'Varieties of naturalism'. In P. Clayton (ed.), *Oxford Handbook of Religion and Science*. Oxford/New York, NY: Oxford University Press, pp. 430–51.

Fodor, J. (1974), 'Special sciences – or the disunity of science as a working hypothesis'. *Synthese, 28*, 97–115.

Foucault, M. (1970), *The Order of Things: An Archaeology of the Human Sciences*. London: Tavistock Publications.

Gasser, G. (ed.) (2007), *How Successful is Naturalism?* Frankfurt/Paris: Ontos Verlag.

Gazzaniga, M. S. (2005), *The Ethical Brain*. New York, NY/Washington, DC: Dana Press.

Hauser, M. D. (2006), *Moral Minds: How Nature Designed Our Universal Sense of Right and Wrong*. London: Abacus.

Horst, S. (2007), *Beyond Reductionism: Philosophy of Mind and Post-Reductionist Philosophy of Science*. Oxford/New York, NY: Oxford University Press.

James, W. (1985 [1902]), *The Varieties of Religious Experience*. Cambridge, MA/ London: Harvard University Press.

Kant, I. (1992 [1795]), *Perpetual Peace: A Philosophical Essay*. Bristol: Theoemes Press.

—(1998 [1793]), *Religion within the Boundaries of Mere Reason and Other Writings*. Cambridge/New York, NY: Cambridge University Press.

Kundt, R. (2007), 'Can cognitive science of religion help us to better understand the reasons for Nestorius' downfall?' *Sacra, 5*, 56–64.

Luhmann, N. (2000), *Die Religion der Gesellschaft*. Frankfurt: Suhrkamp.

McCutcheon, R. (1997), *Manufacturing Religion: The Discourse on Sui Generis Religion and the Politics of Nostalgia*. Oxford/New York, NY: Oxford University Press.

Norenzayan, A. and Shariff, A. F. (2008), 'The origin and evolution of religious prosociality'. *Science, 322*, 58–62.

Oaksford, M. and Chater, N. (eds) (2008), *The Probabilistic Mind: Prospects for Bayesian Cognitive Science*. Oxford/New York, NY: Oxford University Press.

Olivetti, M. M. (1995), 'Filosofia della religione'. In P. Rossi (ed.), *La filosofia 1*. Torino: UTET, pp. 137–220.

Oviedo, Ll. (2006), 'Religious experience: first-, second, and third person accounts'. *Archive of Philosophy, 74*, 391–401.

Putnam, H. (2004), 'The content and appeal of "naturalism"'. In M. De Caro and D. Macarthur (eds), *Naturalism in Question*. Cambridge, MA: Harvard University Press, pp. 59–70.

Sawyer, R. K. (2005), *Social Emergence: Societies as Complex Systems*. Cambridge/ New York, NY: Cambridge University Press.

Slingerland, E. (2008), 'Who's afraid of reductionism? The study of religion in the age of cognitive science'. *Journal of the American Academy of Religion, 76*, 375–411.

Sosis, R. and Alcorta, C. (2003), 'Signaling, solidarity, and the sacred: the evolution of religious behavior'. *Evolutionary Anthropology, 12*, 264–74.

Stark, R. and Finke, R. (2000), *Acts of Faith: Explaining the Human Side of Religion*. Berkeley, CA/London: University of California Press.

Taves, A. (2009), *Religious Experience Reconsidered: A Building-Block Approach to the Study of Religion and Other Special Things*. Princeton, NJ/Oxford: Princeton University Press.

Taylor, C. (2007), *A Secular Age*. Cambridge, MA/London: Harvard University Press.

Turner. M. (ed.), *The Artful Mind: Cognitive Science and the Riddle of Human Creativity* (Oxford/New York, NY: Oxford University Press.

Weber, M. (1993 [1906–18]), *The Sociology of Religion*. Boston, MA: Beacon Press.

7 What's Religion For? A Dilemma for the Scientific Investigation of Religion

Dirk Evers

When we ask – from the perspective of empirical science in general, and of evolutionary psychology in particular – whether religion is natural, we ask about its functional use within the biological constitution of human beings. Sometimes such a view on religion goes together with a criticism of religion. If religion as a human phenomenon can be 'explained' by the evolution of the human brain and of human behaviour controlled by the laws and requirements of natural selection, then religion is unmasked as nothing but an adaptive behaviour devoid of any relation to super-natural entities. To avoid or even counter such criticism of religion, others claim that an empirical survey of religion as a phenomenon of human behaviour is merely descriptive and cannot question religion in its semantics. I want to question this move, both from within science and from within religion. I will do so in three steps:

1   I will question the label 'natural' and will try to show how it is charged with normative connotations. I want do this by reconstructing the history of the term 'natural'.
2   I will then point to the fact that religion is far too complex a concept to be referred to by mere descriptive means which claim to dispense with semantics.
3   In my concluding remarks I would like to point to a fundamental dilemma of any functional approach to religion.

I. What do we mean by 'natural'? Hidden sub-texts in the Western notion of 'nature'

The term 'natural' in Western philosophical and theological thinking has adopted a whole variety of meanings that share a family-likeness in some respects, but nevertheless are quite distinct in others. With regard to the term nature, the great Scottish philosopher David Hume claimed 'that there is none more ambiguous and equivocal' (Hume 1992b: 249). He distinguished three meanings of nature: as opposed to miracles or the supernatural, as opposed to the rare and unusual (which according to his observation is the common meaning), and as opposed to artifice. Today, there are even more different contrast classes in regard to which 'natural' denotes one side of the alternative, like natural vs. cultural, natural vs. forced or laboured, natural vs. unnatural (in the sense of inappropriate), and so on.

In some of these pairs of contrasting terms, 'natural' is associated with a normative meaning – positive as well as negative. Etymologically the root of the term 'natural' goes back to the Latin word *natura*, which originally referred to the properties which beings have not acquired but which they possess by birth (*natus* = born). Soon the term *natura* adopted the meaning of essence or substance, thus *natura* came to mean that set of indispensable properties which qualify an entity as an exemplar of a natural kind. Cf. Augustine: 'Nature is nothing other than that thing which is understood to be something.'[1] A natural being is something which has a nature[2] and therefore is a really existing thing of its kind. In the traditional understanding, the nature of a thing or being is described in terms of its inherent and essential qualities or dispositions, which a being exemplifies through its existence. Furthermore, medieval philosophy commonly distinguished between natural beings, as created in their essences by the divine being, and things produced by the created intelligence of human beings, which were products of an art and therefore not natural but artificial (*non naturale sed artificiale*).

Created by God, natural beings do not simply have a nature, but they strive towards actualizing their nature, their natural disposition, which is bestowed on them by the creator. Thus a *natural order* of beings, the order of their dispositions and ambitions, and of the rules they follow in order to realize their existence according to their nature, is established. This realm of striving and moving beings later became the object of empirical science. From the natural order and course of beings a voluntary, *artificial order* designed by human beings was distinguished, as well as a *supernatural order* or course through which the divine being interferes with the natural course of creation by miracles and revelation (which fell into two categories: *contra naturam*, acting against the course of natural beings, and *supra naturam*, bringing about something which is beyond the powers of natural beings). Thus, Thomas Aquinas defined as the purpose of the philosophy of nature the rational consideration and investigation of the *ordo rerum naturalium*. It is worth noting, that in this concept the *living being*, the organism, is the paradigm for what is called natural.[3]

---

[1] '*Ipsa natura nihil est aliud, quam id quod intelligitur in suo genere aliquid esse.*'
[2] Cf. Thomas Aquinas, Summa contra gentiles (ScG), book IV, ch. 35: '"Natura" est secundum quam res aliqua dicitur res naturalis: It is [its] "nature" by which something is called a natural thing.'
[3] Cf. again Thomas Aquinas, ScG IV, 35: 'The name "nature", moreover, in its first imposition had as meaning the very generation of things being born. Thence it was carried over to meaning the principle of this kind of generation, and then to signifying the principle of motion intrinsic to the moveable thing. And because this kind of principle is matter or form, nature is further called the form or matter of a thing which has in itself a principle of motion. And since form and matter constitute the essence of the natural thing, the name

At the beginning of modernity, the concept of nature underwent severe changes. In the Renaissance with its strong reference to ancient arts, the distinction between the natural and the artificial course of things was transformed into a difference within the concept of nature. The neoplatonic humanist philosopher Marsilio Ficino (1433–99), founder of the Florentine Academy, wrote:

> What is human art? A nature, which deals with a certain matter from the outside. What is nature? It is an intrinsic art forming matter from the inside [...] What is a work of art? The mind of the artist in separate matter. What is a work of nature? The mind of nature in incorporated matter.[4]

Nature now is like an artist, although it does not form a thing from the outside by extrinsic force, but by a force operating from within that thing. What seems to be eliminated is the traditional notion of the supernatural. Miracles become natural in the sense of *mirabiliae naturae*, i.e. novelties of nature, and change their meaning from an extrinsic divine interference with the course of nature to an intrinsic manifestation of hidden potentials of nature: Mother Nature becomes the creator (*creatrix*). This understanding of nature provides the background for natural studies in early modernity, giving priority to the method of induction and to cataloging phenomena, as well as using alchemy, medicine, mechanics and other arts to imitate and even accomplish nature by using its hidden forces.

But the most revolutionary shift in the understanding of nature was the reconstruction of the order of nature through geometry. While Copernicus spoke of the 'prudence or sagacity of nature (*naturae sagacitas*)' (De revolutionibus I, 10) which brings about complex cosmic phenomena by using a few simple geometrical principles, it was Kepler who combined and united celestial and terrestrial mechanics into one order of nature characterized by its geometrical structure and laws. With reference to Plato, Kepler states that the creator is always applying geometry. Nature is a manifestation of geometrical and mathematical principles which exist in the primordial mind of the creator and which we can reconstruct in our mind by finding the mathematics behind the phenomena[5]. Galileo agrees when he states:

> Philosophy is written in that great book which ever lies before our eyes – I mean the universe – but we cannot understand it if we do not first learn the language, and grasp the

---

was extended to meaning the essence of everything whatsoever which exists in nature. As a result of this, the nature of a thing is called "the essence signified by the definition".

[4] 'Quid est ars humana? Natura quaedam materiam tractans extrinsecus. Quid natura? Ars intrinsecus materiam temperans [...] Quid artificium? Mens artificis in materia separata. Quid naturae opus? Naturae mens in coniuncta materia' (M. Ficino, Platonica Theologia de immortalitate animorum, IV, 1).

[5] Cf. J. Kepler, Harmonia mundi I, Prooemium: 'The figures [of nature] are earlier in the archetypical mind than in [its] works, earlier in the divine mind than in the creatures: Primo autem figurae sunt in Archetypo quam in opere, prius in mente divina quam in creaturis.'

symbols, in which it is written. This book is written in the mathematical language, and the symbols are triangles, circles and other geometrical figures, without whose help it is impossible to comprehend a single word of it; without which one wanders in vain through a dark labyrinth.[6]

Inspired by the Newtonian concept of laws of nature, Immanuel Kant generalized this notion of nature by defining it as the comprehensive and systematic realm of all experience, and separated it categorically from the noumenal world of morality and freedom. Like Descartes, Kant wanted to salvage freedom from being dissolved into the deterministic net of mechanical cause and effect with which the modern sciences described the natural word, and he did so by exempting human agency from the context of natural causes. The price they both had to pay was the reduction of nature to a machine-like material world, a *machina mundi*.

Others tried to integrate human agency and existence into the concept of nature. For example, David Hume tried to show that the way we understand nature by interpreting it in terms of natural laws and the way we understand human agency and decision-making are essentially the same. Natural and moral evidences rest on the same principles, i.e. experience, custom and habit:

And indeed, when we consider how aptly *natural* and *moral* evidence link together, and form only one chain of argument, we shall make no scruple to allow that they are of the same nature, and derived from the same principles. (Hume 1992b: 90)

Although Hume was a sceptic with regard to the absolute demonstrative powers of human reasoning, he was also confident that the 'operations of mind' (Hume 1992b: 83) function in the same way as the 'operations of matter' (Hume 1992b: 93) or the 'operations of bodies' (Hume 1992b: 29). Nature is not made in the image of reason (be it divine reason or its human reflection), but nature is using human reasoning as a tool which is helpful as it is 'renouncing all speculations which lie not within the limits of common life and practice' (Hume 1992b: 41). And, insofar as nature as such is already beyond the scope of our understanding, the 'supernatural', that which might be seen as the source and inner meaning of nature, is completely inaccessible to the human mind.

Although 'a human body is a mighty complicated machine', there is 'no proof that the laws of nature are not observed with the greatest regularity in its internal operations and government'. The same applies 'to the actions and volitions of intelligent agents [...] The internal principles and motives may operate in a uniform manner [...]; in the same manner as the winds, rain, cloud, and other variations of the weather are supposed to be governed by steady principles; though not

[6] G. Galilei, Il saggiatore (Galilei 1968: 232): 'La filosofia è scritta in questo grandissimo libro che continuamente ci sta aperto innanzi a gli occhi (io dico l'universo), ma non si può intendere se prima non s'impara a intender la lingua, e conoscer i caratteri, ne' quali è scritto. Egli è scritto in lingua matematica, e i caratteri son triangoli, cerchi, ed altre figure geometriche, senza i quali mezi è impossibile a intenderne umanamente parola; senza questi è un aggirarsi vanamente per un oscuro laberinto.'

easily discoverable by human sagacity and enquiry'. Hume's conclusion is that 'the conjunction between motives and voluntary actions is as regular and uniform as that between the cause and effect in any part of nature' (Hume 1992b: 87s); and this regular conjunction has been acknowledged by common sense throughout human history. Nature as such is beyond our comprehension, but our comprehension is a part of nature: 'Nature, by an absolute and uncontroulable necessity has determin'd us to judge as well as to breathe and feel' (Hume 1992a: 474s).

For Hume nature is everything which is the case, but it is deprived of all normative principles. That becomes clear in a letter to Hutcheson, whom Hume intensively studied while working on the third book of his Treatise:

> I cannot agree to your sense of *Natural*. 'Tis founded on final Causes; which is a Consideration, that appears to me pretty uncertain & unphilosophical. For pray, what is the end of Man? Is he created for Happiness or for Virtue? For this Life or for the next? For himself or for his Maker? Your Definition of *Natural* depends upon solving these Questions, which are endless, & quite wide of my Purpose. (Hume 1932: 33)

As a result, nature loses its function as a norm for moral action, for vices and virtues: "Tis impossible, therefore, that the character of natural and unnatural can ever, in any sense, mark the boundaries of vice and virtue' (Hume 1992b: 251).

This provides the starting-point for Hume's enterprise to reformulate moral concepts in terms of the pleasure and pain with which we react to, and thus evaluate, human actions. They are part of 'the secret springs and principles, by which the human mind is actuated in its operations'. Therefore we can hope that one day, just as Newton revealed the laws and forces by which the planets are governed, we might discover the laws and forces of 'the mental powers and economy' (Hume 1986: 14).

Kant argued that the most fundamental laws of nature, which account for the possibility of natural phenomena as such as well as for the uniformity of our experience, are identical with the *a priori* structure of our mind, so that in a sense everything which is natural is rational. Hume's argument, however, refers to the sceptical assumption that nature is always greater and more powerful than our reasoning (*natura semper maius*, in a way). The human mind is a toolbox for coming to terms with what we experience, and reasoning is only a small part of it. However, both agree on the fact that nature is a closed, self-sufficient system which allows for no super-natural interference from the outside.

However, there was a third alternative to the *rationalist's* and *empiricist's* account, namely the *materialist's* view of the identity of nature and its mechanical laws. In that view, the scientific methods of measuring and quantification are sufficient to understand nature and its course. The primary qualities of material objects such as spatial form, momentum, mass and number, are seen as the inherent and therefore 'real' qualities of nature, while the secondary 'mental' qualities like colour, smell, sounds, etc. are understood to be products of the human mind.

The nineteenth century also saw a return of a qualitatively rich concept of nature. In the late enlightenment and the rising *romanticism*, nature became the source of profound aesthetic experience. In political philosophy, as well as in education, a state of nature was assumed in which human beings were essentially innocent, having neither vices nor virtues. While some saw this as the starting point of cultural refinement, others, such as Jean-Jacques Rousseau, pleaded for a 'return to nature'. He saw bad habits as the products of civilization, while the natural represented the unspoiled. Nature became the antonym of society or culture.

Along with this trend in philosophy, a new aesthetic perception of nature developed. Wild nature was not seen anymore as nasty, dangerous, monstrous and hostile to human beings, but as beautiful and sublime. For example, the artificial French garden was superseded by the ideal of the English 'natural' garden, the rough mountains and the stormy sea became the objects of paintings, and the infinite universe, even the still eerie comets, became a matter of awesome reverence and public attention. Of course, this attitude towards nature and the natural was only possible because human beings lived at a certain distance to it and with a certain degree of independence from it. The modern idea of nature as unspoiled and authentic is a concept that in the West only came up when the cultural and technical hegemony over nature was already established.

In German philosophy, it was Friedrich Schelling who put a new qualitative notion of nature as *the* creative force of reality at the centre of his Naturphilosophie, trying to overcome the traditional dichotomy of spirit and nature. The ideal, which is the object of rational thinking and consciousness, develops out of the real; the real cannot be deduced from the ideal. His philosophy had a strong impact on the natural sciences in the nineteenth century, inspiring research into magnetism (e.g. by Hans Christian Ørsted), electricity, chemical action and the chain of organic beings.

We have to stop our historical reflections at this point. Much could be said about the concept of nature in the twentieth century, especially about constructivist and deconstructivist notions of nature and about the dissolution of the natural through virtual reality. But we must refrain from doing so, and list some of the connotations and normative subtexts of the modern concept of nature and the natural. 'Natural' is what:

- is definable as a being of a kind;
- is determined by the order of things;
- is brought about by laws of nature;
- is not intentionally generated, constructed or cultivated by human beings;
- usually is the case;
- does not transcend space, time and matter;
- …

All notions of 'nature' or 'naturalness' only make sense against the background of a specific contrast (for example, with the non-natural, cultural, supernatural, etc.), and all these contrasts come along with more or less obvious normative meanings. If someone is claiming religion to be 'only' natural, this might be understood as the refutation of the supernatural origins or powers of religion, such as revelation or miracles. Or it might be understood as the claim that religion is part of the full and sane nature of human beings, and is therefore indispensable. In the form of an appeal to nature, the inference 'Religious behaviour is natural; therefore, religion is morally acceptable' can be regarded as valid, while others can argue for its counterpart 'Religious behaviour is unnatural; therefore, religion is morally unacceptable'. These different options cannot be decided by answering the question whether or not religion is natural, but only by discussing the understanding of nature which is behind the question.

One might try to avoid the inference from what is natural or unnatural to normative concepts like acceptability. But as was shown, the term 'natural' does not refer to properties which can be determined by empirical investigation, but to the methods of empirical investigation as such, so that what is unnatural is outside the accessibility of science. This conviction can come in two versions. One might say that what is outside the accessibility of the scientific method is only virtual, but not really existent. This is the argument of *naturalistic reductionism*: everything of which one cannot give a clear and distinct account, i.e. an account which makes a reproducible difference in reality, is either non-existent or irrelevant for existence (because it makes no regular difference). Or one might say that what is outside the accessibility of the scientific method really exists, but cannot be explained or investigated by empirical, scientific methods. This is the argument of *non-reductionists*, who claim that there really are relevant matters of fact outside the realm of the scientific method. But then the question of whether or not something is natural, in the sense that it can be explained or understood by empirical, scientific methods, becomes irrelevant as soon as it is seen to belong to that realm inaccessible by science. If we see religion as a behaviour that is essentially related to questions of norms and values, and hold the view that norms and values are outside of what we can describe as natural processes, then the question of whether or not religion is natural is irrelevant for religion. Insofar as that which is described by science is natural it cannot be part of religion, while what is essentially religious cannot be described as natural because it is, by its very character, not natural.

To ask whether religion is natural makes sense only if one clarifies which aspects of religion are accessible by scientific methods. The claim that the alleged naturalness of something does not imply a normative concept is itself a normative claim, insofar as it is a normative decision to restrict the natural to what can be described by certain methods. That leads us to our next section: What actually *is* religion – a spontaneous behaviour, a belief system or a cultural entity?

II. What is religion?

One can distinguish between two main trends within scientific descriptions of religion, a *substantial* one that defines religion with regard to certain beliefs which are qualified as religious, and a *functional-empirical* one that focuses on certain forms of behaviour and refrains from all substantial descriptions (Kehrer 1998: 422). Substantial definitions of the general term 'religion' usually distinguish religious sets of belief from other beliefs and convictions by their relation to some kind of supernatural agency, and see religious sets of belief as formative for devotional and ritual observances as well as for the moral codes governing the conduct of the respective religious communities. A classic example of such a definition of 'religion' by referring to the specific differences of its beliefs is that of Lord Herbert of Cherbury who, in his major work *De veritate* (1624), formulated five fundamental principles of all religions, namely: (1) there is a supreme God, (2) God has to be worshipped, (3) virtue and piety are the most important parts of religious practice, (4) there is an obligation for humans to repent of wickedness, and, (5) there is reward or punishment after this life (Harrison 2002: 67–9). These five essentials (the so-called "Five Articles" of the English Deists) constitute the nucleus of all religions and of Christianity in its 'natural', uncorrupted form. Natural religion, in this early enlightenment sense, is an anthropological constant.

Only with such a general definition can the term 'religion' be used in the singular, claiming that there is a natural kind of which all historical religions are exemplifications. With the notion of a core concept of 'natural religion' in the enlightenment, religion was conceptualized for the first time in history as a universal, as a natural kind which comes in variations. Immanuel Kant wrote:

> *Difference of religion*: a strange expression! as if one were to speak of different kinds of *morality*. There may indeed be different historical *forms of belief*, – that is to say, the various means which have been used in the course of time to promote religion, – [...] but there is only one *religion* binding for all men and for all times. (Kant 1923: 367)

Schleiermacher's 'sense and taste for infinity (*Sinn und Geschmack fürs Unendliche*)' (Schleiermacher 1984: 212), Rudolf Otto's sense of the holy and numinous or William James's religious genius are all successors of this kind of approach, which remained pre-dominant until the twentieth century: a substantial essence of religion is defined, and then the different historical religions are reconstructed as various exemplifications of this essential idea.

In the twentieth century, however, it became obvious that such a substantial definition of religion faces major difficulties: religion is too complex a phenomenon, and a substantial definition cannot be easily operationalized for empirical studies. Since 1912, when James Leuba extracted 48 different definitions of religion from the literature of his time (Leuba 1912: Appendix) which he categorized in three main groups, namely 'intellectualistic', 'affectivistic' and 'voluntaristic' views of religion, religious studies have more and more renounced the possibility of a commonly acceptable definition of religion. Wilfred Cantwell Smith and others have even argued that we should give up the use of the term religion for scientific or theological theories, because when we define religion by means of a reference to a supreme being or any other set of certain beliefs, we usually exclude some historical religions on that basis. On the other hand, more formal and broad definitions are not selective enough and cannot identify religion as a distinctive phenomenon in contrast to non-religious systems, such as superstition, magic, ideology, sports,[7] theatre or media.

However, not many are ready to follow this suggestion, because we have reliable intuitions about what we regard as religious, although we may not be able to define the phenomenon clearly and distinctively. Thus, although they use the term 'religion', most scientists nowadays agree that a universally valid definition of 'religion' in the singular is impossible. No definition was able to integrate all historical religions and at the same time to distinguish distinctively between religious and non-religious phenomena. What we call 'religion' is a human phenomenon that is by far too complex, and too intensely connected to other phenomena, to be isolated and captured into a simple notion or general term by assessing its semantics. The question whether or not religion is natural as such is meaningless as long as it applies a normatively charged, dubious property to an artificial, historically contingent and phenomenologically inadequate concept. Any answer to this general form of question will reveal more about the inquirer than about the object of investigation.

As a consequence, a *functional* approach to the study of religions was established in the twentieth century in order to avoid discussions about the 'essence' of religious beliefs or the semantics of its practices. Emile Durkheim is usually considered one of the first to have taken a step in this direction with his theory of religion. He saw the elementary function of religion to be an indispensable contribution to the maintenance of social order and social identity. Religion is an expression of social cohesion by distinguishing between the profane and the sacred, and it does so by setting free disciplinary, cohesive, vitalizing and euphoric energies. This elementary form and function of religion allows for a variety of realizations, and Durkheim was of the opinion that though the function which religion serves is indispensible, its concrete form can be substituted by secular equivalents of civic morality.

The functional approach to the study of religion also opened ways for an empirical assessment of religion in a scientific perspective. In the view of a scientist, religion is a form of observable human behaviour and it is distinguished from other forms of behaviour by the specific function it serves. The question of its nature or essence is empirically irrelevant and undecidable by empirical means. Within the framework of evolutionary biology religion as a cultural phenomenon is seen as natural if its functionality is brought about by biologically basic forms of human behaviour and cognitive human faculties, and if its functionality enhances the biological fitness of the respective individuals and communities. In a biological perspective religion is a function of the relation between the environment of human beings and their individual and social needs. Religious behaviour is generated in response to certain constellations of outer demands and inner conditions of socially living human beings. We explain how religion can be natural when we understand the demands and needs to which it is an answer. However, even this concept of naturalness has

[7] In an interview, the successor of Richard Dawkins on *The Simonyi Professorship Chair for the Public Understanding of Science* at the University of Oxford, the mathematician Marcus du Sautoy, described his religion as 'Arsenal – football'.

its normative aspects, although it is reduced to a quantitative notion of adequacy: That is natural, which usually is the case and which either serves a relevant function or is a by-product of it (no. 5 in our list of meanings of 'natural').

This methodology has two consequences:

1   Religious semantics are relevant for such an analysis only to the degree that they contribute to the functionality of religion. Insofar as scientific methods rest on methodological atheism, science can investigate only the way in which beliefs function for the well-being of individuals or groups: it cannot assess the beliefs themselves when they refer to super-natural categories.

2   Since historical religions have so many aspects (doxastic dispositions, belief systems, rituals, social norms, etc.) and are so multi-functional, the functional approach to religions must reduce their complexity to a convenient set of separate functions and assign them to a variety of faculties (cf. the so-called 'Swiss army knife' approach in evolutionary psychology). Eckart Voland, a leading German researcher in the field of the evolutionary study of religion, identifies six aspects of religious behaviour which refer to six core components of the mental ability to be religious, which he calls religiosity. Religiosity consists of a cognitive, a spiritual, a socially binding, an identity-forming, a communicative and a moral component (Voland 2009: 11–21). In five of these domains, religious behaviour can be explained as a functional adaptation. Interestingly enough, it is the first domain, the cognitive side of religion, which Voland regards as a non-functional by-product of evolution, while for a religious believer this is at the centre of his or her belief. But for all other elements of religiosity Voland claims that they are 'biologically functional on average. That is why religiosity can be regarded as an evolutionary adaptation which belongs to universal human nature as a genetically fixed component' (Voland 2009: 21).[8] What qualifies all these functional adaptations as 'religious' Voland does not say. But he seems to suggest that in our societies the same adaptations which bring about the traditional religions can also manifest forms of 'religious' behaviour which are very different from what we usually call religious.

In my view, the example of Voland points to a fundamental issue of any scientific description of religion: Science must reduce nature to functionality with regard to observable factors in order to be able to describe it by empirical methods. But any function can be dissociated from the form of its realization as long as its functionality is maintained. With regard to religion this was the approach developed by Durkheim: the function of religion is creating social identity by establishing and processing the difference between the holy and the profane. But different religions fulfil this function by using very different concepts. If functionality is the point of reference for the scientific study of religion, then religious semantics is of interest

---

[8] For Voland human 'nature' is the sum total of all genetically fixed adaptations, cf. Voland (2009: 19): 'the adaptations of *Homo sapiens* overall form what is called "human nature".

only insofar it contributes to this functionality and mediates between observable factors. In the self-perception of religion it is the other way around: at the centre of religion are semantics and content, while its functionality with regard to the group's coherence or the individual's wellbeing is a secondary side-effect. Religions seek to relate their followers to that which transcends experience and to what is, by definition, not observable or quantifiable; and exactly that makes a non-functional difference in reality. It will have measurable side-effect in empirical reality, but precisely these side-effects allow for no inference to the reality which religion sees behind them. If functionality is the point of reference of science, science will systematically miss the point of religion – at least in the view of religion itself.

III. Conclusion

If this is correct, then a gap opens between the convictions of believers and the functional role of religion, with two consequences: religion can play a functional role without the individual religious follower knowing about it, and the functional role of religious behaviour allows for functional equivalents which semantically might not have much in common with traditional religion. The first consequence of a strictly functional approach can be easily illustrated: for example, celibacy is seen as a 'functional' behaviour because it strengthens group fitness, but it does so without intending it. The second consequence may need a little more clarification, because it is closely connected to recent social developments.

In modern societies the personal identity of an individual is disconnected from the individual's functional role within the different contexts of society. For example, in pre-modern societies marriages were not only personal options, but also part of the political, economic and religious order. The development of modernity is the differentiation and decoupling of these sub-systems according to their specific functionality. Economics functions on the basis of money and markets, marriage and love relationships function on the basis of love and affection, while politics functions on the basis of governance and formal regulation. The process of differentiation is still going on. At present, love relationships are beginning to dissociate from family relationships.

But what is important for our subject is the fact that basic universal contexts in modern societies, like politics, education, economics, law, etc., function independently of the individual's personal convictions, while religion, like the arts, has become a matter of private opinion, irrelevant for the functional coherence of society. While no individual can refrain from participating in economical, juridical and educational contexts, and can even be forced to participate in them, individuals can ignore religion, the arts, etc. An individual in a Western society can be born, can live and can die ignoring religion. It is part and parcel of modern societies that medical aid, marriage, law, money, economical transactions, etc. function independently of religion and according to their own rationale, while the functional roles of traditional religion can be substituted by a variety of equivalents which include art, sports and even science itself in the form of 'scientism'. In any case, the option of a life devoid of institutional religion as well as religious semantics is an empirical fact. In modern societies religion does not solve the necessary problems of society, especially when societies differ more and more in their individual forms. What is left in some societies is a rudimentary form of so called 'civil religion' (Bellah 1967), by which politics is decorated with a certain ceremonial reference to religious notions while at the same time secular practices like singing the National Anthem acquire a quasi-religious status.

The often claimed renaissance of religion seems to me to be an effect of the functional independence of religion connected with its irrelevance for other functional systems within modern societies. Religion can now be designed according to specific needs, both social and individual, and according to specific individual receptiveness with regard to certain religious practices with no immediate consequences for the individual's functionality in other contexts of society. Once religion is deprived of its political, juridical and social role, it might even be converted into a kind of psycho-sanitary technique (or an anthropo-technical exercise, as the German philosopher Peter Sloterdijk 2009 puts it). For others it might turn into a marker of identity, a kind of folklore, consisting mainly in rites, festivals, music, certain dresses for certain occasions, etc., which help forming, expressing and securing cultural identity.

Where does this lead us to? Apparently we are in a dilemma. Either we ask whether religion is fulfilling an indispensable functional role in a scientifically meaningful way, in which case we miss the point of religion, at least of traditional religious semantics.[9] Or we ask what is at stake in religious semantics. Then we enter into hermeneutical and theological categories which are not accessible by empirical research, but which are, so to speak, always behind the back of the observer. One has to give up observing and must suspend the empirical approach in order to discuss matters of religion in a religiously meaningful way, and this cannot be done without getting involved on a personal level. Concepts that claim to have overcome this dilemma covertly (and usually unconsciously) introduce hidden normative sub-texts with their notion of the natural, thus stating either that religion is good because it is healthy or that it is an illusion because, insofar it makes a difference in reality, it can be cut off from its semantics and substituted by functional, non-religious equivalents. At present, I do not see how we can reconcile science and religion by bridging this gap.

---

[9] Cf. Augustine in his *De doctrina christiana* book I, chs 3–5, who distinguished between a being that is to be enjoyed (*res quibus fruendum est*) and a being that can be used (*res quibus utendum est*). To enjoy something means to adhere to it in love for its own sake, while to use something means to make use of it in order to reach that what is to be enjoyed. God is the highest good, which is only to be enjoyed but which cannot and must not be used in order to achieve something else.

References

Bellah, R. N. (1967) 'Civil religion in America'. *Dædalus, 96*, 1–21.

Galilei, G. (1968), 'Il saggiatore'. In *Le opere de Galileo Galilei (Edizione Nazionale)* VI. Firenze: Unione tipografico-editrice torinese, pp. 197–372.

Harrison, P. (2002), *'Religion' and the Religions in the English Enlightenment.* Cambridge: Cambridge University Press.

Hume, D. (1932), *The Letters of David Hume,* vol. I. Oxford: Clarendon Press.

—(1986), *Enquiries Concerning Human Understanding and Concerning the Principles of Morals.* 3rd ed. Oxford: Clarendon Press.

—(1992a), 'A treatise of human nature book I. In T. H. Green (ed.), *The Philosophical Works,* vol. I. Aalen: Scientia, pp. 301–560.

—(1992b), 'A treatise of human nature book II+III'. In T. H. Green (ed.), *The Philosophical Works,* vol. II. Aalen: Scientia, pp. 1–374.

Kant, I. (1923), 'Zum ewigen Frieden (1795)'. In *Gesammelte Schriften* Abt. 1: Werke. vol. VIII. Berlin: Reimer, pp. 17–385.

Kehrer, G. (1998), 'Art. Religion, Definitionen der', *HRWG, 4,* 418–25.

Leuba, J. (1912), *A Psychological Study of Religion.* New York, NY: Harcourt & Brace.

Schleiermacher, F. D. E. (1984), 'Über die Religion. Reden an die Gebildeten unter ihren Verächtern (1799)'. In: H.-J. Birkner, G. Ebeling, H. Fischer, H. Kimmerle and K.-V. Selge (eds), *Kritische Gesamtausgabe.* Erste Abteilung: Schriften und Entwürfe. Vol. 2. Schriften aus der Berliner Zeit 1796–1799. Berlin: de Gruyter, pp. 185–326.

Sloterdijk, P. (2009), *Du mußt dein Leben ändern. Über Anthropotechnik.* Frankfurt am Main: Suhrkamp.

Voland, E. (2009), 'Evaluating the evolutionary status of religiosity and religiousness'. In E. Voland and W. Schiefenhövel (eds), *The Biological Evolution of Religious Mind and Behaviour.* Heidelberg: Springer, pp. 9–24.

8 Why Religious Experience is Considered Personal and Dubitable – and What if it Were Not?

Angela Roothaan

Introduction

One of the major assets of modern Western culture is what one could call its democratic model of knowledge. Whereas 'knowledge' signifies the body of ideas and practices that gives us true insights about the world, the democratic model counts those insights to be true, the proof of which is in principle accessible to anyone. Proof is usually understood to be any sound logical argumentation or any conclusive result of empirical research. No special gifts or revelations are considered necessary in the art of gaining knowledge. This was and is different in other times and cultures, where knowledge was and is considered to be a gift from the gods or from God, allotted to persons with special characteristics, and moreover with a special personal destiny.

In the modern democratic model, however, the possibility of acquiring proof is only granted to scientific knowledge. Artistic production and inspiration on the one hand, and religious experience or inspiration on the other, are exempted from the demand to prove their truth. In contrast to the scientist, who is supposed to follow the universally valid and certain steps of reason that determine the method of his or her repeatable empirical research, the artist is considered to make use of unique talents, of the right situation, and to open him- or herself to the powers of the imagination. The religious person, analogically, is considered to open him- or herself to insights and feelings that come only in unique situations, in unexplainable ways, according to his or her own account, and from a dimension which surpasses the one in which we live.

Although the modern Western view of knowledge rests on the idea of democratic access, the preconditions for gaining access exclude large parts of humanity as, since Descartes and Kant, it is silently assumed that the knower is rational and self-sufficient. As soon as emotional, economic or other dependencies come into play, one is not supposed to be able to access real knowledge. This makes the possible knower a virtually non-existent ideal mind. Although we have seen a lot of criticism of the modern epistemological model in recent decades (e.g. in socio-logical deconstructions of science, as well as in feminist epistemological critiques[1]), it still functions in public denunciations of religious experience as a source of knowledge.

In the following paragraphs I will challenge this model. First I will present the dominant view of religious experience as personal and dubitable. Then I will show how religious experience ended up in this corner, by presenting two authors, William James (1842–1910) and Spinoza (1632–77). Both of them stood firmly in the secularizing currents of the Western philosophical tradition, but tried to do justice to religion and religious experience as important anthropological phenomena all the same. They hold the importance of religious experience to be moral and spiritual (giving meaning to life), but deny it descriptive or explanatory power in an epistemological sense.

The denial of the possibility of being a source of knowledge to religious experience, as well as to other kinds of experience which rely on imagination, on feeling and on unique situations of revelation, has several negative consequences. First, as mentioned above, if we keep to the modern epistemological model at all times, it makes it impossible for us to live up to the democratic ideal, since most of us most of the time live on experiences that are not logical and repeatable. In popular culture this has long since been recognized: for instance, the character of Mr Spock in the famous TV-series *Star Trek* showed the 'inhumanity' of acting only on scientific knowledge. Second, it does not do justice to the actual processes in which scientific knowledge originates (Latour 1987). Third, it discriminates against entire commu-nities who have not yet adopted the modern model of knowledge and who suffer the consequences, as is shown in the difficult struggle of indigenous peoples for the protection of natural environments, which they often indicate to be 'sacred'. And fourth, it expels all experience which gives human action direction and motivation from the domain of knowledge, and directs it to the domain of subjective values.

To correct these negative consequences, one should investigate what would happen if religious (and artistic) experience could be included in the realm of knowledge. In so doing, it would have to be submitted to certain critical principles, which demarcate valid knowledge from invalid. In this article I will try out this possibility – but in order to do so in a fruitful manner, I will propose an alternative epistemological model to the prevailing modern Western one, which brings along alternative critical principles. Thus, the alternative model will be able to criticize religious experience (and other kinds of imaginative experience) as a source of knowledge.

Before presenting the new epistemological model, however, I will broaden the discussion by including the case of so-called shamanistic experience. The reason for doing so is that, while shamanistic experience makes use of the same cognitive powers as religious experience (imagination and intuition), it has a more direct link to the practical orientation of life. This makes its claim to be a source of knowledge more obvious. Shamanistic experience provides those who have it with knowledge

---

[1] To name just some, cf. Latour (1987) and Walker (2007).

of medicinal plants, orientations in space (places of water and food, shelter for temperature, etc.) and time (knowledge of the messages of the ancestors, as well as of ways into the future) while these 'practical' insights may be understood not only to come directly from plants, animals or material forces, but also to come from certain spirits or gods.[2]

To come closer to shamanistic experience, I will, by way of example, present its description and interpretation by psychologist Robert Wolff, who several decades ago spent prolonged periods of time with the Malaysian Sng'oi. This people lived in the jungle, without agriculture, industry or commerce, and relied for directions in leading their daily life largely on what we would call intuitive and imaginative sources of knowledge.

The alternative epistemological model that I will consequently introduce, I will call 'pragmatic-interactive epistemology'. It grounds the possibility of knowledge not in a self-sufficient rational subject, but in the interactions between human individuals, as well as between human beings and other beings. The view of knowledge as interaction I derive from symbolic-interactionist authors George Herbert Mead and Charles Horton Cooley.

To conclude, I will be considering the consequences of adopting such an epistemology. Consequences could be that (a) religious (as well as shamanistic) experience can be understood to provide knowledge, and should be criticized as such (although the principles for criticism will be in conformity to the alternative epistemological model, and not to the classical modern Western model); and that (b) because the range of possible cognitive ways of relating to the world is significantly widened, culturally and individually differing ways of experiencing, knowing and living can come to be understood as varieties of the 'normal'.

I. Studying religious experience

The central question is whether the content of religious experience is open to private, personal experience only, or rather to shared experience – and, if so, under what conditions. But first one has to ask how religious experience is normally defined. Since its origins in the early nineteenth century, the study of religion distances itself from 'metaphysical' questions and holds a phenomenological point of view. This means it forecloses questions regarding the reality of things as such (independently of human designation of meaning, or: '*an sich*'), and only recognizes questions regarding the appearance of things to us ('*für uns*'). It only counts as real the workings of religious phenomena on the human mind and emotions, and keeps an agnostic position towards the reality of the sources of these phenomena. This precludes defining religious experience by its content (e.g. as being a message

---

[2] The inclusive manner in which mythical songs might contain all kinds of practical knowledge is beautifully shown in the philosophical travel stories that Bruce Chatwin presents in *The Songlines* (1988). Ground-breaking on a theoretical level, while introducing similar insights, was the work of Claude Lévi-Strauss (1966).

from God, from gods or from spirits), while it keeps itself to the effects of religious experience on its receptors – human beings.

This epistemological approach was gradually developed from the approach of the eighteenth-century philosopher Immanuel Kant. This philosopher, who so profoundly influenced modern epistemology, wrote a short but most critical book on his contemporary, the visionary Swedenborg. There Kant claimed to have ended all research into the reality of a spiritual and/or a religious realm, when he wrote of spiritual beings:

> [Their study] may be complete, but in the negative sense, by fixing with assurance the limits of our knowledge, and convincing us that all that is granted to us is to know the diverse manifestations of life in nature and its laws; but that the principle of this life, i.e., the unknown and only assumed spiritual nature, can never be thought of in a positive way, because for this purpose no data can be found in the whole of our sensations [...] And now I lay aside this whole matter of spirits, a remote part of metaphysics, since I have finished and am done with it. (Kant 1900: 89–90)

This 'principle of life', the 'spiritual nature' could, according to Kant, not be studied under the demands of a critical philosophy and science. Holding a critical position means to reflect on the conditions of possibility of one's research. It entails that all claims to knowledge that do not reckon with the transcendental principles of time, space and causality cannot be taken seriously.

Kant considers as religious or spiritual all experience related to the idea of an invisible, individual soul, which might survive material existence, and which might have access to a spiritual realm, now or after life. It is important to note here that for Kant the religious and the spiritual (which are often distinguished as having to do with God or rather with spirits, and thus as relating to two distinct spheres) fall into the same category. Both phenomena violate the principles of space, time and causation, by drawing on data that cannot be empirically validated.

Kant, however, was not an anti-religious thinker. He acknowledged the importance of religious experience for the domain of hope, but thought it should be banned from the field of knowledge. People, he maintained, should have hope of an afterlife, of the continued existence of the soul in this afterlife, and of spiritual blessings to be deserved by leading a good life. Nowadays, we would call having such hopes giving meaning to life. And giving meaning is not the same as acquiring knowledge. It is rather the irrational, but functional, activity of human beings which allows them to bear with the sufferings and hardships of life.

The Kantian point of view was still neatly reproduced nearly one and a half centuries later, in the then new science of the psychology of religious and spiritual experiences. One of the founders of this new field, Carl Gustav Jung, wrote in the foreword of his dissertation (defended in 1902):

> Psychology cannot establish any metaphysical 'truths', nor does it try to. It is concerned solely with the *phenomenology of the psyche*. [...] Only a rather stupid mind will [...] venture an opinion on whether immortality does or does not exist. [...] it misses the essential point, which is the functional value of the idea as such. (Jung 1977: 3–4)

In the same year that Jung defended his dissertation, the 'father' of the psychology of religion, William James, published his classic *The Varieties of Religious Experience*, the result of the Gifford lectures he gave in Edinburgh. Here he defined religion as

> [...] the feelings, acts, and experiences of individual men in their solitude, so far as they apprehend themselves to stand in relation to whatever they may consider the divine. (James 2002: 26)

No judgement is thus made on the content or the source of religious experiences, the only reason for calling those experiences religious being that the person who has them relates his feelings to a divine source.

Ever since the appearance of James's work, the study of religion has used a hermeneutic-pragmatic approach for its method. This means that, even though researchers of religion might use natural scientific methods, as for instance brain research, they aim at a *hermeneutic understanding* of the phenomenon of religion, wanting to know what it *means* to be religious. In doing this they are studying the effects of meanings on human sociality, as well as on human dealings with the world: that is, they want to know the *pragmatic effects* of religiosity. Thus religious experience is studied still within the bounds of the Kantian epistemological position.

II. The moralization of religious experience through Spinoza and James

To trace the origins of the phenomenological approach to religion that we find in Kant and his successors, one has to go back to seventeenth-century philosopher Descartes. Descartes, who was trained in the classical authoritative model of knowledge, emancipated himself from the scholastic approach, and dismissed learning and tradition as trustworthy roads to certain knowledge. He replaced these long trusted roads by a new approach, which was based on the combination of mathematics and experimentation. He placed this new method for the sciences under the critical regime of what was later called 'natural light', the inborn rational faculty available to any free and mature person.

The new method immediately excluded important domains of human knowledge, i.e. knowledge of how to lead one's life in connection with others, and in the light of ultimate questions of meaning. It excluded religion, spirituality and morality, which before modern times were included in the sciences, and which were even considered to provide the highest principles of knowledge. As the new experimental sciences showed themselves to be quite successful in producing new practical knowledge of natural phenomena, Descartes' philosophical preference for 'natural' sources of knowledge became unchallenged, forming the ground on which Kant later built his critical epistemology.

Being a contemporary of Descartes, the Dutch philosopher Baruch Spinoza critically received his work. He differed greatly on specific ontological matters, but adopted Descartes' high valuation of mathematics as an example of certain knowledge. Being more interested in sources of meaning than Descartes, Spinoza searched for 'mathematical' guidelines for the moral and spiritual life – thus filling in the gap which Descartes' work had left behind.

Still, although Spinoza saw the importance of philosophy expressing a road to 'wisdom', he had a hard time critically assessing the epistemological value of those non-rational religious beliefs and experiences from which ordinary people build their moral and spiritual life. In his *Theological-Political Treatise* (1991) he wrote that religious experiences cannot claim mathematical certainty, and only have moral certainty. The last mentioned does not refer to the possibility of logical or empirical proof, but is good as long as it leads people to being good, that is, moderate, wise, social, etc..

While introducing the opposition of mathematical and moral certainty, Spinoza, in the same movement, categorizes religious experience as moral or practical knowledge, which is no 'real' knowledge after all, but just, in some mysterious way, beneficial to leading the good life. Here we see the origin of the opinion that spiritual and moral experiences and beliefs should not be tested by their rationality or coherence, but by the way they direct behaviour. Religious experience becomes moralized. We already see the foreshadowing of later psychology, which, as indicated above, judged the relevance of religious experience only by its function-ality for human life.

Spinoza was only one of the inspirational thinkers for the pragmatist philosopher and founder of modern psychology of religion William James. But we recognize his influence when we read James remarking, like Spinoza, that we test our ideas through the way they work in human actions. The main contribution of James was that he founded this idea in an elaborated philosophy of effectuating or working: in *pragmatic* philosophy, which he developed with his friend and colleague Charles Sanders Peirce. James captured the main epistemological tenet of this philosophy in the somewhat cheesy slogan 'truth is what works'.

At the end of his *Varieties of Religious Experience*, we see how James's pragmatic view is put to use to assess religious experience:

> That prayer or inner communion with the spirit thereof – be that spirit 'God' or 'law' – is a process wherein work is really done, and spiritual energy flows in and produces effects, psychological or material, within the phenomenal world. (James 2002: 340)

Although James, just like Jung, did not want to claim anything metaphysical about religious experience, he does take seriously the claims of believers as to the reality of their experiences. He accepts that 'work is really done' – which means that insofar as religious practices and experiences change one's psychological state, or even one's health, their effects are to be considered real, within the limits set by the modern epistemological model. Those researchers who nowadays do experimental research on, e.g., the brain functions of meditating nuns, actually are doing work of which James would have approved: testing experimentally the pragmatic truth of religious and spiritual experience.

Thinkers such as James and Spinoza, who held a favourable stance towards religion and spirituality, were important in 'saving' religious experience as an important subject for psychology and for the study of moral life in the modern age, an age in which science and philosophy mostly aimed to shut out any human experience which is not straightforwardly testable from being a potential source of real knowledge. Spinoza and James achieved this, however, at the cost of lifting any harder epistemological demands on religious experience.

It is my view, though, that any intuitive and imaginative experience, be it artistic, religious or shamanistic,[3] should be put under more critical epistemological pressure. I am convinced that we need to do so, and to restore the possibility of asking serious questions of these kinds of experience, instead of leaving them to the soft regime of 'as long as it helps you to lead your life, it's okay'. More serious episte-mological demands on religious experience can be reintroduced, by developing the new epistemological model which I will introduce below. It rests on an expansion of the pragmatic epistemological approach, which James applied primarily to the individual life, to the domain of the social. But before I come to that, I will broaden the field of investigation by calling attention to what has been called shamanistic experience.

III. Natural messages

In his book *Original Wisdom*, psychologist Robert Wolff presents experiences with different ways of knowing from his long career in so called 'developing countries'.[4] In his collection he does not discuss religious experience as it is defined in the modern world through a long heritage of theological interpretation, but the visions, miracles and other anthropologically possible messages from the spiritual world, as they are understood by the peoples he encounters. While he tells of the ways in which his life and views are altered by these encounters, his personal narrative simultaneously sheds light on how imaginative, non-rational experiences can be seen as real knowledge by those who receive them: as knowledge that is not only trustworthy enough to act upon, but which can also be easily shared with others.

The substantive part of Wolff's book relates of his encounters with the Sng'oi, hunter-gatherers whom he met in some jungle areas in Malaysia. As he describes his encounter with them, they appear to have ways of making themselves unfindable when not wanting contact with the outside world. Wolff first met them through an intermediary, and was gradually taken up more and more closely into their community, which resulted finally in his being initiated into seeing beyond normal experience, a kind of knowledge which for lack of a better term we will call shamanistic.

---

[3] It would go beyond the limits of this paper to argue for the thesis that these kinds of experience have more in common than just their epistemic characteristics. I intend to include this question in my future research.

[4] I am grateful to Robert Wolff, who by way of email corrected some misrepresentations of his book in the earlier version of my paper.

What strikes and bothers Wolff, according to his account of his contact with the Sng'oi, is that when he is about to reach one of their settlements, there is always someone waiting on the path to greet him. And this happens without him having made an appointment – which would also have been impossible, since they have no clocks, phones or agendas – although he receives messages from other Sng'oi about where to find the next settlement. Only after a long time, and learning more of their language, does Wolff find out how this might work. The welcoming person does not have telepathic knowledge of Wolff arriving then and there, nor is there a 'watchman' always sitting at the boundary of the Sng'oi territory.

> Someone would have an inspiration, let's say to follow one of the many paths in the jungle. […] and whatever he or she would find – a particular wonderful fruit, or a visitor to the village, or an animal, that became the reason for coming that way. (Wolff 2001: 119)

In fact all villagers, when awakening at dawn, take time to tell each other what fragments of their dreams they remember or consider important. In what one could call a hermeneutic dialogue they figure out the meaning of the dream language; and although the outcome may still be vague, it indicates to them what is important for that day. In the same way someone might get the hunch to go and wait at the territory border, expecting someone or something to come.

The Sng'oi explain the possibility of acquiring this kind of action-guiding knowledge to Wolff by referring to the experiences of the dream life as coming from the real world, while day-time experiences are thought to take place in the shadow world. This is, very literally, upside-down from what Kant said of dream life, when, in his book on Swedenborg and spiritual experience, he calls the dream experience the untrustworthy one, and the daytime experience the only real and trustworthy one. Wolff explains what he learns about the Sng'oi:

> They did not think that they were sharing dreams as we think of dreams. The Sng'oi believe that the world we live in is a shadow world, and that the real world is behind it. At night, they believe, we visit that real world, and in the morning we share what we saw and learned there. (Wolff 2001: 88)

Wolff relates also other intuitive or imaginative ways in which the Sng'oi attain knowledge. He tells of the occasion when he takes the local 'shaman' with him on a trip out of the forest to the sea, where not one of his people has ever been. This man, after returning home, relates to his fellow villagers detailed scientific knowledge about the sea, its undercurrents, depths and inhabitant creatures, which he claims to have received from 'the spirit of the sea'. Afterwards, the shaman explains to Wolff that this claim is just a metaphor: 'I did not see a person. I find the Great Ocean in my heart' (Wolff 2001: 142).

Finally Wolff tells of the way he himself learns to receive information from plants about their medical and other possible uses. This is part of the experience he receives after his 'initiation' in intuitive contact with plants and animals in the jungle. It is important to note here that he gets the information from the plants themselves! Directly, in a kind of vision, they let him see what possible use he can make of them.

In order to make sense of these claims to intuitive and imaginative ways of knowing our world, I propose that we bring shamanistic experiences and religious experiences (which James distinguished sharply from religious belief, which one can adopt on hearing the experiences from some trusted other person!) under the same epistemological regime. In the classical modern epistemological model, this would mean that both kinds of experience could not be considered a source of real knowledge. All the same, looking at the stories of Wolff and others in an unprejudiced manner they seem to be perfectly trustworthy for those who act on them; so why do we not call them knowledge? To be able to do this in a sensible manner, we would need another epistemological model of understanding for those kinds of experience: a model which would also make it possible to critically distinguish between sense and nonsense in this wider field of understanding the world.

IV. Cooley and Mead: knowledge of the social self

The reason why the classical modern model of knowledge is so restrictive is that it focuses strongly on the autonomy and rationality of the knower. The dependent and imaginative aspects of the human condition (as they appear in sleep/dreams, in emotional disturbance, and in our general bodily dependency on the world around us) are correspondingly allocated to the private and the dubitable. In the twentieth century, however, this allocation has been challenged, by some social psychologists belonging to the direct surroundings of pragmatic philosophy.

George Herbert Mead (1863–1931) and Charles Horton Cooley (1864–1929), both working in the wake of James's *Varieties*, as well as of his work in general psychology, understood the human self integrally, as an acting, feeling and knowing being – unthinkable without its relations to others.

Correspondingly, they viewed human knowledge as communicative and as functional to the constantly changing position human life will be able to hold amidst the forces that surround it.

Knowledge, both thinkers hold, enables people, in their communicative networks, to get a grip on the world, as well as upon themselves and each other. In his classical work on human nature, Cooley does not primarily identify the self with its beliefs or cognitions, but with a specific feeling, called the 'my-feeling or sense of appropriation', in which the relation to the others is present from the beginning (Cooley 2009: 169). And he cites James also:

> As Professor James says in his admirable discussion of the self, the words 'me' and 'self' designate 'all the things which have the power to produce in a stream of consciousness excitement of a peculiar sort'. (Cooley 2009: 170)

He stresses that the self is not just a feeling, but that it is most easily experienced as this feeling of appropriation. Here we see once more the phenomenological approach – favouring access through experience above metaphysical theorizing about the nature or essence of the supposed self.

Individuality is explained by Cooley as the sense of freedom, of being able to act in the wider world of individual forces, the social reality.

> Self-feeling has its chief scope *within* the general life, not outside of it; the special endeavor or tendency of which it is the emotional aspect finds its principle field of exercise in a world of personal forces, reflected in the mind by a world of personal impressions. (Cooley 2009: 179)

What we see as 'mine' is thus not primarily private and personal, it is the appropriation of aspects of the world that we share with others. For instance, when I say 'my friend', or even 'my house', the mentioned person and object are in no way only elements of my personal worlds of experience: they are in the world at large, and in principle accessible to anyone or anything. What I do when I say 'my house', according to Cooley, is experience 'me' by expressing my feelings of attachment to this thing. There is no 'me' outside these 'appropriations', and the appropriations are only a way to strengthen the psychological sensations of my being in the world.

Mead sees the meaning of individuality, just like Cooley, in the social life. He elaborates on this social aspect, adding the theoretical distinction between 'I' and 'me'. We find his thoughts on this theme in his work *Mind, Self, and Society* (1967), which was put together by his students from their course notes. In this work, he characterizes the 'me', the reflective aspect of the individual that coincides with the social picture I have of myself, with what Cooley calls the 'looking-glass-self'. 'Me' indicates how I perceive myself to be perceived by others, as a result of my interactions with them: as a mother, a lower-class person, a trustworthy person, etc. Mead calls it the social situation which is internalized in the individual.

In each person the social situation is present as a general situation, as well as in the form of an individual perception of it, and an individual reaction to it: 'The attitudes of the others constitute the organized "me", and then one reacts toward that as an "I"' (Mead 1967: 175).

The 'I' is just that aspect of the individual which can be understood as its choosing and acting – which one does as 'me', however, on the basis of one's perceived social self. Insofar as one is a free, acting being, one can not characterize oneself – if one does that, one has again returned to the 'me', which is not so much the free as rather the predictable side of an individual. The 'I' is the unpredictable: 'That movement into the future is the step, so to speak, of the ego, of the "I". It is something that is not given in the "me"' (Mead 1967: 177).

Thus although one is free in acting, this unpredictable free 'I' is only one of the phases of the self, according to Mead, since in so far as this acting is *my* acting, it arises as a response to the attitudes the others have taken toward me, from my social self. For both thinkers, thus, the self can not be taken apart from the life we are leading in a field of experiences shared with others. Other people – and, one could add, other beings like plants and animals (as we also interact with them). These thoughts on the social character of the self provide an opening for our epistemological problem. They imply the presence of freedom in the self, of being able to act and to originate, and simultaneously explain this self in its being rooted in relations, in communication. Consequentially, we can no longer divide the self into an objective knower on the one hand and a private believer on the other. All knowledge must be acquired in a situation of dependency and of emotional relatedness, including our most serious 'scientific' knowledge.

The modern epistemological claim of the possibility of rational and objective knowledge, which can be separated from the normal interests and imaginations of everyday life, is therefore false. All knowledge should be seen as related to what we try to achieve in our adaptations to the world, and as acquired by beings who constantly (re)define themselves in their interactions with others. In line with these views, I propose to develop a new epistemological model, drawing on James as well as on Cooley and Mead, which I will label pragmatic interactive. This model, as I will argue in the final section of this paper, should preclude the objections to the classical model that I raised in the introduction. Also it should be able to distinguish between sense and nonsense in all kinds of supposed knowledge.

V. A pragmatic-interactive epistemology

The pragmatic interactive view, as it is found with the thinkers discussed above, provides foundations for a critical epistemology while it characterizes knowledge as arising in the shared human realm of conscious and reflective interactions, in the realm of symbolic communication. Mead writes:

> If mind is socially constituted, then the field or locus of any given individual mind must extend as far as the social activity or apparatus of social relations which constitute it extends; and hence it cannot be bounded by the skin of the individual organism to which it belongs. (Mead 1967: 223, note 25)

We can expand on this idea of Mead in the following manner: if mind is where our relations are, why should we understand the scope of mind to be only as wide as the humanly social? Why would it not extend to every being with which we experience ourselves to be in an interactive relationship? Why would mind (that is, the capacity to understand and to know) not extend to God for the believer, and to plants and animals for the one with a 'jungle' attitude? All the same, according to interactive thinking, there must be real interaction to speak of a relationship, and therefore of understanding and knowing. To borrow the expression of James, 'work really has to be done', something really has to happen – like the Sng'oi who goes out on a hunch, and really meets something or someone important, or like the engineer who tries out some experiment on a chemical substance, following a hunch how it might react, and really meets with its reaction as suspected.

A new epistemological model, to be developed on the basis of these thoughts, would be able to recognize any kind of pragmatic relational and reflective experience, experimental and scientific, as well as hermeneutic and religious, as potentially providing knowledge. The critical boundaries of knowledge would cease to be the Kantian ones of space, time and causality, but could be found in the possibility conditions of the actual interactions which constitute relations.

When we apply these new critical boundaries to the realm of human relations we are led to an assessment like the following: social systems (i.e. systems that produce a certain kind of knowledge) which are rich and diverse allow more individual expression and development, and therefore more real interaction; whereas those that are narrow and repressive allow less growth for the individual, and therefore stifle interaction – that is, encounter, 'work', effect.

Our new critical apparatus therefore also has political implications, judging societies that promote a richness in relations as well as in individuality as making sense from an epistemological view, while judging those that are repressive as making no sense. It would, for example, allow the visions of the Sng'oi to be real knowledge, but dismiss Stalinist ideology as fantasy. It would acknowledge scientific results that illuminate (as well as allow for) the diversity of (human) life, but dismiss those that simplify and restrain it.

The same would go for religious experiences which relate messages from God or gods, from spirits or angels. When they stem from, reflect and promote encounter, relation, interaction, they make sense. When they are blind to and preclude these, they make no sense – from a pragmatic-interactive point of view. Here we see the first possible consequence, mentioned in my introduction, of adopting the proposed epistemological model. In its terms, religious experience can be critically assessed as a form of knowledge, instead of as being just personal and dubitable.

Whereas Cooley and Mead did not write about non-human symbolic interaction (keeping to the traditional divide between humans and animals supposedly separating symbol users from non-symbol users), new research into animal behaviour stimulates extending our epistemology to the interactions between human beings and animals, looking at the ways in which they are reciprocally and dynamically involved in furthering (in more or less successful ways) life as it is shared, and at the same time individually enjoyed.

It is thinkable to extend pragmatic-interactive epistemology to non-animal beings too. Then the messages as they are related by 'shamanistic' peoples from over the world – the ones given to humans by trees and rocks and other natural phenomena – could be included too in what we demarcate to be knowledge. This would open up entirely new (or perhaps very old …) possibilities of critically assessing understandings of our natural environment which are not based on objectifying rationality, but on interactions with the natural beings with which we are in relation.

Finally, I would like to call to mind the second possible consequence of adopting the proposed new model of understanding knowledge, mentioned in my introduction. This urges that a wide variety of culturally different ways of relating to the world may be considered within the varieties of the 'normal', instead of discriminating against them in quasi-colonial and patriarchal modern Western ways of thinking. That this is a real consequence is shown, I think, extensively by the above.

References

Chatwin, B. (1988 [1987]), *The Songlines*. New York, NY: Penguin Books.

Cooley, Ch. H. (2009 [1902]), *Human Nature and the Social Order*. New Brunswick, NJ/London: Transaction.

James, W. (2002 [1902]), *The Varieties of Religious Experience. A Study in Human Nature*. London/New York, NY: Routledge.

Jung, C. G. (1977), *Psychology and the Occult (From Vols 1, 8, 18 Collected Works)*. Princeton, NJ: Princeton University Press.

Kant, I. (1900 [1766]), *Dreams of a Spirit-seer Illustrated by Dreams of Metaphysics*. London: Swan Sonnenschein.

Latour, B. (1987), *Science in Action. How to Follow Scientists and Engineers through Society*. Cambridge, MA: Harvard University Press.

Lévi-Strauss, C. (1966), *The Savage Mind*. Chicago, IL: The University of Chicago Press.

Mead, G. H. (1967 [1934]), *Mind, Self, & Society from the Standpoint of a Social Behaviorist*. Chicago, IL/London: University of Chicago Press.

Spinoza, B. De (1991 [1670]), *Tractatus Theologico-Politicus*. Leiden: E. J. Brill.

Walker, M. U. (2007), *Moral Understandings. A Feminist Study in Ethics*. Oxford: Oxford University Press.

Wolff, R. (2001), *Original Wisdom: Stories of an Ancient Way of Knowing*. Rochester: Inner Traditions.

9 The Religion of Science

Alfred Kracher

I. Introduction

The roles that religion and science play in the lives of individuals and in the functioning of societies are manifold and subject to many different interpretations. Here I would like to focus on a particular question about their relationship: can science generate or sustain its own kind of religion and, if so, is this something to welcome or resist? I will refer to such a newly conceived, science-derived religion as *religion of science* and contrast it with *traditional religion*. In the context of my examples *traditional religion* refers primarily to Christianity and to some extent Judaism, but the argument is not confined to any particular faith.

Religion-and-science inquiries are often undertaken from an apologetic motivation (Drees 2010), in the case of the present issue it is particularly to argue either for or against the validity and functional usefulness of religion. My own intention, however, is to be fair to both the positive and negative aspects of attempts to create a science-based religion. As a scientist I empathize with colleagues who find meaning and fulfillment in their professional commitment. At the same time I see problems and potential dangers in turning this individual devotion into a model recommended to the public at large as a substitute for traditional religion.

II. The scope of 'religion of science'

Individual humans and human societies rely on a range of interconnected processes in order to function and flourish. The words *religion* and *science* mark out large domains within this necessary functional nexus, so large in fact that common usage of these words rarely covers their entire scope. Consequently their meaning in a particular situation is usually context-dependent. For example, we speak of science as a subject taught in public school, or science as the activity of scientists, or as a more abstract notion of a particular kind of knowledge. A similarly wide scope attaches to the word religion. The justification for using such sweeping terms at all is that the various aspects covered by them are functionally related to each other within the larger social nexus. Keeping this wide scope of meaning in mind is important for any functional analysis, if it is to avoid undue focus on one particular function and thereby miss the inherent complexity of the phenomenon.

For the following discussion it will also be important to keep in mind the distinction between *religion* as a social and individual phenomenon, and *theology* as an intellectual endeavour. To the extent that religion and theology belong to different categories, different levels of discourse and practice, the meaning of 'science' in the phrase 'science and theology' has to be different, albeit perhaps subtly, from 'science and religion'.

The concept of functionality is used here in an innocent sense, meaning that religion and science have a reason for existing and play important roles in society. It is not meant to imply that either one can be *reduced to* particular social functions. It does, however, follow from it that at least some functions of religion are indispensable for society, and that therefore all societies have a functional equivalent of religion. Giambattista Vico (1668–1744) is commonly credited with being the first to realize this (Preus 1987: 59–83). Since then many theories have been advanced regarding what exactly these functions are, which ones are primary and how they could be maintained in a society without traditional religion. Stewart Guthrie, who develops a theory of his own in *Faces in the Clouds* (Guthrie 1993), devotes an entire chapter to a comprehensive review of philosophical, psychological, anthropological and sociological theories. Today we should perhaps add neurophysiological ones as well.

What these theories have in common is that there is a *natural role* for religion within societies. The beliefs and practices of various religions or their substitutes may fulfil the social functions required of them to a better or worse extent. Once a function is identified, all religions can no longer be equal. To make a judgement as to what is natural or unnatural about a particular religion is linked, at least in part, to how well or how poorly it fulfils its function within society as a whole. This is the social counterpart to evaluating how healthy or unhealthy particular beliefs and practices are for the individual believer; making such a judgement with respect to society is subject to an analogous balancing act between analysis from outside and beliefs from inside a faith as it is for individuals (Kracher 2000).

My interest in the religion of science then amounts to evaluating the claim that science, or something directly derived from science, is capable of taking over the functions of religion and might even do a better job at fulfilling them. The claim in explicit form belongs to the nineteenth century, and the motivation behind it is intimately connected with the functional view of religion. As the Enlightenment began to treat religion as on object of study (Preus 1987) the initial hope or fear, depending on one's viewpoint, was that the study of nature would make religion superfluous. On the Enlightenment side, expressions of religion were seen as superstition, which would eventually be replaced by correct knowledge. However, the realization that religion had social functions which could not be eliminated, but had to be replaced with some kind of functional equivalent, meant that the possibility and nature of a *religion of science* had to be considered. Auguste Comte made what was perhaps the most far-reaching effort in this direction in the nineteenth century, whilst many of his contemporaries looked for similar functional replacements without specifically labelling them as 'religion'. The label matters because referring to it as religion aims for a double legitimation of the enterprise. On the one hand the new faith would derive its fundamental tenets from science, so that its doctrine would share in the certainty (as the nineteenth century saw it) of scientific discovery. On the other hand it would also be a religion, adopting features that legitimize religions in the eyes of their followers. In other words, one could 'convert' to the new religion rather than simply giving up one's faith.

Of course, calling it a religion may not be an asset in the eyes of those for whom all religions are equally odious. For them the functional substitute would have to come under a different label. I will return to this quandary and its contemporary application at the conclusion of this paper. In its main part, however, I will deal with functional alternatives that explicitly style themselves as new, science-based religions and claim to be superior to traditional ones.

Before investigating this claim two preliminary remarks are necessary. The first is that many findings of science are of course relevant to religion of any kind. How far this relevance extends, and whether it gives science a privileged place, would need a separate discussion and is not my point here. In any case, admitting that science is relevant is obviously quite different from claiming that science could or should replace religion.

The second preliminary comment is more directly germane to the present topic. Whatever the social role of religion, the need for spiritual fulfilment of individuals can certainly be answered in other ways than by traditional religion. If this fulfilment is centred on practising science we would probably say that for such persons science *is* their religion. This is intelligible, in a way that, for example, making the collecting of celebrity trivia one's religion is not. The difference is that science covers a large area, and its results in many cases affect society at large. To make science the centre of one's life is, exceptions notwithstanding, not merely a personal idiosyncrasy but an act with socially relevant consequences.

Not only can scientific practice become the spiritual focus of an individual life, there is also a community of scientists providing a social environment. This community, however, is not the equivalent of a community of believers. It is the community of insiders, the equivalent of an exclusive priesthood. As Gillian Beer has noted, writing about Victorian literature and science, '[w]e unselfconsciously use the term 'layman' to describe the relationship of a non-scientist to the body of scientific knowledge. The suggestion of a priestly class ... goes mostly unremarked' (Beer 1983: 7). The very idea behind a religion of science is rooted in this analogy of the scientific community to a religious body. In this sense the following examples deal with scientists who have deliberately taken on the role of priest or prophet in order to promote their ideas. Later we will need to return to the question to what extent the efforts of these priests and prophets were capable of acquiring a 'lay' congregation for the religion of science.

III. Auguste Comte and the Religion of Humanity[1]

1. Humanity as the New Deity

As mentioned, Auguste Comte (1798–1857) was one of the first who consciously tried to create a religion of science. He conceived the field of sociology and hoped to derive from this new science an ideal society for which he also needed this new religion. A number of Comte's contemporaries likewise developed a comprehensive blueprint for an ideal society, but Comte will provide the best example here because of his explicit attempt to include a new religion, specifically invented for the purpose, in this effort.

Auguste Comte also coined the words *positivism* and *altruism*, but it is for his *Law of the Three Stages* (or *Three States*) that he has become most widely known. He claimed that civilizations as well as individuals progress through the stages of *theological, metaphysical* and *positive* world views. The final and *positive* stage (hence the label of his philosophy as *Positivism*) was originally conceived as scientistic. But in his later life he came to see religion as socially indispensable and proposed to create a new one based on science. A flourishing society could in his view not be sustained by scientific knowledge and expert practice alone; it also had to answer spiritual needs and provide for public worship and ritual. In his later works Comte went on to specify the latter in more and more detail, sometimes to the point of absurdity (Wernick 2001).

Comte emphasized the already mentioned distinction between theology and religion, and it became oversharpened in his later philosophy. Religion is necessary for a functioning society, but in his words '[t]he theological and the positive forms of knowledge … are inherently incompatible forms' (quoted in Gane 2006: 26). Therefore the social progress he conceived is not from religion to science, as is characteristic of scientism, but from a religion of theology to a religion of science. The latter was to be the *Religion of Humanity*, in which Humanity (with a capital initial) took the place that God had occupied in Christianity.

Like many other nineteenth-century thinkers, Comte was much taken with the idea of an inevitable course of history. In this view the underlying reason for social upheavals was an insufficient understanding of social progress, particularly by the common people (Comte was haunted by the aftermath of the French Revolution). It was the purpose of science, especially Comte's sociology, to find out exactly how society could comply with its destined progress. In effect Comte proposed to discover, and to teach his fellow citizens, how to 'stay on course', to cooperate with destiny in bringing about the proper future in which the Religion of Humanity was to play a central role.

Once the notion of a discoverable and predictable trajectory of societies is accepted, all that is unpredictable and contingent becomes the enemy, a source of evil. Susan Neiman, in her reconstruction of modern philosophy in light of the problem of evil (Neiman 2002) particularly identifies the necessity to eliminate

---

[1] Historical material in this section is from Gane (2006), Wernick (2001) and the chapter on Comte in Preus (1987, 107–30).

contingency with Hegel's view of history. It is not clear that Comte, who mostly detested German philosophy (Gane 2006), studied Hegel, but in any case the idea in its practical aspect was ubiquitous in Comte's day.

This makes it clear why traditional Christianity, for which the future was in God's hands, was no longer the appropriate religion for the positive stage of society. Traditional religion always must be, at least to some extent, on the side of wildness, of openness to surprise, of letting go of the desire to control everything (Kracher 2008). Comte's deified Humanity could be scientifically investigated and analysed in a way that the God of tradition could not, and was therefore the proper object of worship in his philosophy. Its trajectory in history could be discovered by reason rather than having to rely on God's promise of salvation.

2. Problems with Comte's Religion

Comte's attempt to consciously create a religion of science already displays for us some pitfalls of the project. First, the driving force for his project of augmenting his earlier scientism with a religion of science by what he called his *subjective method* seems to have been largely his own personal experience. Modern critics of religion have often followed Comte in thinking that traditional religion had outlived its usefulness for society at large, but have jettisoned his perceived need for a *subjective method* to construct a new religion of his own. And indeed it is hard to see how the experience of a single individual, Auguste Comte, and his personal relationships (primarily with the two women of his life, Caroline Massin and Clotilde de Vaux) can logically compel the rest of us to accept and adopt a subjectivity that somehow manages to be sufficiently intersubjective to merit being called a *method*.

Even if worship and ritual are necessary for the health of society, not everyone's subjective need calls for the same form and intensity of these. This is problematic, since Comte's Religion of Humanity demanded stringent moral standards and a high level of asceticism, which he modelled in part on medieval Catholicism. These demands apparently stem from his conviction that Catholicism acted as a stabilizing underpinning of society during the *theological stage* of Western culture, giving way only at the beginning of Modernity to the upheavals of the *metaphysical stage*. But the Religion of Humanity differs from medieval Catholicism in that theistic religion could derive moral standards from God's will. This claim is amenable to theological discussion in a way in which subjective experience is not. Furthermore, replacing God with a quasi-divine Humanity does not really make the divine will any clearer, nor does it prevent the abuses committed in its name. The fate which the ideas of Comte's contemporary Karl Marx suffered in the twentieth century makes that all too obvious.

Second, there is a mismatch between the analytical nature of science and the holistic nature of religion. Scientific investigation directs the exploring mind to detail, intentionally ignoring those aspects that are deemed irrelevant. Comte thought that in the science of sociology, which he invented and named, he had found a bridge across this methodological chasm. When applying the idea in practice, however, the sociological aspect came to dominate all other potential functions of religion in what Comte himself called *sociocracy*. It could potentially sustain society as Comte conceived it, but it was unclear how it would serve individual needs, neither could it easily be integrated into conceptions of society that differed from Comte's own.

The existence of such differences reveals a third problem that affects conceptions of society in a more general way. As Andrew Wernick notes, Comte as well as most of his contemporaries thought of society as a quasi-organism, and '[i]f society is an organism, sociology provides a scientific understanding of the conditions for its health' (Wernick 2001: 57). But this metaphor conceals a fundamental flaw, and it was G. K. Chesterton who pointed it out at the beginning of *What's Wrong with the World* (1994: 15–17). We have, Chesterton argued, a common-sense notion of health for an individual, but when it comes to society, there are widely divergent ideals. Does 'health' for societies mean libertarianism? Communism? Distributism (Chesterton's own preference)? With such lack of consensus we cannot expect a single functionally integrated entity to have universal support, such as Comte envisioned for the Religion of Humanity.

Chesterton thought that his Catholicism committed him to supporting distributism, an almost forgotten early version of the 'small is beautiful' view of society. But traditional religion, whether Catholic or not, can survive in societies not following its ideal, because it has its own autonomous role in the social nexus. The Religion of Humanity, being dependent on a functional role within the particular society envisioned by Comte, cannot.

Finally, a fourth problem is that every religion implies some kind of promise for a better life to those who follow it. For a religion of science this must necessarily be some kind of immanent paradise – in Comte's case the well-ordered and peaceful 'positive society', in Marx's the classless society of the final stage of communism. At first glance the quest for an ideal society here and now would seem an improvement over doing nothing about injustice while consoling believers with otherworldly ideals. But when the promise of an immanent paradise remains unfulfilled, we tend to get not only individual disappointment, but often more widespread suffering and injustice, which tends to lead to the social upheavals that Comte sought to prevent in the first place.

Religions are more realistic; they usually do have stories that explain why society is not perfect. And most religions do not in fact ignore existing suffering and injustice, but tend to balance worldly charity with the proclamation of a transcendent ideal. Much can go wrong with the balancing act, but when it does there is no inherent reason why the balance cannot be restored from within. By contrast, the Religion of Humanity and other forms of a religion of science cannot even admit the reality of such a balance. Because they rule out by definition the existence of an ideal that is transcendent in the religious sense, there is nothing to be balanced, only an immanent goal that must be achieved in order for society to be 'healthy'. This one-sidedness affecting a religion of science can have much more tragic consequences, as we can see from the example provided by the history of the eugenics movement (Black 2003).

IV. Eugenics

It seems almost too easy to bring up eugenics as example of how a populist science movement can go wrong. But its history illustrates so many of the dangers that may corrupt a religion of science that it is worth a closer look. The eugenics movement began in the late nineteenth century when early insights about genetics and heredity became known to the general public. Its goal was at first to discourage, and later to prevent, procreation by those parts of the population that were deemed 'undesirable', a concept whose very vagueness seems in retrospect to have invited the abuses that actually occurred. In spite of the nineteenth-century advances in understanding heredity, the crudely mechanistic view that many eugenicists had of society was in some ways a step backwards from the elaborate sociology of Comte. Unfortunately it may have been exactly this simplification that made it so much more successful.

At first glance eugenics seems such a narrowly focused issue that one might question the label of 'religion'. Yet that is precisely how its founder, Francis Galton, saw it: eugenics 'must be introduced into the national conscience, like a new religion'. This and similar quotations prompt Christine Rosen to write that 'descriptions of eugenics resembled an evangelical vision as much as a science' (Rosen 2004: 5).

If the scope of this 'new religion' was so much narrower than Comte's grand vision, the root cause of this narrowness is the analytical, subject-oriented nature of science that we have already noted. The reason, I believe, why such a comparatively narrow issue could make itself into a new religion is that many people find it easier to adopt as 'their religion' a particular cause rather than the comprehensive view of life demanded by traditional religion. And precisely because of its narrow focus the aim of eugenics eventually managed to overpower and swallow up, as it were, all the other aspects that a healthy and mature religion should have displayed, foremost among them the moral reflection on its own methods. To put it bluntly, eugenics turned into a classic example of ends justifying means.

Initially the majority of eugenicists advocated only a minimum of coercion, or none at all, and in this form the movement found many supporters among progressive Christians, particularly in the United States (Rosen 2004). Many scientists who favoured eugenics were prevented by their own moral standards from advocating radical measures such as forced sterilization (two examples are narrated by Gould 1995: 285–308). Yet the movement developed its own moral, or rather amoral, intrinsic dynamic, and today we largely think of it in terms of its large-scale sterilization campaigns in the early and mid-twentieth century (Black 2003). The personal moral standards of its academic members turned out to be an insufficient brake on the train that ran on the power of a narrowly focused 'scientific' motivation.

Among the few early opponents to eugenics who apparently had foreseen this development was G. K. Chesterton (2009), already on record here as an opponent to the scientific criterion of a 'healthy state'. There is an inner logic tying the two cases together. Just like the promoters of the organismic metaphor sought to eliminate contingency from the purportedly inevitable progress of society, so the eugenicists sought to narrow the scope of contingency inherent in genetic diversity and procreation by restricting personal partner choice and reducing the gene pool. In the first case the goal was an ideal society, in the second the ideal human race of the future. In both cases it was ultimately the uniformity, the lack of allowance for the unexpected, to which Chesterton, lover of paradoxes and defender of quirky individuals, objected.

But Chesterton also foresaw that once the movement toward forced sterilization was set in motion, it would be difficult to stop, no matter what qualms its originators might later have about it. And, in fact, the political movement to promote sterilization laws did indeed gain momentum in the 1920s and 1930s, at just about the time when its support from both scientific and religious communities waned. Newer genetic research had cast doubt on the assumption that heredity had much to do with many of the conditions that were enumerated in eugenics laws, such as feeblemindedness, pauperism and racial inferiority. Likewise religious groups, who might have found it morally acceptable to regulate marriage for those parts of society supposedly unworthy of procreation, balked at the idea of mutilating substantial sections of the population.

It was too late. Campaigns of forced sterilization on a large scale were carried out not only in the US, but in at least a dozen other countries around the world. Only the extremes which the eugenic campaign reached in Nazi Germany finally made the idea abhorrent. Even so it appears that forced sterilization continued into the 1970s in some states of the US and possibly elsewhere (Black 2003: 400).

Today we are facing ethical questions of a similar nature over the possibility of directly manipulating genetic material. The issues are more subtle than simple coercion, and the eugenics-as-religion rhetoric of the original movement is for the most part noticeably absent among proponents. This may be a sign that the explicitly religious language of earlier times has lost its usefulness for rallying non-scientists to the cause. As I argue below, however, it is quite likely that the substance of the idea behind the religion of science is still present to varying degrees in these debates, but it is dressed up in a different language that appeals to people for whom 'religion' has negative connotations or no meaning at all.

V. Traditional religion and the religion of science

For all its excesses, the example of eugenics merely shows that a religion of science can be misunderstood, hijacked by base motives and abused for political ends. Any look at world religions will tell us that most of them have been similarly instrumentalized in such a political way. Of course, showing that a religion of science is no more abuse-proof than any other faith is significant in itself, because surely abuses in and by traditional religions were one motivation for thinking that a religion of science could do better.

But in fact a religion of science is in a worse position than this, and a reflection on our examples tells us why. Whatever other functions religion may have, a central one is surely moral orientation. Science, in the usual sense of the word, can provide 'positive knowledge', but by itself this knowledge does not tell us how to act on it. In philosophical terms, a religion of science is only conceivable if the move from the scientific *Is* to the moral *Ought* can be made without committing the naturalistic fallacy. Thus a religion of science would need an additional ingredient, a moral compass to tell us which uses of knowledge are beneficial and which ones destructive.

There are three different possibilities to consider when thinking about how such a moral compass could be inserted into a religion of science. First, it might come from the morality of its founding individual(s). Second, a particular scientific discipline might be discovered or developed which actually tells us how we ought to behave. Finally, the totality of science might give rise to a general acceptance of moral principles.

We have already seen that the personal moral standards of scientists were powerless to prevent the abuses of their eugenic ideas once the science had been turned into a quasi-religious movement. The abuse of lofty theoretical ideas once they become mass movements is by now so familiar from numerous historical examples that one can only wonder how thoughtful people can still put forward concepts of an ideal society without paying the slightest attention to safeguards against corruption. At least Comte, who had the example of the French Revolution before his eyes, was mindful of the danger, even if his solution of a scientific priesthood was wildly unrealistic.

As for particular scientific disciplines, Comte did expect that his 'science of man', which he called at first *social physics* and later *sociology*, would provide a kind of scientific morality. Other students of humanity, however, had a view of future society radically different from Comte's, which naturally led to very different moral precepts. It is difficult to see how science by itself, even a science of society, could arbitrate among these rival ideals. More recent hopes about a scientific morality, e.g. on the basis of evolutionary psychology or neurophysiology, have likewise failed to find a convincing way to derive an *Ought* from an *Is*.

This leaves us with the third possibility, which was the great hope of the Enlightenment: that a general belief in science would create a congregation of the church scientific with a morality superior to that of traditional religions. And so it might, if there were efficient ways to curb abuses. Comte might have installed a priestly caste of scientists to rule the masses and watch over their moral purity, a proposal in keeping with his scepticism about democracy. In the actual societies of the twentieth century, whether democratic or not, neither scientists from within nor religious critics from outside could do much to keep the eugenics movement from going awry, however informed or misinformed about science its followers might have been.

In the face of this scepticism that any of our alternatives can provide an adequate foundation for morality within a religion of science, we may ask whether the very idea that a moral compass is something to be 'added on' to a comprehensive notion of how to organize the world is perhaps misguided from the start. Surely a source of morality has to be in a sense foundational, not posterior to knowledge about function. There is reason to think that on an individual level morality is in a sense *prior to* knowledge, but, even if this claim is rejected, something like a co-evolution of the two seems to be required to maintain individual sanity and social balance.

VI. Conclusions

A number of conclusions can be drawn from this look at attempts to create new, science-based religions. Although the time when this was done deliberately and explicitly seems to be over, what we can learn from the examples remains important in our day. The need to have a functional equivalent of religion has not disappeared, even if today it may be packaged under a different label from the one used by Comte and Galton. It will remain a challenging project to apply the conclusions of this study to our present situation in which the religious dimension of social proposals is implicit rather than explicit.

1. Religion and the power of self-correction
A critical difference between traditional religions and religion(s) of science stems from the fact that science is a very deliberate activity by a limited number of individuals, and hence a religion of science has to be deliberately designed and specified in some detail. Thus the French rationalists at the end of the eighteenth and early nineteenth century took great pride in the fact that their designs did away with the messy and sometimes self-contradictory aspects of tradition, as demon-strated for example by the persistent, albeit resoundingly unsuccessful, efforts to invent a 'rational' calendar.

But the richness of tradition, which looks so frustratingly messy to a rationalist eye, is what enables religions to correct course from within. It is unfortunately true that historically this has happened less often than one would wish, and frequently more as a result of outside pressure than due to awareness from within that things have gone wrong. Even so, the very capability of self-correction is a stabilizing feature which, properly understood, is itself one of the social functions of religion. The preceding analysis raises doubts whether a religion of science would ever be capable of fulfilling this particular function. In general, it did not occur to the nineteenth-century social reformers that their own ideas might some day be themselves in need of reform. In keeping with the century's optimism that its scien-tific accomplishments were true 'for eternity', the ability of self-correction was to them of secondary importance.

2. The 'optimization' of religion
It is of course true that religions function within societies in ways that sociology can and does analyse. But it does not follow that this analysis exhaustively explains the nature of religion. There is no algorithmic procedure to devise the 'ideal religion' by optimizing it for its known functions (Kracher 2000: 842). Traditional religions have a multitude of functions, and different ones can take precedence at different times and under different circumstances. It is doubtful that any sociological

theory can arrive at a comprehensive list, which is why there seems to be so much disagreement as to what the 'real' function of religion is (cf. Guthrie 1993: 8–38). And it is even more doubtful that all human experience, and therefore all functions of religion, can be formalized in such a way that my hypothetical optimization algorithm would accomplish anything useful in the real world.

This is why it makes little sense to 'invent' a religion out of the idea of one person or a few individuals. All traditional religions have grown in some long social process: through debates, through popular practices that have developed with little or no conscious design, and through the efforts of a great number of individual intellects. In a few words, religions are products as well as sources of tradition. This is perhaps the reason why Comte's contemporary Alexis de Tocqueville (1805–59), famously more sympathetic than Comte to that messy form of government called democracy, sought to retain traditional religion as a stabilizing force in society rather than trying to invent a new one himself (Meyer 1972).

3. Science and spirituality

All the same, it would be a mistake to deny the spiritual power of science, and we should not ignore its potential for inspiring moral as well as practical achievements. But science, as it is usually understood, cannot on its own fulfil and sustain the functions of religion. We have previously considered the possibility that the pursuit of science can become a person's 'religion', but this it mostly limited to practising scientists. Building the church scientific for the masses, of which secular thinkers of the Enlightenment dreamed, turned out to be unexpectedly difficult. On the one hand there is the danger that the original idea becomes, as it were, too popular in the wrong way, by developing a more or less uncontrollable vicious dynamic. We have seen this in the case of eugenics, but it is something very familiar from the history of world religions as well. And, as far as Comte is concerned, his older contemporaries could still recall how the worship of Reason descended into mob hysteria during the Reign of Terror.

On the other hand, historically the church scientific in its uncorrupted form turned out to have fairly limited public appeal. To be sure, there is interest in science events for the public, science museums, etc., but these seem to fall far short of performing the social functions that for example Comte envisioned for his science-based religion. Comte himself spent much of his life developing comprehensive science courses, not for specialists but for the general public. Nonetheless only a small circle of admirers took his proposal for a Religion of Humanity seriously.

When we talk today of non-traditional ways of fulfilling the spiritual needs of individuals, it is not science that comes to mind, but a range of movements such as Eastern meditative practices, New Age, etc. While their attitude towards mainstream science may vary, none of them have a close connection with it, and some of them are downright hostile or pseudo-scientific.

Where some kind of integration among the various social and individual functions of religion and science is attempted at all, it still comes mainly from traditional religions, however strained the relationship may be. Our look at potential science-based alternatives probably gives us some clue why this is so. Any attempt to reduce the richness of tradition to one or a few explicitly specified social functions ends with such a spiritually impoverished structure that it is either no longer attractive, or too easily hijacked by base motives.

4. The need for dialogue

Rather than inventing a religion of science, then, a continued dialogue is necessary that draws on the assets present on both sides: on the side of science in particular those branches of knowledge that affect individual spirituality; on the other side religions that are friendly to this aspect of science and willing to embrace new knowledge as part of their own tradition.

Unfortunately not all is well. Looking at the present situation I cannot see that what might be called 'a comfortable match' has so far been found. On the side of science reductionism still rules the day. As a methodological habit of scientists this is understandable, but in dialogue with religion it ultimately precludes understanding. On the side of religions, at least their official representatives, the spiritual impact of science is still not taken seriously enough. And in addition to their own difficulties both sides have a problem with their camp mates who are viciously hostile to the other side.

To close, however, with a sign of hope, there is no reason why the dialogue should not make progress. There are scholars who are trained in both camps and can therefore see both sides of the issues. There are also mediators outside the realm of formal academic scholarship, such as artists and visionaries, who can be appreciated by both sides. Some day these may bring us to the point where science-oriented minds no longer consider it necessary to invent their own religion or substitute thereof, because the resources of the traditional kind will be completely open to them.

References

Beer, G. (1983), *Darwin's Plots; Evolutionary Narrative in Darwin, George Eliot and Nineteenth Century Fiction*. London: Routledge & Kegan Paul.

Black, E. (2003), *War Against the Weak*. New York, NY: Four Walls Eight Windows.

Chesterton, G. K. (1994 [1910]), *What's Wrong with the World* San Francisco, CA: Ignatius Press.

—(2009 [1922]), *Eugenics and Other Evils*. Charleston, SC: Seven Treasures Publications.

Drees, W. B. (2010), 'The multiplicity of purposes of "religion and science"'. In D. Evers, A. Jackelén and T. A. Smedes (eds), *How Do We Know?* London: T & T Clark, pp. 121–41.

Gane, M. (2006), *Auguste Comte*. London: Routledge.

Gould, S. J. (1995), *Dinosaur in a Haystack*. New York, NY: Random House.

Guthrie, S. E. (1993), *Faces in the Clouds*. New York, NY: Oxford University Press.

Kracher, A. (2000), 'Phenomenology and theology – reflections on the study of religion'. *Zygon, 35,* 827–48.

—(2008), 'The diversity of environments: nature and technology as competing myths'. In W. B. Drees, H. Meisinger and T. A. Smedes (eds), *Creation's Diversity: Voices from Theology and Science.* London: T & T Clark, pp. 78–88.

Meyer, J. P. (1972), *Alexis de Tocqueville.* (3rd rev. edn. Munich: C. H. Beck).

Neiman, S. (2002), *Evil in Modern Thought.* Princeton, NJ: Princeton University Press.

Preus, J. S. (1987), *Explaining Religion.* New Haven, CT: Yale University Press.

Rosen, C. (2004), *Preaching Eugenics.* New York, NY: Oxford University Press.

Wernick, A. (2001), *Auguste Comte and the Religion of Humanity.* Cambridge, UK: Cambridge University Press.

Part III

The Nature of Religion – Theological Perspectives

10 The Religion of Nature and the Nature of Religion: Theological Perspectives on the Ambiguities of Understanding Nature and Religion

Christoph Schwöbel

Is it possible to give a complete and coherent account of religion in naturalistic terms? Is it possible to 'naturalize' religion? And, conversely, does nature in this way acquire a somewhat religious significance? Is it, in this sense, possible to conceive nature religiously? Can one talk in a meaningful way, if one does not eschew the inelegant neologism, about 'religionizing' nature? These questions do not arise from idle speculation. The development of the cognitive science of religion in the last 20 years has, in fact, been based on the claim that it is possible to explain *The Naturalness of Religious Ideas*, as the title of Pascal Boyer's seminal work underlines (Boyer 1994) or to answer the question *Why Would Anyone Believe in God?* (Barrett 2004). Furthermore, the advent of the so-called 'neurotheology' has not only attempted to point to the correlations (and, according to some practitioners of the new brand of theology, causal links) between neural phenomena in the brain and religious experiences, but has also emphasized the significance of these findings for a new universal spirituality. If religion is universal in the sense that it is based on panhuman properties of the human mind that can be correlated to specific neural phenomena which are open to empirical testing, it would seem possible, on the one hand, to account for the significance of religion in the process of human evolution and, on the other hand, it opens up vistas where the differences between religions can be overcome by a new unitary framework of natural religion. The Enlightenment idea of natural religion, i.e. a religion that is based on the common properties of human nature, and the hope that natural religion would provide a basis for peaceful human interaction where the historical religions have tended to lead to conflict and strife would gain new credibility.

However, if one explores the 'naturalness' of religion and, conversely, the 'religiousness' of nature much depends on one's understanding of the key terms 'nature' and 'religion'. What one understands by 'nature' or 'religion' is not an empirical question. It is a conceptual question about the categories that one already presupposes in the design of empirical research. These conceptual pre-understandings have a decisive influence on the questions that are being asked in empirical research on what could be given as an answer to these questions and on what could be seen as data for the verification or falsification of a hypothesis. The concepts one employs also have a decisive influence on communication across disciplinary boundaries, and it is here that hermeneutical questions of trans-disciplinary understanding need to be clarified.

One further issue immediately arises when we reflect on the question of the 'naturalness of religion' or the 'religiousness of nature'. For the term 'nature' it would seem preposterous to employ the term in any theoretical context without consulting natural scientists, because in some way what we understand by nature should be connected to what they do and how they understand nature in this context. However, if one looks a little more closely at the history of science, the ambiguity of the term nature seems to have played a major role in the constitution of modern science. The 'Father of modern chemistry' Robert Boyle even recommended refraining from using the term 'nature' at all (Boyle 1688; cf. Spaemann 2010). Similarly, it would seem at least problematical to investigate religion without being in conversation with those who see themselves as adherents of a particular religion. This would seem to be necessary in order to see how certain features of religion that play a role in research on the 'naturalness of religion' are perceived by believers. How are these features located in the doctrinal schemes that are seen by believers as central in their religion? How do these beliefs structure the lives of religious people in their own view, and how are they interrelated with their participation in certain ritual, their spiritual practices or their overall interpretation of reality. It may be granted that adherents of a particular religion might have problems with the concept of religion. But these difficulties – one only has to think of Karl Barth in the context of twentieth-century Protestant theology – would then have to inform the way one uses the concept of religion, just as the natural scientists' reservations about the meaning of 'nature' would have to come into a conceptual inquiry of what it means to employ the concept of nature. Even at first sight the notions of nature and religion seem to be highly complex and their employment fraught with difficulties.

The title of this chapter contains an intended ambiguity. In the first half 'nature' refers to what is 'natural', i.e. given in the material, physical, chemical or biological structure and organization of entities that are not primarily the product of human activity and in this sense artificial. In the second half of the title 'nature', is employed in the traditional philosophical meaning of denoting the essential characteristics and intrinsic properties of an entity. In the first half of the phrase what should be understood as 'religion' is clearly dependent on the understanding of nature; in the second half what is to be seen as the nature of religion depends on what is understood by religion. These ambiguities are not necessarily detrimental. Rather, they serve to indicate the peculiar character of concepts such as 'nature' and 'religion' in that they contain layers of meaning which cannot simply be reduced to a clear cut definition. W. B. Gallie has called such concepts – his own examples are 'work of art' and 'social justice' – 'essentially contested concepts'. These are concepts that involve disputes among their users as to how they should be understood, disputes which cannot easily be settled by appeals to logic, empirical evidence or common sense. Dogmatic solutions insisting on the correctness of only one usage are just as little helpful as sceptical proposal, simply leaving the dispute unsettled, or an eclecticism which declares it to be a matter of choice to select one of a variety of meanings. Essentially contested concepts need to be contested: they need to be tested in conversation in order to tease out the significance of the disagreements that surround them. Essentially contested concepts confront us with the challenge to reveal the framework within which these concepts function and to describe their function in different frameworks in order to have a meaningful conversation about disagreements, agreements and possible convergences in the process of understanding. They open up the possibility for different understandings to complement or correct one another. The concepts of 'nature' and 'religion' therefore seem to be very suitable candidates for a conversation on the relationship between science and theology.

In this chapter I would like to illustrate in a first step what is understood by 'religion' in some of the theories of cognitive research in religion and some of the new neurotheologies. This involves the question of what is understood by 'nature' in phrases such as the 'naturalness' of religion or in talk about the 'naturalization of religion'. In a second step I will try to point out some features of religion as it is understood from the perspective of the self-understanding of people participating in a religion. Third, I will make some remarks on how the notions of religion and nature can be interpreted from the perspective of Christian faith. Both concepts 'religion' and 'nature' appear to be contextualized in the doctrinal scheme of Christian faith. I suggest that paying attention to the particularities of the way nature and religion can be understood from the perspective of Christian faith opens up interesting areas for dialogue between the experimental neurosciences of religion and the cognitive science of religion and Christian theology, while critically challenging views on the naturalness of religion or the religiousness of nature.

I. The religion of nature: Are we hard-wired for religion?

For almost 50 years C. P. Snow's metaphor of the 'two cultures' of science and what he termed 'literary intellectuals' in his 1959 Rede Lectures has dominated public debate on the relationship between science and culture (Snow 1959). Today it seems that the demarcation lines between the two different territories have broken down. The current scientific and public interest in the relationship between science and religion is a good example of the overcoming of a metaphor that gradually became more problematical, the more it was abstracted from its original setting: a critique of the British education system favouring familiarity with the literary canon over scientific knowledge.

Of particular interest for the question of the 'naturalness' of religion is, on the one hand, the development of the cognitive science of religion and the development of the so-called neurotheology in the experimental neuroscience of religion. Since its inception 20 years ago research on religious concepts and representations in the cognitive sciences has developed rapidly, and in 2000 E. Thomas Lawson introduced the term Cognitive Science of Religion as the programmatic name for the new discipline (Lawson 2000). With the foundation of the International Association for Cognitive Science of Religion in 2006 it has gained an institutional forum for the collaboration of researchers from different disciplines.[1] Cognitive science of religion treats the study of religion as an explanatory exercise. It questions the standard view of cultural anthropology that meaning-systems must be understood as cultural phenomena which are distinct from physical processes and therefore not susceptible to causal explanation. The proponents of the cognitive science of religion emphatically see religious meaning systems as manifestations of physical phenomena, open to causal explanation and accessible to empirical testing. Therefore they work on the basis of a cognitive psychology, which has its primary field in the areas of intuitive knowledge, employing the notion of the modularity of mind as it was developed in faculty psychology and evolutionary psychology (Fodor 1983). Religious representations are specific selections and configurations of those ideas which humans apply in all areas of knowing. Cultural and public representations are based on individual mental representations, and these are the primary focus of empirical research. Religion can thus be traced back to a number of recurrent patterns of representations which we find, so it is claimed, in all human cultures.

Pascal Boyer explicitly rejects monocausal attempts at explaining religion. Religion is a diverse phenomenon and cannot be explained by a single factor. Indeed, it remains questionable, as Boyer admits, whether the term 'religion' should be used at all as an umbrella term for such a complex phenomenon. Far more relevant is the cross-cultural recurrence of certain ideas in religious contexts. They include the assumption of non-observable agents, the idea that a person survived death and the notion that persons can receive some kind of 'supernatural' inspiration or are in communication with a 'spiritual', i.e. non-physical, world (cf. Boyer 2001: 5–34). Such beliefs, so the representatives of the cognitive science of religion hold, are the by-products of mental tools that have evolved in the process of human evolution. On whether religious beliefs should be seen as a real adaptation and in this way the result of natural selection or whether religious beliefs should be seen as a 'spandrel', a trait that is a by-product of evolution but is not selected for an increase in biological adaptation (Gould and Lewontin 1979), remains an open debate among different representatives of the cognitive science approach. A common element of their view is, however, an account of religious beliefs as a counter-intuitive 'violation' or extension of our everyday intuitive thinking. Our intuitive knowledge, so they hold, is normally organized in basic categories, e.g. person, animal, natural object and tool (cf. Boyer 2001: 64–5). Religious beliefs take up one or more of those categories and then correct them in a way that runs

---

[1] A comprehensive overview on the philosophical issues raised by the Cognitive Science of Religion is provided by Visala 2008.

counter to the expectations usually connected with that particular category. The notion of an omniscient God can therefore be understood as being based on the category of person, but extending it to include special cognitive capacities, thus violating the everyday expectations connected with the category of 'person'. Minimally counterintuitive concepts are, on this view, most successful. They can easily be recalled because of the 'violation' element that they contain, but can also easily be employed because they leave a large number of standard expectations, belonging to a given ontological category, intact. Since our minds tend to deal with the world by identifying agencies, some proponents of cognitive science of religion claim that our minds have a Hyperactive Agency Detecting Device, a mechanism designed to identify agencies, which, in the absence of natural agencies (hyper-actively), tends to ascribe certain events as effects to supernatural agencies, i.e. gods or God. In this way, religious notions are 'parasitic':

> Because the concepts require all sorts of specific human capacities (an intuitive psychology, a tendency to attend to some counterintuitive concepts, as well as various social mind adaptations), we can explain religion by describing how these various capacities get recruited, how they contribute to the features of religion that we find in so many different cultures. We do not need to assume that there is a special way of functioning that occurs only when processing religious thoughts. (Boyer 2001: 196)

It is therefore not necessary to inquire into the historical origin of religion. It originates at all times and in many places through the selection of concepts and memories (cf. Boyer 2001: 33). To understand the way this selection works we need no historical information, and even less a religious account, but simply an empirically testable view of how religious concepts are formed through the counter-intuitive extension of everyday concepts. The evidence produced in this way is considered to be strong. Belief in God appears to be as an almost automatic consequence of the way the mind works on a level below consciousness, a view that is held to be compatible with Christian theological accounts of the existence and the agency of an all-powerful, all-knowing God (cf. Barrett, 2004).

When we turn from cognitive science of religion to neurotheology we are entering another sphere of scientific inquiry into religion. These developments, which have received much public attention, were made possible through the development of imaging technologies measuring the blood flow in the brain.[2] SPECT (Single Photon Emission Computed Tomography), PET (Positron Emission Tomography) and fMRI (functional Magnetic Resonance Imaging) are among the most popular. The appeal of these imaging technologies, which create the impression that we can watch the brain at work, is also one of the factors in the public interest in neurotheology. Although the term had already been used in the 1962 novel *Island* by the English writer Aldous Huxley of *Brave New World* fame,

---

[2] An excellent overview of current research is provided in Schjoedt 2009. His presentation of the methods, procedures and research results (and their problems) offers a clearer picture than the popular books by the neuroscientists referred to in the text.

the term received a new significance through James B. Ashbrook's programme of correlating the working brain and the work of theology (Ashbrook 1984) and was popularized by Laurence O. McKinney's book *Neurotheology* (1994), establishing the connection to meditation techniques and Buddhism in the West. Michael Persinger's experiments with the 'God-helmet', stimulating the brain through the skull using TMS (Transcranial Magnetic Stimulation), which results, as Persinger claims, that 80 percent of the population have the experience of a 'felt' presence of another being received widespread attention (Persinger 1987). However, his thesis that the stimulation in the temporal lobe could account for a feeling of the presence of God (or other profound spiritual experiences) was severely questioned, when a group from Uppsala University led by Pehr Granqvist replicated the experiments under double-blind randomized conditions and found no comparable effects of TMS but only the effects of susceptibility to suggestion (Granqvist et al. 2005). Scientific kudos was given to the enterprise of neurotheology by the work of Andrew Newberg and Eugene d'Aquili of the University of Pennsylvania, presented for a wider audience in the *The Mystical Mind* (d'Aquili and Newberg 1999) and *Why God Won't Go Away* (Newberg et al. 2001). According to their theory, religious experience is caused by an overload of stimuli in the limbic structures of the brain, in the hypothalamus and amygdala. This blocks perceptual input which in turn leads to an interruption of afferent nerve impulses in the associative areas. The result is an altered state of consciousness. If input to the posterior superior parietal lobe (PSPL), where the processing of representations of spatial distinctions and distances between the self and others occurs, is blocked, this induces a state which Newberg/d'Aquili call Absolute Unitary Being (AUB). There are two ways in which this may occur. In rhythmic practices accompanied by rich sensations the brain is flooded with sympathetic and parasympathetic activity leading to a direct blocking of PSPL. Here decreased activity in the prefrontal cortex can be shown, which leads to increased activity in the superior parietal lobe (SPL). This pattern could be shown in a study of five volunteers from the Pentecostal movement during glossolalia where the decrease of prefrontal activity may be connected to loss of control during the experience of speaking in tongues (Newberg et al. 2006). Focused attention in meditation leads according to d'Aquili and Newberg to the activation of the sympathetic processes of the autonomous nervous system through hippocampus and amygdala. The consequent increase of activity in the prefrontal cortex blocks the PSPL, the distinction between self and others is transcended. Increased activity in the dorsolateral prefrontal activities leads to decreased activity in the SPL. This Newberg's team could show both in a study with eight meditators in the Tibetan Buddhist tradition (Newberg et al. 2001) and with three Franciscan nuns and their prayer recitation (Newberg et al. 2003). All studies were conducted by using the SPECT technology of brain imaging.

While Newberg's and d'Aquili's findings are suggestive for the way in which experiments can be designed, combining the competences of a radiologist and a research psychiatrist, in order to show the correlation between specific kinds of religious experience with neural processes, many of their assumptions concerning the existence of functionally specialized systems in the associative areas of the brain, e.g. their location of the subjective experience of the self/other dichotomy in the PSPL, remain so far conjecture (Schjoedt 2009: 316–17) . These difficulties not withstanding, d'Aquili and Newberg have already in *The Mystical Mind* developed a vision which direction the development of neurotheology should take, if their assumption that religious experience is based on universal brain mechanisms is correct. They envision a 'metatheology' which 'can be understood as the overall principles underlying any and all religions and ultimate belief systems and their theologies' (d'Aquili and Newberg 1999: 195). On the basis of these principles they hope to show how and why myths are formed, how and why they are developed in complex theological systems, and how and why their insights can be performed in ceremonial rituals. While 'metatheology' in their sense abstracts from the content, and focuses on the how and why of the mechanisms of elaboration, they also envisage a 'megatheology' which 'should contain content of such a universal nature that it would be adopted by most, if not all, of the world's great religions as a basic element without any serious violation of their essential doctrines' (195; cf. Peters 2001). This heady vision of a shared future of the neurosciences and theology would seem to transcend the expectations of most scientists working in the field (cf. Geertz 2009) *and* of most theologians (cf. Evers 2006).

What then is the view of 'religion' presupposed in the accounts of the cognitive science of religion and neurotheology in the way described by some experimental neuroscientists? And on which understanding of 'nature' is this view based? From the perspective of cognitive science of religion the thoughts and acts that are deemed natural are those that rest on 'noncultural' foundations (cf. Boyer 1994). What is natural in this sense is not dependent on a particular cultural input, in the sense of an acquired competence that presupposes a particular symbolic system, and does seem to occur in all cultural situations. To learn a language, to have some sort of understanding of the behaviour of physical objects in spaces, to deal with basic distinctions such as edible and inedible, animate and inanimate, to be able to relate to other people as conscious agents, etc, are all capacities which seem to be spread across all cultures. It is therefore reasonable to suppose that the underlying cognitive processes and representations therefore have a cross-cultural universality because they are based on noncultural foundations. Actions based on these cognitive capacities are performed almost automatically and with ease, requiring little or no explicit tuition and they do not seem to vary much between cultures. These capacities seem to be acquired at an early stage in human development, which is one of the reasons why empirical studies with children play such an important role in the cognitive science of religion. Although these capacities seem pretty basic, they nevertheless have a cognitive function. They are ways of explaining the world in such a way that human agents can move in it with ease and confidence. If 'natural' means 'doing what comes naturally' then religion must be understood exactly in this sense (cf. McCauley 2000). Religion seems to rest on fundamental forms of behaviour which we find already in prehistoric cultures. The ways in which religion is practised show a large degree of recurrent patterns and no unilinear development. And, finally, it occurs in all cultures at all stages of cultural development. It relies on standard human cognitive equipment and mental tools, its assumptions are intuitive and wide-spread across cultures. The most conspicuous element is the identification of agents and their actions which is the most basic way in which humans interact with one another and with the world around them. This is the reason why religious explanations normally refer to superhuman agents as explanatory factors and why religions normally operate with anthropomorphic cognitive strategies whatever their reflective, cultural 'theologies' may be (cf. Barrett and Keil 1996). In this sense religion is natural as opposed to science or theology which, because of their reliance on cultural inputs, must be regarded as 'unnatural'. For cognitive scientists of religion this also explains the extraordinary persistence of religion in human history. In contrast to the view of the early positivists, like Auguste Comte, where religion is superseded by the scientific exploration of the world, they hold that it is very unlikely that religion will ever be superseded since religion relies on the natural 'wiring' of humans far more than elaborate cultural activities.

What about neurotheology? In the version of neurotheology we have briefly sketched, the natural is the neural as it can be imaged by an imaging technology measuring the brain's blood flow (like SPECT). Religion is natural insofar it has clear and clearly imaged neural correlates. It is interesting that we have here a similar reduction of the significance of the cultural diversities in the sign systems of different religions. Natural universality which is claimed on the basis of the neuroscientific evidence is contrasted with cultural diversity which we find in different religious traditions. The focus on religious experiences and the subsequent narrowing of religious experiences to extraordinary experiences such as meditation and glossolalia has as its correlate the focus on mystical notions of unity. The underlying argument runs as follows. Since religious experiences even in very different traditions, like those of Tibetan meditation and Franciscan prayer practice, can traced back to the same neural mechanism, the blocking of PSPL, the orientation area, through the increased activity of the prefrontal cortex, they offer the same kind of experience. Mystical experiences are understood to be on the one end of a continuum, at the other end of which are baseline experiences. In the most profound form, mystical experience is a state of the experience of absolute unitary being where, because of the blocking of the processes of differentiation of self and non-self, the meditator is being absorbed into a state of non-differentiation which is experienced as ultimate reality: more real than the baseline experience of reality. There is an interesting contrast to cognitive science of religion here for which religion is natural because it is interwoven with the *most basic* cognitive functions of intuitive knowledge. For neurotheology, universality appears as the transcendence of baseline experience in the suspension of everyday modes of knowledge through complex cognitive tasks in meditation. For a world that is confronted with potentially violent conflicts apparently rooted in or supported by religious diversity, the vision of overcoming these divisions by a unifying experience of absolute unitary being seems to have considerable attraction. In their view of metatheology, developing the universal principles underlying all religious experiences by discovering the neural mechanisms of religious experiences can lead to a megatheology which – on the basis of these principles – can even produce a new religious content which overcomes the divisions of religious traditions.

From the perspective of the study of religion, it is interesting to note that cognitive science of religion tends to lead to a theistic understanding of religion focusing on an acting God or gods, whereas neurotheology tends to focus on a mystical understanding of religion, interpreting theistic religion along these lines, i.e. union with God as a state of absolute unitary being.

II. The nature of religion: Amazed by Grace

We now turn to the understanding of 'religion' and 'nature' as they appear from the perspective of the understanding of the religions. This is, of course, an abstraction. In the context of the living religions, the self-understanding of religion is always the self-understanding of a particular religion and, within that particular religion, of a reconstruction, based upon a particular individual vantage-point within a particular religious community. The procedure from which a description of religion is suggested is therefore always one of controlled analogical generalization which requires testing against the evidence of the religious self-understanding offered from other perspectives. Paul Tillich has argued as early as 1919 that in systematic cultural studies the standpoint of the investigator belongs to the subject matter itself and every proposal is an oblique normative concept (Tillich 1975: 13). This may, in fact, be helpful to avoid the one-dimensional reductionism, wide-spread in many popular accounts of neuroscience, which, by bracketing the standpoint of the investigator, also abstracts from the natural and cultural embodiment of the subject-matter under investigation. If 'religion' and 'nature' are 'essentially contested concepts', it would appear as an advantage to identify the positions on the basis of which the contest is conducted. This is especially important since 'religion' has a complex history and only gained its significance as an umbrella term for inquiries into the variety of religions and their possible common focus around 1750. Therefore the view, also embraced by Boyer (2001: 6–31), that definitions of religion are mostly mini-description which point to elaborate theories is helpful in identifying the issues which are contested (and perhaps need to be contestable) if one wants to advance the understanding of religion in the conversation between scientific approaches to religion, religious studies and theology.

The starting point from religion as a kind of anthropological constant, as a kind of 'religious a priori' (E. Troeltsch) that is simply given in the natural condition of humans, is, from the perspective of the religions, a problematical presupposition. It conflates the prevalence of religious phenomena in all cultures we know with a particular view of its anthropological genesis. The universal prevalence of religion is generally not challenged by the religions, although it is heavily qualified by notions such as idolatry and delusion. However, it is not explained by understanding religion as actively produced by humans. There is a significant consensus among the religions that religion is not a product of human nature, but granted through the passively experienced disclosure of the Sacred (if one wants to use this

rather ominous term as place marker for that which is ultimately real, the supreme
godhead or the true character of reality). This emphasis on the passive disclosure
of insight into the true character of reality can also be seen as the distinguishing
feature of religions over and against ideologies. Ideologies (such as scientism,
nationalism, communism, etc.) generally presuppose that the truth can be actively
acquired through the engagement of our cognitive capacities. Therefore the truth
about reality can be taught and learnt. Whoever does not accept it, is either stupid,
deluded or a malevolent obscurantist, or a combination of those. In contrast, what
unites the religions is the emphasis on the gratuitous and free disclosure of true
insight: it cannot be produced, it must be granted. Numinous (or theistic) religions
speak in this context of the revelation of a deity, mystical religions of the passive
illumination in mystical experience which is not an achievement but a gift. This
passive experience of disclosure or spiritual illumination occurs in the context of
our active engagement with the world and it becomes the foundation for a new
policy of activity, but it is not constituted by human activity. What the religions
have in common is the emphasis on the gratuitous character of the foundational
event of the epiphany of a deity or of the fundamental experience of illumination
which shapes all dimensions of religion. If we want to express this in Christian
terminology: the religions are amazed by grace.

What can be suggested as the dominant features of what should be called
'religion' on the basis of the self-understanding of religions, as it is documented and
manifested in religious traditions, beliefs systems, rituals, ethical practices, forms
of community organization and aesthetic perceptions? I suggest the following
(incomplete) list of features:

1   Because they understand themselves as passively constituted by the disclosure
     of the godhead or by the event of ultimate enlightenment the religions are
     characterized by a categorical difference between the absolute reality of deity
     or the true reality of the goal of the mystical path and the relative reality of
     everything else. Whereas in 'primal religions' (cf. Smith 1991; Sundermeier
     1999: 34–50) the relationship to the divine forms an undifferentiated unity
     with the relationship to the world and to oneself which has been aptly called
     '*unio magica*' (Ratschow 1947), the religions (sometimes called 'secondary
     religions', including the world religions) make a categorical distinction
     between the relationship to the godhead as the ground and goal of everything
     there is (or the goal of the mystical path) and everything else. In the relational
     being of humans and the world everything is to be understood in the light of
     the relation to the ultimate ground and ultimate end of all being. This has the
     consequence that the attributes of the deity or the state that is seen as the end
     of the mystical path forms the framework of everything that is not God or that
     lies before the goal of the mystical path. This is important for understanding
     the relationship between the 'supernatural' and the 'natural' in the religions.
     The 'supernatural' is not a parallel world of spiritual being but it forms the
     framework within which the 'natural' is to be understood. In this sense, God's
     omnipotence is not seen as an extension of finite power, but as the infinite

ground of all power. God's omniscience is to be understood as the ground of the possibility of every form of knowledge. What belongs to God is unconditioned in the sense that it is only conditioned by God's being and essence. It is the ultimate condition for the being and meaning of everything else. Similarly, the goal of the mystical path illumines every step and stage before that path is reached. In this sense it is the ultimate reality that gives meaning to all other reality, or rather reveals it as a delusion which has to be overcome. One can therefore speak of God or the ultimate reality by negation, denying the attributes of finite reality (*via negationis*) or by superlatives pointing to something beyond every ontological comparative (*via eminentiae*). In the same sense, divine agency in theistic religions is the ground of all other forms of agency in the world and neither an agency arbitrarily intervening into the patterns of finite agencies nor an agency which is invoked when all other explanations fail. The godhead as well as the goal of the mystical path are both beyond the categories with which we name and structure finite beings. Analogical language of God or of the goal of the mystical path therefore traces the analogy between what is ordered in categories through greater dissimilarity to the ground of what is ordered in categories which itself is beyond categories.

2   In all dimensions of the religions which can be analysed as a multi-dimensional complex reality (cf. Smart 1998), comprising the dimensions of symbol, myth, doctrine, experience, ritual, ethos, social organization and aesthetics, religious activity is seen as a response to the disclosure of the deity or the granting of enlightenment is a semiotic activity, employing signifying acts and objects which point to the ultimate referent beyond all signs. While theistic religions understand revelation as an act of sign-giving, providing the constitutive signs for the right worship, mystical religions employ signs as pointers to a reality beyond signification as means for transcending what can be signified. These signs are, however, not seen as cultural constructions in the religions. Rather, they participate in the reality of what they signify. They are reconstructions in the created medium that point to the creative reality of the godhead. They are stepping-stones on the mystical path which point to the ultimate goal by being transcended. Holy Scripture is therefore understood in important strands of the monotheistic traditions as the book of the testimony of revelation which discloses the meaning of the book of nature (cf. Peacocke 1979: 1–49; Dalferth 1988: 67–75). It is in the correspondence of both books that the ultimate referent is known.

3   All religions claim soteriological significance. They all present a transformative dynamics from a state which is experienced as calamitous, a state of the absence of salvation, to a state of salvation. This transition can be envisaged in many forms, from a state of bondage to a state of redemption, from a state of injustice to a state of justice, or from a state of delusion to the disclosure of true insight. Religions claim to lead from a state of dissociation and estrangement of humans from the ultimate source of being to a new communion with the ground of being, from being immersed in illusion and misguided desires to

attaining a new state of bliss. This soteriological dimension which shapes myths, rituals and community structures has profound anthropological dimensions. The religions agree in the assumption that humans are highly ambivalent beings which in their 'natural state' are conscious of their ambiguity, of their having to die and having to kill plants and animals in order to survive, of their bondage to death and their inability to attain life that is not touched by the shadow of death (Ratschow 1987: 133–42). The reasons given in the religions for this negative view of factual human existence fall roughly into two groups, either seeing humans as deeply divided beings because good and evil deities contributed their gifts to their creation, or understanding humans as being guilty of a primordial crime which has affected their existence since then and which is experienced as estrangement from the source of life. Because of this ambiguity, humans have to transcend their natural state in order to be saved from their bondage to death. The religions offer mainly four strategies of transcending the negativities of the natural state: ecstasy, asceticism, knowledge and the law (Ratschow 1987: 142–63). They all strive for the transcendence of the self; they enact in religious practices the death of the natural self in order to achieve real life that is no longer threatened by natural mortality and natural desires which have lead humans astray in the first place. The 'natural state' needs to be transcended so that humans can realise their true destiny.

4   The soteriological dimension shapes the social dimension of the religions. Religious forms of community organization that have a principle of cohesion which is based on the transition from the 'old' life to the 'real' life. Religions reshape the sociality of humans by forging new links that replace biological patterns of belonging or give them (as in Judaism) a new soteriological significance which transcends biological family relationships.

5   What further characterizes religions is an emphasis on the particularity of each religion which is understood as the gateway to universal insights. Friedrich Schleiermacher already admonished the cultured among the despisers of religion in his speeches *On Religion* that *religion* should be discovered in the *religions*: ('... in den Religionen sollt Ihr die Religion entdecken' [Schleiermacher 1799: 238; 1969: 158]) and he concluded from that that religion can only be understood through itself ('... daß auch Religion nur durch sich selbst verstanden werden kann' [286; 190]). In theistic religions this seems most obvious, since the meaning of all theistic statements depends on the identity of the God one is talking about. As Robert Jenson has shown, 'X redeems' only acquires specific meaning if X is replaced by the proper name of a particular God. If we substitute the variable X with the proper name 'Baal', it is quite clear that 'redeem' means 'sends rain' (Jenson 1984: 83–4). The identity of a 'theistic' religion is constituted by the identity of the particular deity it worships. There also seem to be similarities in mystical religions, although it is often claimed that mystical experience transcends the particularity of religions. If I share the insight of the *sunyata* of all phenomena in the context of Mahayana Buddhism, I may be able to re-identify this insight also in the

writings of Meister Eckart, although it remains an open question whether I thereby move in the same field of ontological commitments. This emphasis on the particularity of religions results in an epistemic perspectivism which is, however, very different from the kind of relativistic perspectivism that is often ascribed to Friedrich Nietzsche (Clark 1990: 127f.). Religious knowledge is participatory knowledge and privileges the internal perspective over against external perspectives. However, since the religions claim that their insights are not only true for adherents of their particular religion but for everyone, this is a perspectivism with universalist implications. This implies, as I have mentioned at the outset of this chapter, that these suggestions about common features of the self-understanding of religions are highly abstract and are based on analogical generalizations from a particular standpoint. However, they serve to illustrate in which areas the notions of what is 'natural' and what can count as 'religion' differ considerably in an account based on the self-interpretation of the religions from the views of the cognitive science of religion and of neurotheology in the way it is suggested by Newberg and d'Aquili.

At first sight the account given of 'religion' when religion is explained by cognitive science of religion or neurotheology based on empirical neuroscience on the basis of specific conceptions of 'nature' and the description of some constitutive elements based on the self-understanding of the religions and their view of nature, differ so extensively that one feels tempted to ask why anyone should want to try to compare and contrast scientific theories of 'the religion of nature' with accounts of 'the nature of religion' based on the self-descriptions of the religions. The answer, however, is clear. Offering a scientific account of religion without consulting the views of people who are engaged in religious practices and try to give a reflective account of them would be tantamount to offering an account of science in the philosophy of science without consulting people who are engaged in the practice of the sciences and without paying attention to their descriptions of what they do. On the other hand, it seems reasonable to suppose that people who are engaged in religious practices and hold religious beliefs have an interest in the way their activities and commitment are viewed from the perspective of people who conduct empirical research on what to them, the people participating in religious practice, is of utmost importance. This alone should provide for an interesting contest in the interpretation of 'religion' and 'nature' as essentially contested concepts. If one tries to compare both accounts, in spite of all their differences, some aspects seem quite obvious:

1   The research programmes and explanatory hypotheses of cognitive science of religion focus on elements of numinous or theistic religious traditions, like notions of divine agency, and the anthropomorphic images of a super-natural agent whereas neurotheology seems to be especially concerned with a particular strand of the mystical tradition. In trying to provide evidence for the 'naturalness' of religion, research focuses on those areas that are most

160   *Christoph Schwöbel*

accessible for the methods employed in the cognitive sciences and empirical neuroscience. Compared with the richness of the multi-dimensional reality of religions as they come to the fore in the self-interpretation of the religions it seems reasonable not to extrapolate from these relatively restricted areas by offering a comprehensive account of 'religion explained' or a complete vision of neurotheology as meta- and mega-theology. In order to avoid the charge of *premature generalization*, it would seem more helpful to embark on a more modest strategy of connecting the areas of relatively secure research results to fit them into the complex overall picture that the religions present in their self-interpretations. This seems to be easier in a trans-disciplinary research strategy.

2   There appears to be a tendency to understand what is 'natural' in religion in terms of what is most fundamental in the respective research strategies. Linking 'religious' forms of explanation to established basic patterns of cognition or trying to validate hypotheses of correlations between certain types of religious experiences and neural processes in isolated dedicated areas of the brain could be seen as a kind of *methodological primitivism*, focusing on that which seems most fundamental, even if it is in itself seen as not unprob-lematic in standard accounts (like the assumption of certain functionally dedicated areas in the brain that can be isolated). To identify the 'natural' with the methodologically primitive may not be sufficient to account for the complexities of religious systems of belief and practice. In any case, it would be worthwhile to investigate the relationship between what is naturally basic and religiously foundational.

3   In both scientific approaches there seems to be a certain *anti-reflective bias*. The concentration on 'what comes naturally' in the cognitive science of religion and the focussing on meditation or phenomena of glossolalia which transcend or suspend reflective engagement seems to be a case in point. Therefore the forms of religious explanations in terms of supernatural agency in the cognitive science of religion seems to be close to phenomena which we find in primal religions, based on the *unio magica*, but less so in secondary religions, like the world religions where reflection is not only an isolated strand (like 'theology') but is also pervasive in many forms seemingly non-reflective religious practices in rituals, etc. In any case, it must be kept in mind that this focusing on 'what comes naturally' is the result of a carefully thought-out research design in the 'unnatural' and highly reflective sphere of science. The same applies to reflective considerations which led to focusing on states of transcending or suspending reflection like meditation or glosso-lalia in neurotheology. This anti-reflective bias cannot be easily found in the religions who are on the whole more concerned with recruiting reflection for the service of God.

4   From the perspective of the religions' understanding of the agency and attributes of God or gods in their self-interpretation, the way in which a supernatural agent is identified by the hyperactive agency detecting device and the way in which divine attributes are interpreted in the cognitive science

of religion (intuitive category plus counter-intuitive violation) seems to present the *danger of displacement* of the notion of God and God's attributes. Especially in the monotheistic religions, God is not to be understood on the basis of categories that fit finite entities. God the creator of all that is not God is beyond the categories that characterize finite existence, and the relationship of God to all that is not God must be understood as the framework in which created beings have to be understood. Similarly, God's power and God's knowledge are not to be understood along the lines of creaturely power or creaturely knowledge but as the ground of all created power and knowledge. This emphasis of the understanding of God is not just a piece of sophisticated 'unnatural' theology but it is religiously important because it identifies the one who alone is to be worshipped. It is at the heart of what the monotheistic religions understand as 'idolatry', worshipping a finite created entity instead of the infinite God. From a religious standpoint in the monotheistic traditions, the view of the development of notions of supernatural agents in the cognitive science of religion seems to offer a good theory of idolatry, it provides a good account why the human heart is an 'idol-making factory' (John Calvin). From the perspective of the monotheistic religions one could ask whether the theory, rather than offering an answer to the question, 'Why would anyone believe in God?', does not, in fact, answer the question: Why would anyone believe in idols? Many believers in the monotheistic religions would probably agree that in the early stages of the development religious ideas can be described in the way cognitive science of religion explains the identification of supernatural idols. However, they would insist that this stage has to be transcended in the process of religious formation, a process which breaks the mould of developing counter-intuitive notions in this way. If the aim is explaining religion and not idolatry the danger of religiously unacceptable displacements must be dealt with.

5   From the perspective of the self-interpretation of the religions the aim of both cognitive science of religion and neurotheology to overcome the dominance of social constructivist views of religion would probably be seen with a lot of sympathy. However, is the only alternative to understanding religion as a social construct interpreting it as an evolutionary spandrel? The interface between the natural, both in the sense of 'what comes naturally' and in the sense of the neural correlates of cultural acts and techniques, seems to be the really interesting question. In cognitive science of religion as well as in neurotheology, what is foundational for religion and therefore explains religious forms of cognition and practices as well as religious experiences is firmly placed on the side of the natural. Religion is not a social or cultural construct, but these cultural constructions can only be explained on the basis of what is given in the basic noncultural structure of cognition or in the neural foundations of experience. However, is the relationship simply a one-directional where the natural is the *explanans* for the cultural *explanandum*? As long as the relationship is understood as a context between competing forms of explanation, naturalism versus culturalism, the problem of how the natural shapes

cultural activity and how cultural activity draws on natural capacities is not yet seen in its full complexity. From the perspective of the religions, human beings in their natural state are deeply ambiguous beings. This ambiguity is only clarified when the disclosure of the godhead or the enlightenment by true insight both illumines the ambiguity of nature and points to a path of transcending it; for the religions 'nature' is neither logically nor ontologically a primitive concept. It is more like an incomplete symbol in logics that is amenable only through a contextual definition. Cultural signifiers may provide this context, but they are only the means through which the ambiguity of nature is overcome by being related to its ultimate ground and goal. This can either be God as the ground and aim of nature or the state in which the illusory self-being of nature wanes away as in the Buddhist understanding of *nirvana*. Both the given character of nature (and culture) and the goal-directness of nature (and culture) are contextualized in being seen as relative to the ground and goal of all existence and meaning. This does not mean that the natural is thereby destroyed, but rather that it is made perfect in that its ambiguity is overcome. As the universally maintained slogan in the Christian tradition has put it: *gratia non destruit sed supponit et perficit naturam.* However, from a religious point of view, the way in which grace supports and perfects nature is not one that can be deduced or empirically explained by the characteristics of nature. In this sense one has to say: Although we may be hard-wired for God in our neural circuitry we will nevertheless be amazed by grace.

III. 'Nature' and 'religion' from the perspective of Christian faith: The word was made flesh

If Schleiermacher's insistence that religion must be discovered in the religions is correct, this implies that what can be said on the concepts of religion and nature in a general sense from a religious perspective, based on the self-interpretation of the religions, is necessarily abstract. The only way to overcome this abstraction is to look at the problem from a particular religious perspective: in my case, that of Christian faith. If we want to clarify the contested concepts of 'nature' and 'religion' it seems required that the contest is conducted from particular identifiable standpoints, which are made explicit in the debate. Talking in general terms about science and religion or theology is in the best case less than helpful and in the worst case misleading in view of the diversity of the sciences and the particularities of the religions.

The stance in the conversation about the relationship of religion and nature I shall take is therefore one of Christian theology, based on the beliefs and practices of the Christian community of faith. This perspective is a particular perspective in the sense that what is seen as Christian, must somehow be constitutively related to Jesus Christ. I shall presuppose without offering further arguments for this presupposition that this identity-defining reference to Christ is at the root of the Christian view of the triune identity of God which is expressed by invoking the triune name of Father, Son and Holy Spirit. The central statements of Christian faith as they are summarized in the classical ecumenical creeds present the ground, meaning and ultimate destiny of the world humankind in terms of the relationship of the triune God to everything that is not God. God is seen as both internally relational in the communion of the persons of Father, Son and Holy Spirit who coequally share in the infinite divine essence as well as relational in God's relationship to everything that is not God. Since it is constituted in God's relationship to all that is not God, the being of the world and of human beings is therefore understood from the perspective of Christian faith as essentially relational (Schwöbel 2002). Its ontological status, its meaning and its ultimate destiny, as it is realized in the process of history, can be summarized under the headings of creation, reconciliation and eschatological consummation. Within this framework human beings are understood as God's created images, sharing the created status and linked in many other ways to the non-human creation. As the created images of God humans are called to find the fulfilment of their destiny in communion with the triune God by exercising their created freedom in accordance with their created status and the will of the creator. As a matter of contingent fact, humans contradict their destiny and become dislocated in their relationship to God the creator and in the relational order of creation by attempting to be like God and assume God's place in the relational order (sin). Through the Incarnation of the second person of the Trinity in Jesus of Nazareth God takes the initiative to restore the relationship of human beings to God by reconciling the world to himself and so relocating humans in their relationship to God (grace). The healing of the disrupted relationship to God and the continuing realization of the communion of the triune God with the reconciled human creation shape the life of the Church in worship, proclamation and in its ethical life until the consummation of God's relationship with the world in the *eschaton*.

It is necessary to remind ourselves, albeit very briefly, of this doctrinal scheme of Christian faith, because from a Christian perspective the understanding of nature and religion is contextualized in the network of relationships which this scheme tries to express. Before we look a little more closely at what this implies for a theological view of the methods and results of the research of the cognitive science of religion and of neurotheology, we must quickly note the peculiar character of these beliefs and of the statements in which they are expressed. This is important for determining their relationship to the methods and findings of the neurosciences. Borrowing categories from Immanuel Kant's *Was heißt sich im Denken orientieren?* (Kant 1958) we can characterize the status and character of these beliefs as 'orientational beliefs' (Dalferth 1988: 204–23; Schwöbel 2007). Briefly summarized, orientational beliefs:

- are perspective-bound, whether they concern a standpoint in physical space or in a symbolic space;
- they relate a particular standpoint to specific goals that have to be reached;
- they integrate standpoint and goals in a relational network;

- specify my location in that network in relation to other coordinates;
- presuppose a unitary reality in which the different vantage-points, goals, coordinates etc. can be located;
- imply a specific a relationship between signifiers and reality which can be expressed in statements with a definite truth-value;
- connect theoretical knowledge and practical knowledge so that theoretical knowledge can become operational and practical knowledge becomes concrete and theoretically transparent practical knowledge;
- form a necessary precondition for the capacity to act in symbolizing, organizing or productive action;
- constitute as such the preconditions for the exercise of finite freedom;
- are constitutive for our social interactions which are based on the (often implicit) recognition of shared orientational beliefs by a plurality of agents;
- are constitutive for our communicative interaction with one another.

It is characteristic for our orientational beliefs that they are situated at the interface of our empirical knowledge, our technical knowledge and our non-empirical metaphysical beliefs. They are presupposed in our empirical and technical knowledge because they concern the foundations of our experience and the modalities of our technical capacities. In the act of finding orientation, all these aspects of orientational beliefs are actualized and put into practice. Our orientational beliefs shape our understanding of the world so that the world becomes an ordered cosmos in which we can live, it becomes our *Lebenswelt*.

If we consider the beliefs of Christian faith as orientational beliefs it becomes immediately clear that they do not only concern a specific sub-field of orientational beliefs, as Kant considered orientation in physical, mathematical and logical spaces. Rather, understood as orientational beliefs, religious beliefs concern the basic orientation which shapes all other forms of orientation. Religious beliefs are concerned with the whole framework of our orientation, since the whole network of relationships is seen as rooted in a basic relationship that shapes all other relationships. They locate our lives in relation to the ultimate beginning and ultimate end of everything and relate the layers of meaning with which we are concerned in our daily lives to the dimension of ultimate meaning. This fundamental orientation is, according to the understanding of Christian faith, the relation to the only Absolute, the triune God, who relates to what is not God in creation, reconciliation and in the eschatological consummation of all things. It is a logical implication of seeing God's relating to what is not God as fundamental for all other created relationships, that this relationship cannot be actively known by created epistemic subjects unless God gives himself to be known. The emphasis on the passive constitution of the fundamental orientation of human life in the self-disclosure of God is therefore systematically implied in the creator–creature relationship. Theologically, it follows from this that the passive constitution of knowledge in revelation is not a special and exceptional case of the constitution of knowledge but concerns the constitution of all knowledge. From the perspective of Christian faith, the orientational beliefs of the Christian tradition are grounded in experience but they are not forms of empirical knowledge based on empirical observation and quantifiable procedures of measuring based on the criteria of reliability, validity and objectivity. As orientational beliefs they concern the basic pattern of relationality, the categories which determine our conceptual criteria for developing strategies of empirical investigation and their interpretation by relating them to an overall understanding of reality.

This is important for conceiving the relationship between the orientational beliefs of Christian faith to other modes of knowledge in the different epistemic spheres and in its different forms of knowledge. Orientational beliefs can neither be directly verified by empirical investigation nor can they be directly falsified by empirical research. They are, however, not unconnected since they shape the *conceptual expectations* we have of empirical knowledge and they can be corrected and modified by the findings of empirical research. The concrete application of orientational beliefs remains open to correction and modification by empirical findings. One only has to remember the adjustments and modifications which the development of our scientific knowledge, exemplified by the changing world-views from Copernicus to Darwin and Einstein, necessitated in the Christian understanding of creation without directly invalidating it – at least not to the extent, that Christians generally stopped believing in creation. The mutual interaction between our orientational beliefs and our empirical knowledge seems to be the field that has to be investigated more closely in the conversation between empirical scientific approaches to religion understood as a 'natural' phenomenon and a Christian theological view of both nature and religion. Let us therefore look a little more closely at the way this relationship appears when we start from the Christian doctrines of creation, Incarnation and eschatological consummation.

The Christian doctrine of *creation* sees the creation of the world as the unconditional and free creative action of the triune God. This creative activity which has no other presuppositions than God's own creativity (*creatio ex nihilo*) and itherefore an absolute beginning is continued through the history of the universe (*creatio continuata*). Its aim is to bring about the communion between the creator and creation in which God's created images, human beings, are taken up into communion with the triune God. The existence and the meaning of creation as well as its inherent creaturely capacities are understood as being constituted by God through the Logos and the Spirit so that the logos-structure of the world is understood as the work of the dynamic ordering of the divine Logos and its vital processes as the result of the activity of the life-giving Spirit (Schwöbel 1997). It is an integral part of the Christian doctrine of creation that the world is to be known, interpreted and shaped by human beings as God's created images.

The decisive question is: What would we expect of the scientific investigation of the world on the basis of the orientational beliefs of Christian faith that we have sketched in their bare outlines? How is the world to be known on this account of the constitution of its existence, order and meaning? Since creation is understood as characterized by contingent intelligibility through the work of the Logos and the Spirit we would expect that the world can be known through experience and through the mechanisms of human biophysical capacities and not by means of logical inference. A contingent order cannot be known by logical deductions, but only through experience and this experience is made possible through the natural cognitive organization of human beings (Foster 1934; Torrance 1981). There is a sharp contrast between the wisdom traditions of the Old Testament where the regularities of nature and the appropriate forms of human conduct are known through experience, and the intellectualist forms of the knowledge of nature favoured by Greek philosophy where experience mediated by the senses is not regarded as a reliable guide to true knowledge. To investigate the world empirically by employing the biophysical structure of human nature seems to be a 'natural' expectation which follows from Christian faith in God the creator. On such an account nature would be understood as the contingent created order which God made possible in creation. Religion would have to be interpreted as an implication of the dependence of human creatures on their creator. As an implication of the created status of humans it is by no means wrong to speak of natural religion.

The Christian tradition also holds that God's human images abuse their finite created freedom by assuming divine creative freedom and so transcending their created status (Schwöbel 1995). By trying to assume the role of the creator, humans are displaced in the order of creation and this affects their relationship to God, to other human beings and to the whole of nature. It also affects human life in all dimensions of its interaction with the world. It is an implication of the asymmetry in the relationship between the creator and the human creatures that human beings cannot restore the relationship to God by themselves. If that were the case they would have the creative status in this restored relationship. The broken relationship between God and the fallen human creatures can only be healed by the creator. Knowledge of the true relationship between God and the creation therefore depends on being disclosed by the creator. What are the conceptual expectations that we have on the basis of these orientational beliefs for the enterprise of human knowing? We would expect all human knowledge to be *fallible* and in need of correction, even to be *fallen* where it interprets itself as the absolute perspective on reality. Pure constructivism appears from a Christian perspective as an exemplification of the human contradiction against the created order.

It is one of the central beliefs of Christian faith, that the creative Logos became human in the *Incarnation* in order to restore the broken relationship between God and God's human creatures. Belief in the Incarnation implies that the creative Logos who creatively determine all intelligible structures in the universe can be known in the material structures of a human life. The principles of the logos-order of the universe are inscribed on the structure of human bodily existence. God communicates through the systems of the natural organization of human life. On the basis of the Incarnation, Christians are committed to expect that the natural organization of bodily existence is the medium of knowledge of the true relationship between God and God's creatures. It is hard to find a stronger religious foundation for the investigation of nature, above all human nature, as the key to the intelligible structure of the material order. If God communicates through the natural organization of human life the material dimensions of existence need not to be transcended in order to find divine truth. God can be found in the flesh and not only in the mind. On the basis of the Incarnation as an orientational belief, we would expect to understand the mind only as an embodied mind and to see the brain as a 'relational organ' (Fuchs 2010), mediating personal, mental and physiological dimensions. It would come as no surprise to understand human knowledge, including religious knowledge, through the correlations between mental acts and states and neural phenomena. The Incarnation does not provide any reasons for expecting a disembodied mind as the instrument of true knowledge and as the core of human identity. On the basis of this view, we would expect to understand the natural mechanisms of knowledge – including religious knowledge – as correlations and constraints of cultural sign systems.

Furthermore, on the basis of belief in the Incarnation we should not be surprised by the fact that the cognitive science of religion presents God-concepts in anthropomorphic forms. After all, the message of the Incarnation is that God wants to be known through the life, death and resurrection of a human being. However, on the basis of the faith in the Incarnation of the second person of the Trinity, the divine Logos, we would also expect that anthropomorphic forms of understanding God do not violate the categorical distinction between the creator and creation. We would expect anthropomorphic God-concepts to become transparent for God as the transcendent ground of all being and meaning and not just present God as superman. The Incarnation, however, reaches its climax in the death and resurrection of Christ and in the assumption of humanity into the divine being. Therefore anthropomorphic God-concepts are not to be understood as an exaggerated concept of a human person (person plus 'counterintuitive violation') but as a 'counterintuitive violation' of the (natural) concept of God. Luther's emphasis on the distinction between a theology of glory (*theologia gloriae*) and a theology of the cross (*theologia crucis*) has its provocative point in this connection. It is at this point that the orientational belief of the Incarnation unfolds its critical power. Worshipping a perfect human being would be idolatry. It is the kind of worship that follows from the promise of the serpent '*eritis sicut Deus*'. Worshipping God in Christ and thereby associating God with weakness and death is the ultimate critique of all idolatry. The orientational beliefs, focussing on sin, Incarnation and salvation, point to the ambiguity of the Christian understanding of nature. From having its dignity as *created nature* it turns into *fallen nature* once it claims absoluteness and self-existence over against God and becomes *redeemed nature* through God's contradiction against human absoluteness in the Incarnation. Nature is restored in its created dignity by being taken up into the unity of the divine person in Christ.

This Christological pattern (spelled out in the patristic doctrine of the *enhypostasia*) is the logic of Christian orientational beliefs about the eschatological consummation of creation. It denies the perfectibility of nature through its inherent 'natural' capacities but promises its perfection through God's grace. This promise offers a radical critique of all notions of the perfectibility of nature on the basis of an assumed capacity for self-perfection. Perfection comes as a gift of grace and not as a natural achievement or as the final stage of natural evolution. Nature will remain imperfect and ambiguous, unable to effect its own perfection, until it is perfected in the eschatological communion of the Triune God with God's reconciled creation. This has profound ethical implications for the application of the results of the empirical neurosciences in programmes of education or genetic enhancement. The perfectibility of nature is not an aim of human development. All that research can do is to contribute to the improvement of the human condition in the management of our natural imperfection. However, the promise of the hope of Christian faith points to the inclusion of nature in the eschatological perfection. If we believe the images in which this hope is expressed it is only at that point, in the Kingdom of God, that religion, the worship of the Triune God, will be completely natural and nature will be perfectly religious. From the perspective of Christian faith, the 'naturalisation of religion' and its implication of the 'religiousness of nature' is an eschatological concept. Until then, the contest about the appropriate understanding of nature and religion will go on, critically and constructively inspired by the interaction between orientational beliefs as they are offered by the insights of Christian faith and the empirical findings of the sciences.

References

Ashbrook, J. B. (1984), 'Neurotheology: the working brain and the work of theology'. *Zygon, 19*, 331–50.

Barrett, J. L. (2004), *Why Would Anyone Believe in God?* Walnut Creek, CA: AltaMira Press.

Barrett, J. and K. Keil (1996), 'Conceptualizing a non-natural entity: anthropomorphism in god concepts'. *Cognitive Psychology, 31*, 219–47.

Boyer, P. (1994), *The Naturalness of Religious Ideas*. Berkeley, CA: University of California Press.

—(2001), *Religion Explained: The Evolutionary Origins of Religious Thought*. New York, NY: Basic Books.

Boyle, R. (1688), *De ipsa natura sive libera in receptum naturae notionem disquisitio*. Geneva: Samuel de Tournes.

Clark, M. (1990), *Nietzsche on Truth and Philosophy*. Cambridge: Cambridge University Press.

Dalferth, I. U. (1988), *Theology and Philosophy*. Oxford: Basil Blackwell.

d'Aquili, E. G. and A. B. Newberg (1999), *The Mystical Mind: Probing the Biology of Mystical Experience*. Minneapoli, MN: Fortress Press.

Evers, D. (2006), 'Hirnforschung und Theologie'. *Theologische Literaturzeitung, 131*, cols 1107–22.

Fodor, J. A. (1983), *Modularity of Mind: An Essay on Faculty Psychology*. Cambridge, MA: MIT Press.

Foster, M. B. (1934), 'The Christian doctrine of creation and the rise of modern natural science'. *Mind, 43*, 446–68.

Fuchs, Th. (2010), *Das Gehirn – ein Beziehungsorgan. Eine phänomenologisch-ökologische Konzeption*. 3rd edn. Stuttgart: Kohlhammer.

Gallie, W. B. (1956), 'Essentially contested concepts'. *Proceedings of the Aristotelian Society, 56*, 167–98.

Geertz, A. W. (2009), 'When cognitive scientists become religious, science is in trouble: on neurotheology from a philosophy of science perspectives'. *Religion, 39*, 319–24.

Gould, S. J. and R. C. Lewontin (1979), 'The Spandrels of San Marcoi and the Panglossian paradigm: a critique of the adaptionist programme'. *Proceedings of the Royal Society of London, (Series B) 205* (1161), 581–98.

Granqvist, P., M. Frederikson, P. Unge, A. Hagenfeldt, S. Valind, D. Larhammer and M. Larsson (2005), 'Sensed presence and mystical experiences are predicted by suggestibility, not by the application of transcranial weak complex magnetic fields'. *Neuroscience Letters, 379*, 1–6.

Jenson, R. W. (1984). 'Second locus. The triune God. In C. E. Braaten and R. W. Jenson (eds), *Christian Dogmatics*. Philadelphia, PA: Fortress Press, pp. 97–192.

Kant, I. (1958 [1786]), 'Was heißt sich im Denken zu orientieren?' In W. Weischedel (ed.), *I. Kant*, Werke III. Frankfurt: Suhrkamp, pp. 267–83.

Lawson, E. Th. (2000), 'Towards a cognitive science of religion'. *Numen, 47*, 338–49.

McCauley, R. N. (2000), 'The naturalness of religion and the unnaturalness of science'. In F. Keil and R. Wilson (eds), *Explanation and Cognition*. Cambridge, MA: MIT Press, pp. 61–85.

McKinney, L. O. (1994), *Neurotheology: Virtual Religion in the 21st Century*. Cambridge, MA: American Institute for Mindfulness.

Newberg, A. B., A. Alavi, M. Balme, M. Pourdhnad, J. Satanna and E. G. d'Aquili (2001), 'The measurement of regional blood flow during the complex cognitive task of meditation: a preliminary SPECT study'. *Psychiatric Research: Neuroimaging, 106*, 113–22.

Newberg, A. B., E. G. d'Aquili and V. Rause (2001), *Why God Won't Go Away: Brain Science and the Biology of Belief*. New York, NY: Ballantine Books.

Newberg, A. B., M. Pourdehnad, A. Alavi and E. G. d'Aquili (2003), 'Cerebral blood flow during meditative prayer: preliminary findings and methodological issues'. *Perceptual and Motor Skills, 97*, 625–30.

Newberg, A. B., N. Wintering, D. Morgan and M. R. Waldman (2006), 'The measurement of regional blood flow during glossolalia: a preliminary SPECT study. *Psychiatry Research: Neuroimaging, 148*, 67–71.

Peacocke, A. R. (1978), *Creation and the World of Science. The Bampton Lectures*. Oxford: Clarendon Press.

—(1979),

Persinger, M. A. (1987), *Neurophysiological Bases of God Beliefs*. New York, NY: Praeger Publishers.

Peters, K. E. (2001), 'Neurotheology and evolutionary theology: reflections on "The Mystical Mind"'. *Zygon, 30*, 493–500.

Ratschow, C. H. (1947), *Magie und Religion*. Gütersloh: C. Bertelsmann.

—(1987 [1972]), 'Das Verständnis des Menschen in den Religionen und im Christentum'. In Chr. Keller-Wentorf and M. Repp (eds), *Carl Heinz Ratschow,*

Von der Gestaltwerdung des Menschen. Berlin/New York, NY: de Gruyter, pp. 133–76.

Schjoedt, U. (2009), 'The religious brain: a general introduction to the experimental neuroscience of religion'. *Method and Theory in the Study of Religion, 21*, 310–39.

Schwöbel, Chr. (1995), 'Imago libertatis: human and divine freedom'. In C. E. Gunton (ed.), *God and Freedom*. Edinburg: T & T Clark, pp. 57–81.

—(1997), 'God, creation and the Christian community'. In C. E. Gunton (ed.), *The Doctrine of Creation*. Edinburgh: T & T Clark, pp. 149–76.

—(2002), *Gott in Beziehung. Studien zur Dogmatik*. Tübingen: Mohr Siebeck.

—(2007), 'Arbeit am Orientierungswissen – Theologie im Haus der Wissenschaften'. In P. David (ed.), *Theologie in der Öffentlichkeit*. Hamburg: LIT, pp. 27–52.

Smart., N. (1998), *Dimensions of the Sacred: An Anatomy of the World's Beliefs*. Berkeley, CA: University of California Press.

Smith, H. (1991), *The World's Religions: Our Great Wisdom Traditions*. (San Francisco, CA: HarperCollins.

Snow, C. P. (1959), *The Two Cultures and the Scientific Revolution. The Rede Lecture*. Cambridge: Cambridge University Press.

Spaemann, R. (2010), 'Natur. Zur Geschichte eines philosophischen Grundbegriffs'. In H.-G. Nissing (ed.), *Natur. Ein philosophischer Grundbegriff*. Darmstadt: Wissenschaftliche Buchgesellschaft, pp. 21–34.

Sundermeier, T. (1999), *Was ist Religion? Religionswissenschaft im theologischen Kontext*. Gütersloh: Gütersloher Verlagshaus.

Tillich, P. (1975 [1919]), 'Über die Idee einer Theologie der Kultur'. In P. Tillich (ed.), *Gesammelte Werke IX: Die Religiöse Substanz der Kultur*. 2nd ed. Stuttgart: Evangelisches Verlagswerk, pp. 13–31.

Torrance, Th. F. (1981), *Divine and Contingent Order*. Oxford: Oxford University Press.

Visala, A. (2008), 'Religion and the human mind: philosophical perspectives on the cognitive science of religion'. *Neue Zeitschrift für Systematische Theologie und Religionsphilosophie, 50*, 431–49.

11 Perspectives on Theomorphism in Islam

Mona Siddiqui

To know himself, man must come to know the 'Face of God', the reality, that determines him from on high. Neither flights into outer space nor plunges beneath the seas, nor changes of fashions and modes of outward living alter the nature of man and his situation vis-à-vis the Real. Nor can biological or conventional psychological studies which deal only with the outward aspects of human nature reveal to man who he is and how he should 'orient' himself in that journey whose end is the meeting with the Real. Man can know himself only by realizing his theomorphic nature. It is only in remaining conscious of the divine imprint upon his soul that man can hope to remain human. Only the attraction of the celestial can prevent man from being dragged by gravity to the abysses of sub-human existence. And it is a remarkable feature of the human state, that no matter where and in what condition he may be, man always finds above him the sky and the attraction which pulls him toward the Infinite and the Eternal. (Nasr, in Chittick 2007)

In this paper I will offer some reflections on interpretations of theomorphic themes in Islamic thought. I have drawn upon the work of contemporary scholars and three areas where the ambivalence of the human-divine make-up emerges most strongly in the history of Islamic thought. First, anthropomorphism/theomorphism and transcendence/immanence; second, humankind/natural world; and third, light as an image and quality of God.

I understand theomorphism, broadly in the religious sense, as humankind having godlike attributes or themselves being reflectors of God's essential nature. In Islam, the themes emerge from those Qur'ānic verses which gave rise to anthropomorphic conceptions of God and theomorphic conceptions of humankind. Indeed many of the discussions around human theomorphism were centred on God's anthropomorphism (tashbīh).

In Islam one dwells on God fundamentally by reading, reciting and listening to the word of God contained for believers in the Qur'ān. The Qur'ān itself as a text emerges in time, but, for the believer, it speaks for all eternity. The Qur'ān like all scriptures both speaks of its own time and retains authority for all time. For Muslims God speaks in the Qur'ān to human beings and speaks of events as if these events exist in our own memories or in a collective human memory as an integral part of our human heritage and nature. As Hussain (2003) writes:

> The Qur'ān asks us to be present, in our own era, wherever truth requires us to be present and it requires that presence to be a deeply rooted presence, not a superficial, ineffective, fleeting presence. It asks us not to regard humanity's past as merely 'tales of the ancients' (Qur'ān 83:13), or as quaint historical footnotes that are irrelevant to our times and our own modern notions about the nature of things, about the nature of society, of humanity, of morality. It presents the world as more than just matter, as more than a chronological string of occurrences. Rather, it posits an essence and reality to certain events that lifts those events out of time, giving them a presence in a higher reality, in a deeper, more substantial layer of existence, and thereby makes their essential truths accessible to all times and places. So when the Qur'ān speaks of Moses and Aaron, of Zachariaha and Maryam, of the various prophets and men of knowledge that have walked the earth it raises their stories out of historical time and into a universal time. It presents them almost as universal memories and then it asks us to remember, to recall.

Thus our understanding of all things immanent and all things transcendent is rooted in the Qur'ān. We are asked not only to learn from the past, but also to keep the morals of past stories alive as repositories of wisdom for the questions of today. How does one approach a text which is understood to be both transcendent and immanent, sacred to the touch yet alive through human interpretation? Norman Calder (1997: 49), a leading scholar of Islamic law, took a literary approach:

> For scholars in religious studies, revelation can never be perceived directly as an act of God, or a fact of history. God's self-revelation to a community can only be accessible to scholarship as a historical process, effectively a literary one, and one in which the community partakes creatively. Irrespective of the degree of metaphor discovered in the notion that God writes himself, it is the writings of God's mediators that are available for analysis. Not even of the Qur'ān is it claimed that God dictated, and merely dictated it. God's revelation is not different from the effort of the community to express its understanding of God, and since that (in all its highest forms) is necessarily a literary achievement, it will be subject to the usual conventions of literary type and genre. To know God, it is reading skills that are required. But the act of reading is a creative one: the message depends on the readers' interaction with the text. God is what the reader makes of his (God's) texts.

Even if this passage overstates the 'reading' of God to know God, belief in God demands an obligation to talk of God; silence, even contemplative silence, is not enough. In this attempt to talk of God we respond to a God who chooses to 'reveal' something of his infinite self in finite time. Revelation belongs to the history of the manifestation of God, and is present in the history of those sent by God. Revelation communicates not only the truth of God in himself but also the truth of man and of history, by telling humankind something different from what they know. In the Qur'ān the Muslim gains a glimpse of the possibilities and realities of God, for in the written word is contained the divine word.

Reflection on God led inevitably to diverse way of understanding God in his being and his essence. The Qur'ān contains abundant imagery describing God's ways and being that reflect human attributes, i.e. those physical attributes which we human beings recognize in ourselves. For example, 'Wherever you turn, there is God's face' (Q2.115), 'God sits on a throne' (Q2.255), 'All bounties are in the hand of God'(Q3.73), 'All that is on earth will perish but will abide for ever the face of your Lord' (Q55.27), 'But construct an ark under our eyes and our inspiration' (11.37); there are also numerous verses which speak of God's speech and God's hearing as well as his knowing. Such verses were understood in very different ways by scholars of the eighth–eleventh centuries who contested, among other issues, how such verses could be understood within the principle of God's one-ness. The most strident debates emerged between those who became known as the Mu'tazilites and the Ash'arites. The Mu'tazilites understood such descriptions of God as metaphors, not as literal descriptions of his being. Literal interpretations of such verses could compromise the very oneness and non-divisibility of God. For the Ash'arites, such verses had to be affirmed as attributes of God even if human beings could not understand how (*bi-lā kayfa*). God's transcendence and immanence provided two alternative models of articulating God's being.

In his work on early Muslim orthodoxy and 'transcendent anthropomorphism' Williams (2002) argues that it was only under Hellenistic influences that Jewish culture expressed anxiety about theophany and *Visio Dei*. This eventually found its parallels in the history of Islamic theology. In 'normative' or 'mainstream' Islam, God's otherness necessitated divine incorporeality and invisibility. But Williams argues that this was not always the case, and analyses the creed of Ahmad Ibn Hanbal as an example of a theological tract very comfortable with corporealist ideas attributed to God:

> God is on the Throne and the Kursi is the place of His feet ... God is on the Throne, and the Throne has bearers carrying it ... He is in movement, He speaks, He looks, He laughs, He rejoices, He loves and He detests, He displays ill-will and kindness; He becomes angry and He forgives ... Every night He descends, in the manner He wishes, to the nearest heaven ... the hearts of humankind are between two fingers of the Merciful; He turns them over as He desires and engraves on them whatever He wants. He created Adam with His hands and in His image. On the Day of Resurrection, the heavens and the earth will be in His palm ... The People of Paradise will look at His Face and see it. God will honour them. He will appear to them and dispense His grants to them. The servants will appear before Him [on] the Day of Judgment. It is He, Himself, who will ask them for their accounts. Other than He will not administer that.

Williams argues that contrary to later Islamic thought, which denied anthropomorphic attributes to God and zealously defended God's divine otherness (*mukhālafa*), formative theology of the eighth–tenth centuries on this issue was far more fluid in its understanding of the divine.

The Qur'ān does not say that human beings are created in God's image even though they are created in the 'best of form' (Q95.4). However one Prophetic hadith from Bukhari's *Sahīh* refers to man being created in God's image: 'God created Adam according to his form.' This hadith was used by eminent theologians such as Ibn Hanbal as one more element to substantiate their anthropomorphic/

theomorphic doctrines. While Ibn Hanbal was careful not to attribute a body
to God, he did attribute God's form to Adam, despite protestations from other
theologians who argued that the 'his' refers to Adam's form, not God's form.
Ibn Hanbal argued that the 'his' could not possibly refer to Adam as he did not
have a form before God created him. He chose the theomorphic explanation and
denounced those who did not believe that Adam's form was based on a divine form
as unbelievers. Ibn Hanbal therefore chose to treat the anthropomorphist descriptions of God as *muhkamāt*, admitting to only a literal meaning. Williams (2002:
443) explains Ibn Hanbal's stance:

> We have a major figure of 9th-century religiosity, highly learned and capable of thinking
> outside the 'literalist box' of his less sophisticated contemporaries, choosing divine
> embodiment as his dogmatic position. A whole generation would subsequently embrace
> aspects of this dogmatic position.

The Qur'ānic world view is essentially theocentric. This may seem unsurprising
given the fact that Muslims believe that the Qur'ān is the direct speech of God, that
the Qur'ān is a book from God always pointing to God. But what is meant here
is that the image of God pervades the whole Qur'ān – nothing escapes God, and
no major concept of God exists independently of God himself. Izutsu (1966: 18)
explores this: 'In the sphere of human ethics, each one of its key concepts is but a
pale reflection or a very imperfect imitation of the divine nature itself or refers to a
particular response elicited by divine actions.'

Christian theological traditions have generally regarded the concept of *imago
Dei*, 'man made in the image of God,' (Gen. 1.26–27) as a central, though not
singular, concept for elaborating the relationship between man and God: 'Then
God said, "let us make humanity in our image, according to our likeness"'.

The phrase signifies that human beings are created by God purposefully, not
just as his creatures but as creatures who themselves are godlike in some way.
The Hebrew word denotes both the sense of likeness and image. Although the
first chapter of Genesis does not speak of God as a visible image, it speaks of a
God who creates and who has created humankind in his own image. However,
there is no precise explanation of what this likeness implies and Middleton (1994:
2–3) has argued that the few biblical references to *imago Dei*, including only two
texts in the New Testament (1 Cor. 11.7 and Jas 3.9), have left the way open for a
wide variety of philosophical and theological interpretations of this concept. This
has included the creation of metaphysical analogies between the human soul and
God's being.

In Islam, the Qur'ānic account of man's creation is simultaneously also an
account of man's vocation in life:

> Behold, thy Lord said to the angels, 'I will create a vicegerent on earth.' They said, 'Wilt
> thou place therein one who will make mischief and shed blood while we do sing thy
> praises and glorify thy holy name?' He said, 'I know what ye know not.' And he taught
> Adam the names of all things. (Q2.30)

Behold, thy Lord said to the angels, 'I am going to create man from clay. When I have finished him and breathed into him of my spirit, fall down in obedience to him.' (Q38.71–2)

We created man in the best of forms. (Q95.4)[1]

These verses indicate multiple perspectives about man, his physical nature and place in creation, and his relationship with God. First, the creation of humans is not a quiet affair, rather announced to the angels as a turning point in the destiny of the Earth itself. Indeed, the objection that the angels raise about the need to bring human life into existence and the consequent destruction on Earth, develops into one of the first Qur'ānic conversations affirming humanity's place in creation. Second, man's relatively lowly but complex nature, i.e. his physical essence which is clay (*tīn*) or dust, contrasts with the lofty moral status God bestows on him, i.e. as a representative (*khalīfa*). God has spent time on the formation and image of humankind, and God distinguishes human beings from other beings by breathing into Adam of his own spirit; thus humanity comes into the fullness of its being only through that final breath, i.e. through the element of divine origin in the human makeup. The anthropomorphic image of a God blowing into a theomorphic human frame remains powerful but mysterious. At the time that Adam was a mere form, body without spirit, it is said that the angels marvelled at Adam's strange form and figure, for they had never seen anything like it before. Indeed Iblīs himself looked at it for a long time before saying, 'God has created this thing for some great purpose. Perhaps he himself has gone inside it.' It is in the *Stories of the Prophets* (Kisā'i 1997: 26) where we have the description of the breath gradually permeating all of Adam:

> They will ask you concerning the spirit. Answer the spirit was created at the command of my Lord (Q17.85). God ordered the spirit to be immersed in all the lights then he commanded it to enter Adam's body with praise and without haste. The spirit seeing a narrow entrance and narrow apertures said, 'oh Lord how can I enter? It was told to enter reluctantly and exit reluctantly.

Exactly what is meant by *khalīfa* or 'representative' in this context is open to interpretation in similar ways to *imago Dei*, except that *khalīfa* does imply some kind of successor or deputy who will settle on earth to realize God's plans which will be done in a relationship with God. Early Muslim commentary also suggested that Adam, implying the generic concept of man, may be God's representative in 'exercising judgement with justice' (Q38.26). The Qur'ān advises Adam and the sons of Adam that the status of *khilāfat* means that they are being entrusted to look after the Earth – the Eearth and its riches are in man's care (*amāna*): 'It is We who have placed you with authority on earth and provided you therein with means for the fulfilment of your life' (Q7.10).

---

[1] Translations taken largely from Ali (1983).

There are verses which explicitly convey the exalted status given to humanity: 'We have bestowed special favours (*karramna*) on the sons of Adam and blessed them with favours above a great part of our creation' (Q17.70).

In the Qur'ānic story of Adam's creation and his eating from the 'tree of knowledge,' Adam's first act of freedom becomes his first act of disobedience. It is this very freedom which gives humankind the moral choice of doing good. In his social relations, in his dealings with those around him, in his stewardship of the Earth, man can find meaning and purpose which allows him to discover God. This was the new beginning which the Muslim philosopher and thinker, Muhammad Iqbal (1958: 8–9) alluded to:

> No doubt, the immediate purpose of the Qur'ān in this reflective observation of nature is to awaken in man the consciousness of that of which nature is regarded a symbol… to awaken in man the higher consciousness of his manifold relations with God and the universe.

The creation of humanity is simultaneous with a given status for humanity for this is part of the gradual unfolding of the divine plan. But, in the act of creation, God himself remains transcendent and untouched. In the Qur'ān at least, human beings carry an inherent dignity and honour conveyed in the very manner of their creation, but God's love (*hubb*) is not expressed as a reason for human creation. Furthermore, while the divine breath is an essential element in the completion of humankind, it does not explain how and if this makes humanity godlike in any way.

This is not because there is no reference to images of God in the Qur'ān, but because the dominant message of the Qur'ān is that 'nothing is like him' [God] (Q42.11). There can be no confusion between the Creator and the Created. The Qur'ānic God speaks only through inspiration, or from behind a veil, never revealing himself directly to humankind. The word Revelation is open to multiple interpretations, but the most popular view is that God's revelations mean God's direct interventions in different forms to humanity. Revelation has been mediated through different books and prophets throughout history. At times, God has made exceptions of some prophets with whom he has shared more intimacy, such as Moses, Jesus and Muhammad, but revelation is construed fundamentally as messages from God to humankind about the truthfulness of God. For this reason, revelation must be understood in the wider context of transcendence and immanence. While a major Qur'ānic theme came to be the absolute transcendence and oneness of God, the fundamental core of Islamic monotheism, as we see Muslim theology from the second/eight century onwards wrestled with how transcendence could be reconciled with immanence and how God, who does not reveal himself in his interaction with humankind, could be known. How could human beings understand a transcendent God who exists in pre-eternity as well as post eternity, whereas human life, intellect and perception are all finite?

The issue it seems is that transcendence does not mean distance, for God does want to be known. God is near man, 'nearer to him than his jugular vein' (Q50.16): he can be known by his attributes (*sifāt*) of which he speaks directly through the

Qur'ān: he is 'light upon light', and he is defined by his 'most beautiful names' (*al- asma al- husna*), traditionally numbering 99. All this formed the basis for a systematic theology about God's essence (*dhāt*) (Bowering 2002: 319). Conversely, even if God wants to be known, humankind is incapable of truly knowing him. Despite a variety of opinions on the knowability of God's essence and God's attributes, the elvenenth-century theologian Abū Hāmid al-Ghazālī (Shehadi 1964: 37), perhaps the most prominent and celebrated theologian of Islam, concluded: 'The end result of the knowledge of the `*arifin* is their inability to know Him and their knowledge is in truth that they do not know Him and that it is absolutely impossible for them to know Him'.[2]

One way of conceptualizing God was by understanding his attributes and the references to his physical being. As noted above, the most celebrated group of people to reject the literal understanding of anthropomorphic verses were the Mu`tazilites, the official court theologians of the early Abbāsids. So strongly did they conceptualize God's divine oneness and freewill, and his unswerving justice, that they propounded the doctrine of the created Qur'ān, i.e. the Qur'ān was created in time and was not the eternal word co-existing with the eternal God – otherwise there would be two divine realities, God and the Qur'ān. If God is just he could not condemn an individual to hell without giving the individual an opportunity to save him- or herself. Therefore the Qur'ān was created in time and the message of the Qur'ān created by God as his guidance for humankind; human being exercised free will in their response to the created Qur'ān. Frederick Denny (1994: 182) writes:

> Ironically the doctrine of the eternal Qur'ān doctrine somewhat resembles the Christian doctrine of the pre-existent and divine Logos 'Word' of God which in the opening of the Gospel of John is characterized as eternal and finally equivalent to God. But the word became incarnate in the life and work of Jesus. The Mu`tazilites were concerned about just this sort of 'incarnationism' slipping into Islamic doctrine and considered the position that held the Qur'ān to be eternal as a main avenue for such a development. In Christianity the Word became flesh; in Islam it became a book.

The insistence on keeping God as 'other' can be seen in other scholars of the time. Baydāwi (2002: 751) writes about the exclusion of resemblance between God's reality and other beings:

> The first topic is that the reality of God most high does not resemble any other being; that is to say his reality in its total quiddity has no commonality with any other being. This is because if his reality should resemble that of any other being, then the factor by which each of the two natures would be distinguished from the other would be both external to their realities.

Yet, in his conclusion to these ninth/tenth-century debates on the conceptualization of God, Williams (2002: 454) writes:

---

[2] The '*arifin* literally means 'those who know' and is used by the mystics in the sense of 'gnostics'. For a detailed analysis of this issue, see Abrahamov (2002).

The God of 9th-10th-century Sunnism was theophanous and corporeal. It was widely believed that an encounter with the divine inaugurated Muhammad's prophetic career. Such a God would eventually be replaced by an invisible, non-theophanous deity, as it was in Judaism, but not before making a significant contribution to the development of Islamic orthodoxy, which has shown itself to be remarkably fluid over the years.

It is important to point out here, albeit briefly, that the tension between self-revelation and complete transcendence has exercised the minds of Christian and Muslim scholars for centuries – reconciling a God who is radically one and trans-cendent, and a God who reveals for a purpose. In both religions, God is not an abstract concept; rather, he reveals himself in diverse ways in history so that we can re-centre ourselves towards him. As Rowan Williams says (1982: 29), 'God is the "presence" to which all reality is present.' In developing the relationship between the divine and the human, Muslims focused on God's modes and purpose in revelation, the human obligation to submit to reading God's presence in the Qur'ān and to obeying God's will in response to a revealed text. Christianity saw in revelation an aspect of God's self-giving so that revelation is seen as 'a happening that settles in the concreteness of events and that finds in Jesus Christ its fullness of meaning' (Dotolo 2006: ii).

Much of the anthropomorphic/theomorphic discussion is held largely in the framework of a particular Qur'ānic verse which pertains to a primordial pledge made between the Creator and his creation: a pledge which cannot be broken. This pact establishes God's sovereignty in the very act of creation, and becomes the essential question-command in God–man relations despite the subsequent alienation of humankind from an Edenic state: 'When the Lord drew forth from the children of Adam from their loins their descendents and made them bear testimony about their souls, he asked, "Am I not your Lord?" They said, "Yes we do testify"' (Q7.172).

Human nature cannot forget this pledge; it is ingrained in our very being or *fitra*, which is why we turn to the contemplation of God as an inevitable in our life. Through this primordial covenant, human beings have testified to their own theomorphic nature in pre-eternity (Haq 2003: 150). There is indeed an interpre-tation from Ibn Abbās that human beings are seen as restless creatures because, though the material world, in the form of earth, becomes their destiny, they are fully aware of their lost perfection which now ultimately resides in a return to their creator. Meanwhile they are God's representatives on a finite earth, 'custodians' of a world which they have promised to look after in their obedience to a cosmological justice. This is a voluntary stewardship in which humankind is of nature as well responsible to nature. Why do I say voluntary? Central to any understanding of man's relationship to God and man's relationship to nature is a curious Qur'ānic verse: 'Look, We offered the *trust* to the heavens and the earth and the mountains, but they refused to carry it and were afraid of it. But man accepted [the challenge]. He has indeed been unjust and ignorant' (Q33.72). It is as if God himself is amazed at man's foolhardiness, his temerity that he can be faithful to this momentous promise of looking after the bounties of creation, especially when all else declined this invitation.

Human freedom is man's biggest gift, not because animals and other life forms are not free but because human freedom is aligned with human accountability. The exercising of this freedom is intrinsic in the very obligation of stewardship. When God offered moral responsibility to the heavens and the Earth but they refused out of fear, yet man accepted, the Qur'ānic world reveals humankind ready to assume their ambivalent role; there is no sense that humanity really understands the onerous responsibility of a just stewardship of the natural world and a just, moral order for humankind. While the Qur'ān repeats, 'To God belong the dominion of the heavens and earth' (Q2.107), there is a transition of responsibility to human beings which becomes a defining moment in human destiny.

Being human in Islam is thus to forever wonder what it is to be human in the presence of God. It is to realize ones desires and to struggle with that which lures us away from God. It is to live with both the faith and the risk God has placed in humanity while all the time reflecting on our final destiny. Believers live with the dilemma of God's nearness to humanity but humanity's persistent failure to turn to God, to recognize the essence of the divine breath which calls us too God. Indeed, the Qur'ānic discourse is firmly rooted in God's intervention and signs in human history as acts of divine mercy. His signs are prophets and books, and while belief has never been coerced upon humanity, belief has always been invited:

> And we have sent down to you the Book in truth, confirming the Book that existed already before it and protecting it … For each one of you [several communities] We have appointed a Law and an open way. If God had so willed, he would have made you all one community, but [He has not done so] that He may test you in what He has given you; so compete in goodness. To God shall you all return and He will tell you [the Truth] about what you have been disputing (Q5.48).

Divine intervention demands that humanity defines a relationship with God through the different modes of revelation. In Islam, the authority of the Qur'ān and the wisdom of the Prophet and prophets offer guidance, but human beings have the freedom not to respond. Against this freedom to reject the signs of God, is the Qur'ānic exhortation to turn to God in worship. Prayer develops a person's sense of themselves and a yearning for God: it is an instinctive desire to speak to someone where the believer is transfixed on a God to whom he hopes to feel intimately connected even though God remains a hidden presence.

The essential premise of worship is not that God gains anything by human obedience, but that humanity realizes its ultimate goals through recognition of the sovereignty of God, rejection of false gods and development of divine-like attributes.

In his seminal work *From the Divine to the Human* (Schuon 1981: 1), Schuon opens with the following paragraph:

> The first ascertainment which should impose itself upon man when he reflects on the nature of the Universe is the primacy of that miracle that is intelligence – or consciousness or subjectivity – and consequently the incommensurability between these and material objects, be it a grain of sand or of the sun, or of any creature whatever as an object of

the senses. The truth of the Cartesian *cogito ergo sum* is not that it presents thought as the proof of being but simply that it enunciates the primacy of thought, hence of consciousness or intelligence, in relation to the material world which surrounds us. Certainly, it is not our personal thought which preceded the world, but it was or is our absolute Consciousness, of which our thought is precisely a distant reflection; our thought which reminds us and proves to us that in the beginning was the spirit. Nothing is more absurd than to have intelligence derive from matter, hence from the greater to the lesser; the evolutionary leap from matter to intelligence is from every point of view the most inconceivable thing that could be.

Human consciousness is blessed with the ability to contemplate the material world and what the material world points to, the Absolute, the Divine or God. For some the material world only points to the material, but in most of the Islamic philosophical tradition human beings are understood in terms of the unity of the human world and the natural world, where knowledge of the transcendent remains veiled but where sacred knowledge speaks from all aspects of nature:

> Because nature cannot explain itself, it stands as a sign of something beyond itself pointing to some transcendental entity that bestows the principle of being upon the world and its objects. Nature then is an emblem of God; a means through which God communicates with humanity. (Haq 2003: 146)

It is said that the Prophet himself constantly prayed for more knowledge of the universe, 'God grant me knowledge of the ultimate nature of things'. There is no place in this tradition to drive a wedge between humans and the cosmos.
  William Chittick (2001: 66) also states:

> In the final analysis the natural world is the externalization of the human substance, and the human soul is the internalization of the realm of nature. Human beings and the whole universe are intimately intertwined, facing each other like two mirrors. The quest for wisdom can only succeed if the natural world is recognized as equivalent to one's own self, just as one must see the whole human race as the external manifestation of the potencies and possibilities of the human soul.

Following Mircea Eliade and Tu Weiming, Chittick calls this intimate relationship shared between self and cosmos the 'anthropocosmic vision'. Since this vision entails a view of self and cosmos as being 'a single, organismic whole', knowledge of one entails knowledge of the other:

> In keeping with traditional Islamic doctrines, the human soul is a microcosm (*al-ʿālam al-saghīr*) and the cosmos proper is a macrocosm (*al-ʿālam al-kabīr*). According to Q41.53, God's signs (*ayāt*) are to be found in both the macrocosm and the microcosm: 'We will show them our signs in the cosmos (*afāq*) and in their souls (*anfūs*), until they know that He is the Real.' Since there is no absolute contrast between subject and object, the more humans study the signs within themselves, the more they will understand the signs in the cosmos. That is, the more we learn about the microcosm, the more we will come to know about the macrocosm. (Rustom 2008: 56)

The Qur'ān itself is replete with verses where the natural world is a sign and human reflection on the natural world is a pathway to the sacred. True knowledge is knowledge of the sacred and the history of the Islamic intellectual tradition is in many ways a history of the search for understanding or reflecting upon God. According to the Qur'ān:

> We have not created the heavens and the earth and whatever is between them in sport; we have not created them but for a serious end (Q44.38);
>   It is Allah who causes the seed-grain and the date-stone to sprout. He causes the living to come forth from the dead and He is the one to cause the dead to come forth from the living. That is Allah, so then how are you deluded from the truth? It is he that breaks the day and makes the night for rest and the sun and moon for the reckoning. Such is his judgement, the Exalted in power and the Omniscient. It is he who makes the stars for you so that you may guide yourselves with their help through the dark spaces of land and sea. Indeed we detail our signs for people who know. It is he who produced you from a single soul and then a resting place and a repository. We detail our signs for people who understand. It is he who sends down rain from the skies. With it we produce vegetation of all kinds.

To be human is to seek that knowledge which enhances our awareness of our self and provides intelligence as to what makes us human. It would seem that even if the concept of the divine breath remains largely elusive in determining theomorphism, monotheism stresses that it is our special relationship with God not our nature that is humankind's distinguishing feature. Nature in the Qur'ān is anchored in the divine both metaphysically and morally.

Finally, I would like to look at Uri Rubin's work on the use of light in the Islamic tradition (Rubin 1975). Drawing upon several Sunnī and Shī'i sources, Rubin shows that 'Light serves as a symbol of the prospective expansion of the Islamic faith' (Rubin 1975: 64). There is God's light, the light of Muhammad's prophetic emergence and the light motif used as representative of divine presence amongst the Shī'a (Rubin 1975: 66). For the Shī'a light is an allegoric symbol of the Prophet, 'Ali, his sons and the rest of the imams. A notable Shī'i tradition says:

> When Allah created paradise, he created it from the light of His face. Then he took the light and dispersed it. One third hit Muhammad, one third hit Fatima and another third hit 'Ali. All people whom this light reached found the right path of loyalty to Muhammad's family; those who missed it went astray. (Rubin 1975: 65–6)

Among all the sects, the Shī'a have made the most of light in the concept of divine light:

> Light as an element of communication between the imams and the rest of humankind is sometimes described as a cosmic column. It is erected as such on the birth of each imam and supplies him with knowledge about the deeds of all people. It also communicates between the imam and the heavenly world. (Rubin 1975: 66)

The prophets too are created with light, and traditions extol Muhammad as being created with a primordial light, a substance which places him above other prophets and the best of Adam's offspring. Muhammad is said to be the 'first prophet to be created and the last to be sent' (Rubin 1975: 70–1).

According to the Shī`a, Ali, as well as his family, was existent before Adam's creation as primordial luminous reflections of their corporeal bodies. These reflections are called *ashbāh* or *ashbāh nūr* and from the clay of these *ashbāh* God created the souls of all the Shī`a (Rubin 1975: 99). But the light motif is complimented by the concept of the pre-existence of divine spirits independent of bodies. The pre-existent spirits of the imams, as well as that of Muhammad, are conceived to possess the essence of their divine features (Rubin 1975: 104). One of the most famous Shī`a traditions says:

> God said to Muhammad, 'I had created you and `Ali as light – that is, spirit without body before I created heaven, earth, the throne and the sea; all that time you kept praising me. Then I incorporated your two spirits into one and it went on praising me.' (Rubin 1975: 105)

The tradition continues to say that God places his hand over Muhammad and his family so that the divine light shines within them. In such traditions, divine light and the holy spirit transmigrate through prophets and into the line of imams, where the light is regarded as source of knowledge. The aim of these traditions is to accord a superior status to Muhammad as a prophet and to `Ali as his rightful successor. Such traditions easily allow divine elements to be absorbed into earthly human existence without any tension as to how far the eternal divine element can enter a finite mortal existence.

Light is also used as a motif for the hidden God who can be discovered. In his esoteric treatise, *The Mishkāt al–Anwār, The Niche for Lights* (Al-Ghazzali, 1924), Al-Ghazālī explores the Qurʾānic Light verse (Q24.35) and the veil traditions as a way of attempting to show how God is the only real actual light in all existence; all other 'is predicated metaphorically and conveys no real meaning' (Al-Ghazzali 1924: 45). This knowledge of God, however, is for the mystical path a way of *being* with God:

> Allah is the Light of the heavens and the earth. The similitude of his light is as it were a niche wherein there is a lamp: the lamp within a glass, the glass as it were a pearly star. From a tree that is blessed it is lit, an olive tree neither of the East nor of the West, the oil whereof were well-nigh luminous though fire did not touch it; light upon light, God guides to his light whom he wills. (Q24.35)

And the Prophetic veil tradition:

> Allah has seventy thousand veils of light and darkness. Were he to withdraw their curtain then would the splendours of His aspect surely consume everyone who apprehended him with his sight. (Al-Ghazzali 1924: 88).

Ghazālī talks about the real light, which is God, and the significance of using light as a theme in human–divine relations. Heavenly realities all have their symbols on Earth, and there is a certain ineffable likeness between man and God, but all of us have only a veiled understanding of God. Al-Ghazālī divides those who are veiled into different groups. Those who are veiled by pure darkness are the atheists and Al-Ghazālī draws on Qur'ānic verses to show that 'They are those who love the present life more than that which is to come' (Al-Ghazzali 1924: 89). This group has subdivisions between those who are preoccupied with finding a cause to account for the world and those who are preoccupied with their own Self (Al-Ghazzali 1924: 89). The second division consists of those who are veiled by mixed light and darkness where people have darkness of the senses 'which veils from them the knowledge that they must transcend the world of sense in this quest (Al-Ghazzali 1924: 92). Ghazālī's taxonomy of the different grades is complex, but his underlying message is that human intelligence has a capacity for perceiving the divine through the stages of contemplation. The Qur'ān contains the vocabulary which allows humankind to identify with God's goodness, and yet ultimately the divine reality may always elude human understanding. Only for the very few will 'nothing remain except the Real'.

Alexander Treiger (2007: 4–5) explains Al-Ghazālī's philosophy in the *Mishkāt* as following:

> The theme of God as the only true existent is central to al-Ghazālī's metaphysics. It occurs, most famously, as the highest stage of confessing God's oneness, *tawḥīd*. In the *Mishkāt*, al-Ghazālī draws a distinction between two types of *tawḥīd*, characteristically of the commoners and of the elect, respectively. The commoners believe in the plain meaning of the *shahāda*, 'There is no god but God.' The elect, by contrast, have a more esoteric version which reads, 'There is no god but he.' An even more esoteric version, 'There is no he but He.' The implication is that this is the *tawḥīd* of the elect among the elect.

The light motif is only one motif used to understand God and the sense of divine presence in this world. The ineffable existence and presence of light becomes closest to the almost unspeakable yet overwhelming existence of God, which should be the believer's true goal in this life. Despite understanding God as the transcendent other, Islamic thought has from the earliest times wrestled with how divine presence manifests itself in this world and how humans can understand themselves as well as God's chosen few as agents of the 'divine breath': although Adam's descent on Earth is regarded as a new paradigm for human existence, it seems that something between the human and the divine has been ruptured in this exile and that the longing for return remain a powerful longing.

In the words of the great Sufis one detects this desperation to be with God again, a restless desire to do away with that which separates humankind from God even in this life. Perhaps nowhere has this been expressed more hauntingly than in the words of the great Muslim Sufi saint Abdul Quddūs of Gangoh whose words allude to the narrative of Muhammad's ascension to heaven: 'Muhammad of Arabia ascended the highest Heaven and returned. I swear by God that if I had reached that point, I should never have returned' (Iqbal 1958: 86).

References

Abrahamov, B. (2002), `Fakhr al-Din Razi on the knowability of god's essence and attributes'. *Arabica, T.49*, Fasc.2 (April), 204–30.

Ali, Y. A. (1983), *The Holy Qur'an* (Brentwood, MD: Amana Publications).

Baydawi, `A. A. (2002), *Tawali `al-Anwar min Matali `al-Anzar. [Nature, Man and God in Medieval Islam]*. Vol. 2, E. Calverley and J. Pollock (eds) and trans., Leiden: Brill.

Bowering, G. (2002), 'God and His attributes'. In J. D. McAuliffe (ed.), *Encyclopaedia of the Qur'an*. Vol. 2. Leiden: Brill, pp. 316–31.

Calder, N. (1997), 'History and nostalgia: reflections on John Wansbrough's *The Sectarian Milieu'. Method & Theory in the Study of Religion, 9*, 47–73.

Chittick, W. (2001), *The Heart of Islamic Philosophy: The Quest for Self-Knowledge in the Writings of Afdal al-Din Kashani*. New York, NY: Oxford University Press.

—(ed.) (2007), *The Essential Syyed Hossein Nasr*. Bloomington, IN: World Wisdom.

Denny, F. (1994), *An Introduction to Islam*. New York, NY: Macmillan .

Dotolo, C. (2006), *The Christian Revelation* (trans. C. Domenica). Aurora: Davies Group.

Al-Ghazzali (1924), *Mishkāt al-Anwār ('The Niche for Lights')* (trans. W. H. T. Gairdner). London: Royal Asiatic Society.

Haq, S. N. (2003), 'Islam and ecology: towards retrieval and reconstruction'. In R. Foltz, F. Denny and A. Baharuddin (eds), *Islam and Ecology: A Bestowed Trust*. Cambridge, MA: Harvard University Press, pp. 121–54.

Hussain, I. (2003). History as memory. Available from http://www.islamfrominside.com/Pages/Articles/The%20concept%20of%20time%20in%20the%20Quran.html

Iqbal, M. (1958), *The Reconstruction of Religious Thought in Islam*. Lahore: The Ashraf Press.

Izutsu, T. (1966). *Ethico-Religious Concepts in the Quarān*. Montreal: McGill University Press.

Al-Kisā`i (1997), *Qisas al-anbiya, Tales of the Prophets* (trans. W. Thackston). Chicago, IL: Great Books of the Islamic World.

Middleton, R. (1994), 'The liberating image? Interpreting the imago dei in context'. *Christian Scholars Review, 24* (2), 8–25.

Rubin, U. (1975), 'Pre-existence and light'. *Israel Oriental Studies, 5*, 62–119.

Rustom, M. (2008), 'Equilibrium and realization, William Chittick on self and cosmos'. *American Journal of Islamic Studies, 25* (3), 52–60.

Schuon, F. (1981), *From the Divine to the Human*. Bloomington, IN: World Wisdom.

Shehadi, F. (1964), *Ghazali's Unique Unknowable God*. Leiden: Brill.

Treiger, A. (2007), 'Monism and monotheism in al-Ghazāli's Mishkāt al-Anwār'. *Journal of Qur'ānic Studies, 9* (1), 1–27.

Williams, R. (1982), *Resurrection: Interpreting the Easter Gospel*. London: Darton Longman and Todd.

Williams, W. (2002), 'Aspects of the creed of Imam Ahmad Ibn Hanbal'. *International Journal of Middle-Eastern Studies, 34*, 441–63.

12 What Could Theologians Possibly Learn From the Cognitive Study of Religion?

Taede A. Smedes

The way you use the word 'God' does not show *whom* you mean – but, rather, what you mean. (Wittgenstein 1980: 50e)

Introduction

Many religious people consider the cognitive study of religion (hereafter abbreviated as 'CSR') to be a threat to religious faith. Undoubtedly, this impression is strengthened by the rhetoric of Richard Dawkins, Daniel Dennett, Sam Harris and other fanatical atheists, who give the impression that to explain religion using principles from the cognitive sciences and/or evolutionary biology is sufficient for making a watertight case that religion is 'nothing but' the misfiring of neurons in the brain or Feuerbachian projection – in sum, that religion is an illusion.

The CSR is thus often perceived to be a reductionist approach. I grant that the CSR *is* reductive, but so is every other branch of science if it wants to be successful in explaining a part of our reality. However, the CSR is often perceived not merely as a *methodologically* reductive approach, but also as a *metaphysically* reductive (and thus 'reductionist'); i.e. the CSR is perceived as being able to make inferences to the existence or nonexistence of God. Someone who takes the CSR as being metaphysically a reductionist approach will then argue that if a naturalistic explanation is given of religious beliefs and behaviours in terms of cognitive and/or evolutionary principles (i.e. if the natural factors involved in religious belief are identified), then this explanation is sufficient to explain why people hold religious beliefs, irrespective of the reasons believers themselves put forward for their beliefs.

Although atheists such as Dennett and Dawkins regard the CSR as being a strong enough approach to warrant metaphysically reductionist conclusions, I believe that such views are unjustified if one takes an honest look at the present status of the field of the CSR. At present, the field of the CSR is methodologically fragmented (i.e. even speaking about 'the' field or 'the' CSR is actually already saying too much, although I will continue to do so throughout this paper for convenience) and many of the claims done by those researchers active in the field as yet lack empirical backing.[1] I acknowledge that the field of the CSR is in the process of becoming and maturing and has tremendous potential. But even if the field were to be fully evolved, I do not share the conviction that the CSR is a threat to religious faith – quite the contrary.

In this chapter I argue that the CSR is extremely useful to theologians in illuminating the human nature of religious faith and the different ways in which religious believers think and speak about God. In the next section, I will give a short and somewhat technical reconstruction of the claims of the CSR concerning the biological and cognitive rootedness of religion in human nature. Thereafter, I will briefly go into the principle of 'theological correctness' to explicate the difference between intuitive or common-sense god concepts and the more abstract god concepts that follow from theological reflection. Among religious believers both the intuitive and the more abstract theological concepts are present simultaneously, and the CSR makes it clear why that is the case. Finally, I will give a theological reflection on how I see the CSR as useful to (in my case Christian) theology.

But I will start with some preliminary methodological remarks. I assume that religious faith, just like every other human activity or trait, is ultimately biologically anchored and constrained, although not (metaphysically) reducible to biology solely. I thereby also assume the validity of the biological narrative of the evolutionary history of *Homo sapiens*. I see no theological reason to reject or modify the biological-evolutionary narrative, although I am suspicious when it comes to metaphysical (whether theistic or atheistic) conclusions being drawn from biological-evolutionary data. Thus, when it comes to the CSR, I have no reason to reject or doubt the validity of the description of the biological and cognitive rooting of religious faith, but I would reject as a *non sequitur* the conclusion that an evolutionary or cognitive description of how religious belief works is sufficient for proving (or at least making highly likely) *either* the existence *or* the non-existence of God. I thus reject the apologetic use of the CSR for either theism or atheism. Instead, I hold that the CSR cannot and does not say anything about God, but is all about *belief in* God.[2]

Introducing the cognitive study of religion[3]

Many working in the field of the CSR use the popular idea that human minds are 'massively modular' (Tooby and Cosmides 1992; Cosmides and Tooby 1994;

[1] For a thorough criticism of the CSR, see Barbara Herrnstein Smith's Terry Lectures (Smith 2009). See also Justin Barrett's plea for scientific rigour in Barrett 2008a.
[2] I thus make a quite rigid distinction between methodological and metaphysical claims and sidestep at this point the issue of whether, in the case of the CSR, methodological and metaphysical issues can be separated as neatly as I assume in this chapter.
[3] For this reconstruction, I lean heavily on Boyer (2001), Barrett (2004) and Tremlin (2006).

Samuels 2000).[4] The modular architecture of the mind has been compared to a Swiss army knife (Tooby and Cosmides 1992), a cathedral (Mithen 1996) and a workshop (Barrett 2004). The different mental modules constitute innate abilities or 'mechanisms' which are evolutionarily designed (i.e. designed by natural selection) to perform domain-specific tasks. Thus humans are said to have mental modules for language acquisition and for facial recognition. The workings of these modules are activated by stimuli in specific environments, e.g. the language module is triggered when a child encounters an environment where there is a language spoken, and the facial recognition module is activated when a baby encounters other humans.

These mental modules yield certain beliefs about the world that enable humans to operate efficiently, flexibly and relatively effortlessly in relation to the world and the agents they encounter (in many cases our fellow humans). Justin Barrett (2004: 2, following Sperber 1997) makes a useful distinction between *reflective* and *nonreflective beliefs*. Reflective beliefs 'are those we arrive at through conscious, deliberate contemplation or explicit instruction', while nonreflective beliefs are 'those that come automatically, require no careful rumination, and seem to arise instantaneously and sometimes even "against better judgment." These nonreflective beliefs are terribly important for successfully functioning in the day-to-day world' (Barrett 2004: 2). These nonreflective beliefs give rise to 'intuitive' or 'folk' knowledge, which refers to 'the several systematic forms of knowledge and thinking that ordinary people use to explain the things, activities, and other individuals encountered in everyday life' (Tremlin 2006: 66). Developmental psychologists have charted out three categories of intuitive knowledge: biology (e.g. essentialism about species), physics (e.g. two solid objects cannot go through each other) and psychology.

Especially the notion of intuitive psychology, referring to 'the natural attribution of mental states to other people and the cognitive skills involved in the ongoing interpretation of those states' (Tremlin 2006: 68), is important, since it affects the way we interact with intentional agents. Two mental modules responsible for intuitive psychological beliefs are the *Hyperactive* (in some papers also called *Hypersensitive*) *Agency Detection Device* (HADD) and the *Theory of Mind Mechanism* (ToMM). These two tools are crucial for the social interaction in everyday life and also seem to be functional in religious belief. Justin Barrett (2004: 33) summarizes the workings of the HADD as follows:

> When HADD perceives an object violating the intuitive assumptions for the movement of ordinary physical objects (such as moving on noninertial paths, changing directions inexplicably, or launching itself from a standstill) and the object seems to be moving in a goal-directed manner, HADD detects agency. Gathering information from other mental tools, HADD searches for any known agents that might account for the self-propelled movement. Finding none, HADD assumes that the object itself is an agent. Until information arrives to say otherwise, HADD registers a nonreflective belief that the object is

---

[4] The modularity thesis is not uncontroversial; however, since the term 'module' means different things to different cognitive scientists. I cannot go into that discussion here.

an agent, triggering ToM [the Theory of Mind] to describe the object's activity in terms of beliefs, desires, and other mental states.

Because of the relevance of spotting the presence of agents in an environment for survival, evolution has selected for minds with an agency detection system that is tuned to efficiently spot agents, or infer the possible presence of agents, from available clues, but at the cost of not always operating flawlessly. Since from an evolutionary perspective it is better to be safe than sorry, the HADD is prone to make misidentifications: it sometimes points to the presence of agents where there are none. This feature of being too eager for finding agents has motivated Justin Barrett to speak about a *Hyperactive* Agency Detection Device. Barrett argues that experiments have shown that when there are hunches that an agent is present, our HADD is activated to actively search for agents and it will not rest until it has found a satisfactory explanation for the presence of the hunch.

As soon as the HADD has settled on an agent the Theory of Mind Mechanism (ToMM) springs into action. The ToMM, according to Tremlin (2006: 80), 'appears to operate on the basis of internal assumptions about how minds work', which entails granting 'feelings, intentions, memories, beliefs and desires to others' to make those agents more intelligible in order to interact with them (2006: 81). The ToMM thus attributes mental states to the identified agent and thus leads to inferences as to its intentions. It operates efficiently in interpersonal communication with other people. Now, the link between the HADD and ToMM and religious belief is that modules may, in ambiguous situations, settle for 'novel or imaginative candidates, particularly those already believed in or seriously entertained by others' (Tremlin 2006: 79). In short: the workings of the HADD and ToMM may lead to inferences as to the presence and activity of gods and supernatural entities.

According to cognitive science, gods and supernatural beings belong to the category of *counterintuitive concepts*. These are concepts that violate our natural expectations about the ways objects behave (e.g. Tremlin 2006: 87; Barrett 2004: 22.). Counterintuitive concepts either *violate* intuitive expectations, which belong to a certain category, or some expected property of one ontological category is *transferred* to another. To take just one example, the story of Balaam's talking ass (Num. 22: 21–35) is interesting and memorable because it violates our intuitive expectations about animals (they do not talk like humans), and also transfers properties belonging to the ontological category of persons (talking, reasoning) to the category of animals.

However, for concepts to be counterintuitive enough to be interesting, they have to be *minimally* counterintuitive (Barrett 2004: 22), which indicates that such concepts should not violate all of our intuitive expectations about ontological categories. As Barrett (2004: 22) describes, minimally counterintuitive concepts (MCIs), are easy to understand, remember and believe, but they violate 'just enough … assumptions to be attention demanding and to have an unusually captivating ability to assist in the explanation of certain experiences'. Moreover, for minimally counterintuitive concepts – among which are god concepts – to be culturally successful, there has to be a *cognitive optimum* (Boyer 1994: 406) balancing the violation or transference of some intuitive expectations while preserving other expectations.

The crux of the matter is that the minimally counterintuitive concepts have to be interesting and attract attention, but most importantly they must have a good *inferential potential*, thus 'activating large numbers of mental tools and exciting reasoning' (Barrett 2004: 25) in order to be culturally successful: 'For MCIs to successfully compete for space in human minds and thus become "cultural," they must have the potential to explain, to predict, or to generate interesting stories surrounding them' (Barrett 2004: 25). This has the important implication that there is a *cognitive constraint*: in the case of religious concepts there can be no unbridled creativity. To be believable, religious concepts are constrained by our imagination. In turn, our imagination is constrained by the biological structuring of our minds.

Underlying many if not most god concepts is the basic ontological category of a person, or as Tremlin (2006: 95) puts it: 'The basic design for building a god is based on the mental blueprint for building a person.' Barrett (2004: 26) underlines the notion that persons or

> Agents have tremendous inferential potential. Agents can cause things to happen, not only be caused. We can explain why things are so by appealing to agents. We can anticipate what an agent might do. We can't anticipate what a rock might do, only what might be done to it. Not surprisingly, then, from space aliens to humanlike animals to cartoon characters to God, intentional agents are the MCIs that people tell stories about, remember, and tell others.

Thus the concept of the Christian God is rooted in the ontological view of a person that people can relate to, but with a counterintuitive twist: God is not visible, has no tangible body and has extraordinary powers no human person possesses (omnipotence, omniscience, omnipresence, etc.). Here we see the HADD and the ToMM in action: God is conceived of as an intentional agent, a being with a mind. Whether or not one prefers to call this 'anthropomorphization' (Guthrie 1993), god concepts are represented and processed by the human mind as representing social agents: 'Gods and humans interact as humans interact, and human interaction takes the form of social exchange' (Tremlin 2006: 113). However, the Christian concept of God is also minimally counterintuitive, giving rise to interesting inferences and fascinating stories and elaborate rituals and liturgies that capture cultures the world over.

'Theological correctness'

Now supposing that the above analysis is valid, what does this imply for theology? As I see it, there are a couple of theological responses possible. The first is rejection, because it seems as if the CSR is explaining away religious faith by uncovering its biological and cognitive roots. However, as I've already said, unless one is a metaphysical reductionist I do not think the CSR logically entails the claim that religious belief is an illusion. The second, opposite response argues that the 'hard-wiring' for religious belief that the CSR uncovers indeed proves the naturalness of religion and the 'unnaturalness' of atheism (cf. Barrett 2004). According to this apologetic response, their biological rootedness may be seen as being evidence for the veracity of religious belief. One could even imagine a creationist approach, which argues that the CSR proves that humans are created in the image of God and are 'intelligently designed' to believe (even though the human cognitive system is corrupted due to original sin). As tempting as such apologetic responses may be for religious believers, I believe any metaphysical claim from the CSR to the truth of religious claims or the existence of God entails a *non sequitur* and strays unjustifiably far beyond the empirical data.

As I said above, the CSR is not about God, but about belief in God. In other words, the results of the CSR merely say something about the way humans believe in God, but say nothing about God him/her/itself. The CSR thus describes the intuitive ways in which humans tend to think about God, their concepts of God, which are cognitive representations that may or may not correlate with how God actually is. The forms of religious belief that the CSR describes are far removed from the abstract forms of thinking one finds in theological discourse. Indeed, as most theologians know from their own experience, there is often a tension between theological concepts and the God-talk of 'ordinary' religious believers. The CSR explains this tension by a principle that Justin Barrett calls 'theological correctness'.

According to Barrett, the phenomenon that 'what we say we think and know and what we think and know in real-time problem solving sometimes are two entirely different things' (Barrett 1999: 325) is not only common to religion but is known in many areas of life. For example, science has shown that the Earth revolves around the sun, and yet in everyday discourse we talk as if instead the sun moves around the earth, which is reflected in most languages who have expressions to 'the sun rises' and 'the sun sets'. And we know that computers are not living, intentional beings, and yet many people will talk about them as evil entities that are always trying to make people's lives as miserable as possible by failing to do what we want them to at crucial moments.

As Barrett (1999: 326) writes, in many cases one can say that there are 'parallel levels of understanding or representation of the same phenomenon that may be contradictory: the theoretical level and the basic level; the level used in formal discourse and careful reflection, and the level used on-the-fly to solve problems quickly'. The CSR holds that religious reasoning is not principally different from reasoning in other contexts, so that in religion the two levels of understanding are also assumed to be present.[5] Barrett therefore argues that in religion there is a 'theoretical or theological level of representation' which is in accordance with

---

[5] Slone (2004: 47) formulates this in a more sophisticated way: 'The cognitive approach to religion is a "naturalness" thesis because cognitive scientists believe that religion is a by-product of the processes of ordinary human cognition. In other words, cognition operates in such a manner that religious representations emerge quite naturally as an aspect of ordinary thinking.'

theological dogma, and 'a basic level of representation' which is more intuitive (1999: 326).

In a different context, Barrett (2008b) used the distinction between 'implicit' and 'explicit' cognition to refer to these two levels. For example: 'While many Therevada Buddhists insist (explicitly) that the Buddha was not divine but only a man, they act and reason (implicitly) that the Buddha is a god' (Barrett 2008b: 292, referring to Slone 2004: 71–84). The official, explicit theology of Therevada Buddhism thus states something different from what the implicit ritualistic behaviour of Buddhists suggests. When given the opportunity to explain (and thus reflect on their behaviour), many Buddhists will acknowledge the apparent discrepancy between their behaviour and their explicit theological beliefs.

These two levels – the explicit theoretical-theological and the implicit basic level – are, according to Barrett, not mutually exclusive, but are connected through a 'continuum of abstractness or cognitive complexity' (Barrett 1999: 326), from more concrete and simple concepts to more abstract and complex ones. Eventually, the abstract and complex theological concepts seem to be the criteria of theological adequacy. There is thus, as Barrett calls it, a criterion of 'theological correctness':

> I term the coexistence of multiple levels of representation of religious concepts or relations 'Theological Correctness' or 'T.C.', because when beliefs about God or other religious concepts are reflected on, they tend to be reported as more similar to dominant theological dogma than the gut-level, basic concepts used in more mundane behavior. (1999: p. 326)

Barrett explains that which god concepts people will use depends on what the situation demands. For example, Barrett and Keil (1996: 224ss; cf. also Barrett 1999: 328s) write about an experiment in which subjects are asked to recount the following story:

> A boy was swimming alone in a swift and rocky river. The boy got his left leg caught between two large, gray rocks and couldn't get out. Branches of trees kept bumping into him as they hurried past. He thought he was going to drown and so he began to struggle and pray. Though God was answering another prayer in another part of the world when the boy started praying, before long God responded by pushing one of the rocks so the boy could get his leg out. The boy struggled to the river bank and fell over exhausted. (Barrett and Keil 1996: 224)

Now, when people were asked to recount the story, many stated that God finished answering one prayer first before attending to the boy – something which is not present in the story. Thus, they turned to a more anthropomorphic god concept in which God, like any other human person, can attend to only one thing at a time. However, in taking a questionnaire (having more time for reflection) the same subjects tended towards theological correctness, thus turning to more abstract theological god concepts. As Barrett (1999: 329) concludes: 'These data suggest that the processing demands of a context might, in part, influence how abstract, or cognitively cumbersome, a concept can be.'

Theological assessment

Slone (2004: 51) writes that one of the key features of contemporary cognitive science is 'that the brain is chock full of structures that constrain the way humans behave'. As the above analyses of the CSR and of theological correctness show, religious belief is also one of the human traits that is apparently constrained by biology. Again, this does not mean that religion is reducible to biological categories – here again we have the *non sequitur* – but that our human ways of talking about the Transcendent are constrained by functions of our cognitive apparatus that have a long evolutionary history.

One could even translate this in Kantian terms. Immanuel Kant's 'Copernican revolution' consisted in the view that our cognitive apparatus does not perceive things as they are; rather, our cognitive apparatus is a filter that not only *constrains* how we perceive things, but – and this is important – that also *makes possible* that we perceive things (and gain knowledge about them) in the first place. Kant was not a Berkeleyan idealist who claimed that the world 'out there' is a mere idea, but neither was he a naïve (or common-sense) realist who claims that our intuitive perception corresponds with how things really are. Our cognitive system functions as a filter that constrains, but also makes possible, knowledge of reality. The cognitive sciences are now starting slowly to unveil the evolutionary development of the structures and mechanisms that make up our cognitive system. And the CSR is attempting to describe how our cognitive system constrains and makes possible ways to talk about a transcendent reality that is somehow encountered in the world around us, although it is said also to transcend that world.

However, Kant also held that, because of cognitive constraints, humans are not able to make any theoretical claims as to the existence and attributes of God, because God is not part of the reality that we normally perceive. God, for Kant, can only be talked about in the context of morality. If humans do make theoretical claims about God (as opposed to speaking about God in practical, and thus moral, terms), they are liable to anthropomorphization, and it is clear that Kant did not have a high regard for anthropomorphic imagery.

On the other hand, the CSR has shown that anthropomorphism – thinking about God in personal and even human terms – is one of the key features of at least the Jewish, Christian and Muslim god concept. By anthropomorphism I do not, however, consider the naïve god concepts that were ridiculed by the Presocratic philosopher Xenophanes, who apparently wrote that

> the Ethiopians say that their gods are snub-nosed and black, the Thracians that theirs have light blue eyes and red hair. But if cattle and horses or lions had hands, or were able to draw with their hands and do the works that men can do, horses would draw the forms of the gods like horses, and cattle like cattle, and they would make their bodies such as they each had themselves. (Quoted from Kirk et al. 1983: 169)

However, that gods are talked about in anthropomorphic terms was, for Xenophanes, no reason to abandon the concept of God altogether. Instead, Xenophanes argued for a theology in which the idea of 'one god, greatest among gods and men, in no way similar to mortals either in body or in thought' (Kirk et al. 1983: 169) was central.

What I have in mind with using the term 'anthropomorphism' is the following. Given the functioning of the HADD and the ToMM, it is not surprising that religious believers speak about God in personal and often even anthropomorphic ways. Apparently, speaking about God in personal terms comes most intuitively to us humans. Speaking about God in personal terms is thus not only biologically and cognitively constrained, but also makes it possible to talk about the Transcendent that in essence cannot be talked about. The implictly used anthropomorphic language in a sense masks the more explicit and reflective understanding of the Transcendent, but because of its communicative function (remember the idea of 'minimal counterintuitiveness') the anthropomorphic language also gives rise to (and thus makes possible) theological reflection.

The more reflective theological approaches within religious traditions have always emphasized that we should not take our intuitive or folk-conceptions of the Divine too seriously. According to the language game of the Christian tradition, we are allowed to talk about God in personal and relational terms, but God *should not be considered as* a person in the sense that humans are persons. As we saw, the principle of theological correctness shows that religious believers ultimately agree to this (because of their explicit theological understanding of the religious discourse), even though in everyday discourse they are more used to using more implicit and intuitive personal language to talk about God.

In other words, our humanity *configures* the way we think and talk about God, even though this configuration also makes it possible to talk about (and, for believers, to experience a personal relationship with) the transcendent God. From psychological studies it was already known that there also exists a 'psychological configuration', because an individual's concept of God is intimately linked to experiences with his or her parents (cf. the classical study by Rizzuto 1979). But now the CSR is slowly uncovering the biological rootedness of religious belief. This says nothing about the illusory or real character of belief, but it confirms that we cannot think and talk about God without our human frame of reference. This obviously confirms the 'projection thesis' that gained prominence in modernity via the works of Ludwig Feuerbach and Sigmund Freud, although I believe their conclusion that *therefore* religion is an illusion does not automatically follow.

I believe the CSR is of tremendous use in that it once again confirms one of the fundamental theological notions of the Judeo-Christian tradition, viz. that if we absolutize our human language and our human images of God, we tend to domesticate God's transcendence. God's 'otherness' or *alterity*, which is expressed by speaking about God's transcendence, is lost when we take our human ways of talking about God too seriously. One could even read the Second Commandment as not only a prohibition on materially graven images, but also as a prohibition on conceptual or linguistic graven images. As Feuerbach and Freud emphasized, such a human-like image of God may be comforting, but if taken too seriously it reduces God to human categories. God is then reduced to what we can comprehend. In that case, God's otherness disappears. As the Swiss theologian Karl Barth argued, this could be considered as a sort of control or power over God in that we make God the object of our cognition, whereas for Barth 'God is known through God and through God alone' (Barth, quoted in Webster 2004: 78).[6]

In this context, the theological concept of *revelation* may become crucial, as William Placher makes clear:

> Human reason cannot figure its way to such a God, since a God we could figure out, a God fitted to the categories of our understanding, would therefore not be transcendent in an appropriately radical sense. We can know the transcendent God not as an object within our intellectual grasp but only as a self-revealing subject, and even our knowledge of divine self-revelation must itself be God's doing. Christian faith finds here confirmation of God's Triune character: we come to know this gracious God not merely in revelation but in self-revelation in Jesus Christ, and we come to trust that we do know God in Christ through the work of the Holy Spirit. (1996: 182)

However, is such a view sufficient? From a theological perspective, it may be. From a philosophical perspective it hardly is, since an appeal to revelation does not guarantee the validity of the various religious truth-claims of a religion. Indeed, one can point to the differences between Judaism, Christianity and Islam to see that the use of the concept of revelation and the content given to it within each of the three traditions leads to incompatible results: Judaism does not accept the Christian claim of God's revelation in Jesus Christ, and in Islam the definitive revelation which overrules all others is claimed to have taken place through the prophet Mohammed.

In other words, even with the claim to revelation, there remains a fundamental uncertainty. Revelation is never sufficient as proof for the validity of claims to knowledge about God and God's will, because revelation itself is perceived and interpreted in human categories. The configuration of religion by our humanity leads to a critical and irreducible hermeneutical moment to all religion. In a sense, as the Princeton philosopher Mark Johnston (2009: 20) argues, all religion itself is always already a way to domesticate and thus to resist the Transcendent:

> To comprehend one's own religion is not just to comprehend its dogmas and rituals. It involves bringing into clear view the religion's characteristic way of resisting the Divine: its way of redeploying its supposed foundational experiences of Divinity in the service of a reinvented worldliness on which one's religious community has itself come to depend.

Thus, as Kierkegaard and other existentialist thinkers have emphasized, a commitment to a religious tradition involves ultimately not certainty, but a 'leap of faith'. This existential leap is irreducible and does not reduce the uncertainty or doubt an individual may feel towards the claims of a religion. For some this leap of faith may lead to existential certainty, but for many more the uncertainty and

---

[6] According to Barth, humans can only know God if God posits Godself as the object for human cognition, and this was done in the Incarnation. Thus for Barth, the Incarnation becomes the lens through which Christian believers look at reality.

doubts remain. This doubt, however, is far from dangerous to faith. A healthy attitude of doubt hovering between and avoiding the extremes of relativism and absolutism is necessary in modern Western society, and religion is not exempt from such doubt (cf. Berger and Zijderveld 2009).

Indeed, the CSR underlines the fact that in religious matters we should always remain suspicious, and theologians should even excel as the masters of suspicion. They should overcome the easy religious complacency that so many people search for, and resist any attempt to domesticate the Transcendent.

References

Barrett, J. L. (1999), 'Theological correctness: cognitieve constraint and the study of religion'. *Method & Theory in the Study of Religion, 11*, 325–39.

—(2004), *Why Would Anyone Believe in God?* Lanham, MY: AltaMira Press.

—(2008a), 'Keeping "science" in the cognitive science of religion: needs of the field'. In J. Bulbulia, R. Sosis, E. Harris, et al. (eds), *The Evolution of Religion: Studies, Theories, & Critiques*. Santa Margarita, CA: Collins Foundation Press, pp. 295–301.

—(2008b), 'Theological implications of the cognitive science of religion' In J. Bulbulia, R. Sosis, E. Harris, et al. (eds), *The Evolution of Religion: Studies, Theories, & Critiques*. Santa Margarita, CA: Collins Foundation Press, pp. 393–9.

Barrett, J. L. and F. C. Keil, 'Conceptualizing a nonnatural entity: anthropomorphism in God concepts'. *Cognitive Psychology, 31*, 219–47.

Berger, P. and A. Zijderveld (2009), *In Praise of Doubt: How to Have Convictions Without Becoming a Fanatic*. New York, NY: HarperCollins.

Boyer, P. (1994), 'Cognitive constraints on cultural representations: natural ontologies and religious ideas'. In L. A. Hirschfeld and S. A. Gelman (eds), *Mapping the Mind: Domain Specificity in Cognition and Culture*. Cambridge: Cambridge University Press, pp. 391–411.

—(2001). *Religion Explained. The Evolutionary Origins of Religious Thought*. New York, NY: Basic Books.

Cosmides, L. and J. Tooby (1994), 'Origins of domain specificity: the evolution of functional organization'. In L. A. Hirschfeld and S. A. Gelman (eds), *Mapping the Mind: Domain Specificity in Cognition and Culture*. Cambridge: Cambridge University Press, pp. 85–116.

Guthrie, S. E. (1993), *Faces in the Clouds: A New Theory of Religion*. New York, NY/ Oxford: Oxford University Press.

Johnston, M. (2009), *Saving God: Religion after Idolatry*. Princeton, NJ/Oxford: Princeton University Press.

Kirk, G. S., J. E. Raven and M. Schofield (1983), *The Presocratic Philosophers*. 2nd ed. Cambridge: Cambridge University Press.

Mithen, S. (1996), *The Prehistory of the Mind: The Cognitive Origins of Art, Religion, and Science*. London: Thames and Hudson.

Placher, W. C. (1996), *The Domestication of Transcendence: How Modern Thinking about God Went Wrong.* Louisville, KY: Westminster John Knox Press.

Rizzuto, A.-M. (1979), *The Birth of the Living God: A Psychoanalytic Study.* Chicago, IL/London: University of Chicago Press.

Samuels, R. (2000), 'Massively modular minds: evolutoinary psychology and cognitive architecture'. In P. A. Carruthers and A. Chamberlain (eds), *Evolution and the Human Mind: Moldularity, Language and Meta-Cognition.* Cambridge: Cambridge University Press, pp. 13–46.

Slone, D. J. (2004), *Theological Incorrectness: Why Religious People Believe What They Shouldn't.* Oxford/New York, NY: Oxford University Press.

Smith, B. H. (2009), *Natural Reflections: Human Cognition at the Nexus of Science and Religion.* (New Haven, CT/London: Yale University Press.

Sperber, D. (1997), 'Intuitive and reflective beliefs'. *Mind & Language, 12,* 67–83.

Tooby, J. and L. Cosmides (1992), 'The psychological foundations of culture'. In J. H. Barkow, L. Cosmides and J. Tooby (eds), *The Adapted Mind: Evolutionary Psychology and the Generation of Culture.* (New York, NY/Oxford: Oxford University Press, pp. 19–136.

Tremlin, T. (2006), *Minds and Gods: The Cognitive Foundations of Religion.* Oxford/New York, NY: Oxford University Press.

Webster, J. (2004), *Karl Barth.* 2nd ed. London/New York, NY: Continuum.

Wittgenstein, L. (1980), *Culture and Value.* Chicago, IL: University of Chicago Press.

13 Natural and Revealed Religion in Early Modern British Thought

Roomet Jakapi

Introduction

The question 'Is religion natural?' can be understood in a variety of ways depending on the intellectual context in which it is asked. According to the current scholarly understanding, the dictum 'religion is natural' suggests that religion can be explained in terms of natural science, or that it is a certain social practice common to all mankind. Discussions on whether religion is a (by)product of biological evolution, whether it somehow results from our physical constitution and behaviour, whether religious thoughts and experiences could be reduced to physical processes in the brain, and many related debates, are in the forefront of contemporary studies of religion. In the long history of pre-Darwinian thought, the word *natural*, when applied to religion, often had rather different implications. Thus it might be useful and interesting to consider some of those implications in detail, and so to add a historical dimension to the present-day terminology and discussion. This paper will reflect on the issue of whether religion is natural in the context of Early Modern views on *natural religion* as distinguished from *revealed religion* and *natural philosophy*. In this context, *religion* and *theology* were not clearly differentiated concepts, since theology was seen primarily as a practical discipline. Explicit terminological distinctions between *natural religion* and *natural theology*, or between *revealed religion* and *revealed theology*, were not yet there (see Gerrish 2006: 645–8). The focus of this chapter will be on British thought between 1650 and 1750.

I. Natural religion

The intellectual world of the Early Modern period was largely shaped by a number of fundamental religious, metaphysical and moral beliefs inherited from the Middle Ages. A set of these beliefs would constitute natural religion; that is, a body of religious doctrines or principles thought to be binding on all rational creatures. These doctrines would include the existence and attributes of God, divine providence, the immortality of the soul, rewards and punishments in afterlife, and a cluster of moral precepts expressing God's will. According to the then standard view, these tenets were universal in the sense that every sane adult human being would, at least in principle, be able to discover them by ratiocination. Whether the principles in question were innate or not became a matter of serious debate following John Locke's publication of *An Essay Concerning Human Understanding* in 1690 (Locke 1979).

The doctrinal content of natural religion was held to be identical, and discoverable, in all places, times and cultures. The known anthropological fact that religious beliefs and practices in distant countries varied a lot from those established in Europe did not weaken the standard belief in the absolute truth, validity and rationality of the principles of natural religion. Polytheism and atheism were usually regarded as irrational, 'contrary to reason', rather than just wrong (see Locke 1979: 687).

Natural religion, then, was considered as the one and only *rational* religion, opposed to all kinds of supposedly irrational religious ideas, but also distinguished from revealed religion, the body of truths supernaturally revealed in Scripture.

The principles of natural religion, furthermore, were held to be capable of strict proof. Philosophers produced new versions of old arguments, as well as some new arguments, to prove the existence, and deduce the attributes, of God. Most influential of these proofs was Samuel Clarke's version of the cosmological argument (Clarke 2000). Monotheism was hardly ever questioned even by heterodox thinkers who challenged or dismissed several other doctrines relevant to the Christian faith.

In the last decade of the seventeenth century, dozens of pamphlets discussing the nature and immortality of the soul appeared. On the standard account, supported by the Church of England, the soul was taken to be a simple, immaterial substance indestructible by any physical processes and thus immortal. The view was disputed by several dissenters both on philosophical and scriptural grounds[1], but the official position remained in force and was restated in various forms.

Finally, the belief in the possibility of turning moral philosophy into a deductive system of axioms and proofs was still in place (see Locke 1979: 548–52). These systems, however sketchy or elaborate, would almost inevitably rely on the premise that God had created humans on purpose and imposed certain moral principles on them. Fair distribution of divine justice seemed to entail God's providence as well as the existence of appropriate rewards and punishments in the afterlife.

To elucidate the implications of the epithet *natural* in these contexts, let us consider, for example, the doctrine of the natural immortality of soul. The

---

[1] Alternatives to the official position included different forms of Christian mortalism. According to these views, immortality cannot be proved by reasoning. The hope for immortality rests solely on revelation. See Hobbes (2002: chs 34, 38), Coward (1702, 1703). Christian mortalists can be generally divided into annihilationists and 'soul-sleepers'. The former deny bodily resurrection and *personal* immortality, the latter hold that, between bodily death and resurrection, the soul either sleeps (psychopannychism) or is dead (thnetopsychism) (Burns 1972: 13–18).

following passage from the *Principles of Human Knowledge*, published in 1710 by the Irish philosopher George Berkeley, may serve as a standard formulation of the then commonplace argument for immortality:[2]

> the soul is indivisible, incorporeal, unextended, and it is consequently incorruptible. Nothing can be plainer, than that the motions, changes, decays, and dissolutions which we hourly see befall natural bodies /---/ cannot possibly affect an active, simple, uncompounded substance: such a being therefore is indissoluble by the force of Nature, that is to say, *the soul of man is naturally immortal*. (Berkeley 1948–57, vol. 2: 106)

What does it mean to say that the soul is *naturally* immortal? The saying implies that, metaphysically speaking, the property of immortality follows from the immaterial nature of the soul. The soul, as a simple immaterial being, cannot disintegrate by virtue of any physical processes and therefore survives bodily death. In other words, the soul is created such that it can exist independently of the body. It is immortal by its very nature. The dictum also suggests that immortality can be discovered and proved by *reasoning* from certain premises. Natural immortality as a tenet of natural religion can be established by rational argument without the help of revelation. The content of this doctrine is transparent to human reason: nothing irrational or supernatural is involved in it. The doctrine could in principle be discovered and proved by any rational creature who uses her cognitive faculties properly.

Similarly, the existence of God, or of future rewards and punishments, could be discovered and proved by proper reasoning from appropriate premises.

In the Early Modern period, natural religion had an important ally in *natural philosophy*, that is, the theoretical and experimental study of the natural world which developed into modern science. Natural philosophers, such as Sir Isaac Newton or Robert Boyle, viewed the natural world as God's creation.[3] Recent discoveries regarding the fine mechanisms of the physical universe, in their view, manifested the power and wisdom of its Creator. So the scientific theories and findings were in effect placed into a broader framework of metaphysical conceptions involving God and his governance of the created world. Furthermore, as will be explained in the following section, knowledge provided by natural philosophy was sometimes used to support and defend biblical revelations.

II. Revealed religion

The tenets of revealed religion were traced back to Scripture. The Christian religion with its specific doctrines and mysteries was conceived of as *supernatural*, that is, 'above' but not 'contrary to' human reason. Such doctrines as the Holy Trinity, the

---

[2] I ignore certain metaphysical aspects and premises of Berkeley's argument as these do not concern us here.
[3] See the General Scholium in the 2nd edition of Newton's *Principia* (Newton 1713).

Incarnation, the Grace of God, the Resurrection of the Dead and other Christian mysteries were seen as revealed truths whose content transcends, but does not contradict, the human intellect. Divines and philosophers on the side of Christian orthodoxy made efforts to show that these mysterious articles of faith are not in contradiction with the findings of natural philosophy or with sound, rational thinking in general.[4] According to the orthodox account, the divine origin of the Christian religion was proved by the miracles and the fulfillment of prophecies reported in the New Testament.

At the same time, some established scholars, including Newton and Clarke, were suspected of holding heretical views on particular Christian doctrines, especially the doctrine of the Trinity. Anti-trinitarianism and other heterodox beliefs could hardly be professed in public.[5]

In Early Modern times, it was still common to believe that Scripture contained not only articles of faith relevant for salvation, but also true and reliable accounts of the beginning, course and end of this world. The stories of the Creation and the Great Deluge were typically regarded as historically true descriptions of events that took place less than 10,000 years ago. Several natural philosophers, accordingly, tried to reconcile scientific evidence with the great biblical narratives (see, for example, Whiston 1696). They combined natural philosophy with biblical exegesis to show the agreement of reason and revelation.

The Christian religion, with its specific supernatural revelations, was in effect considered as a kind of supplement to natural religion. Revealed propositions expressing the truths of Christianity were not to be taken on blind faith. Rather they were to be subjected to the test of reason, for it was assumed that God, as a rational and veracious agent, would not reveal anything that contradicts human reason. Evidently nonsensical propositions could not come from God. As John Locke famously put it, reason is to judge whether the given proposition is or is not revealed:

> it still belongs to reason, to judge of the truth of its being a revelation, and of the signification of the words, wherein it is delivered. Indeed, if any thing shall be thought revelation, which is contrary to the plain principles of reason, and the evident knowledge the mind has of its own clear and distinct ideas; there reason must be hearkned to, as to a matter within its province. Since a man can never have so certain a knowledge, that a proposition which contradicts the clear principles and evidence of his own knowledge, was divinely revealed, or that he understands the words rightly, wherein it is delivered, as he has, that the contrary is true, and so is bound to consider and judge of it as a matter of reason, and not swallow it, without examination, as a matter of faith. (Locke 1979, 694–5)

These developments in philosophy and theology naturally raised the question of the principal function and status of revealed religion. Perhaps the universally

---

[4] See, for example, Boyle's essay 'Some physico-theological considerations about the possibility of the resurrection' in Boyle (1675).
[5] Newton's disciple William Whiston lost his job at Cambridge University because he professed anti-trinitarian convictions (Force 1985: 3).

accessible natural religion is sufficient for salvation? Does the special revelation in Scripture add anything significant to the truths of natural religion, or is it just a means to propagate the latter?

Between 1690 and 1730, the teachings of revealed religion came under serious attack by such *deists*, or *freethinkers*, as John Toland, Matthew Tindal and Anthony Collins.[6] These heterodox thinkers used different strategies to discredit revealed religion as understood by the established churches. Toland, for example, argued in his book *Christianity not Mysterious* (1696) that, in the New Testament, the term *mystery* stands for something that was hidden from us before it was revealed, but now is something we clearly know and understand. For Toland, the Bible does not contain anything 'above reason', since revelation is but a means of giving comprehensible information.

The deists also claimed that revealed religion does not add anything new to natural religion. All the relevant doctrinal points in the New Testament are in fact contained in the principles of natural religion. This position is famously stated in Tindal's *Christianity as Old as the Creation* (1730).

In short, the freethinkers' objections to revealed religion served to demonstrate that natural (rational) religion is in fact the only (true) religion. Revealed religion could be accepted in so far as its content coincided with that of natural religion. Allegedly supernatural, incomprehensible doctrines were to be abandoned. It is no wonder that this adherence to natural religion resulted in anti-clericalism, and criticism of religious ritual and authority. A significant work representing this trend is Collins's *A Discourse of Freethinking* (1713).

So the Early Modern deist's response to the question 'Is religion natural?' might have been 'Yes, of course, religion is natural'. Religion is natural in the sense that a limited set of true religious doctrines is accessible and fully comprehensible to human reason without the help of supernatural revelation. These doctrines are universal, since they could in principle be found out by any rational human being. The alleged mysterious articles of faith that do not pass the test of rational inquiry are simply meaningless and ought to be rejected. There is no other, revealed religion beside the natural.

The deists, furthermore, tended to confine the content of natural religion to a very few doctrinal points such as the existence of God and his attributes, from which our duties could be derived. Thus Tindal states:

> By *Natural Religion*, I understand the Belief of the Existence of a God, and the Sense and Practice of those Duties which result from the Knowledge we, by our Reason, have of him and his Perfections; and of ourselves, and our own Imperfections; and of the relation we stand in to him and our Fellow-Creatures: so that the *Religion of Nature* takes in every thing that is founded on the Reason and Nature of things. (Tindal 1730: 11)

Another distinguishing feature of deism in general is that it 'is frequently silent on the subject of an afterlife' (Stewart 2006: 688).

---

[6] For recent overviews of 'the deist debate', see Gerrish 2006 and Stewart 2006.

The works and views of the freethinkers brought about numerous responses from established divines and philosophers, who decided to write in defense of revealed, as well as natural, religion. Such prominent intellectuals as Richard Bentley, Samuel Clarke, William Derham and many others, contributed to the apologetic lecture series established by, and named after, Robert Boyle: the famous Boyle Lectures (Burnet 2000). Notable books from the orthodox camp include George Berkeley's *Alciphron* (1732; Berkeley 1948–57, vol. 3), William Law's *The Case of Reason* (1732), and *The Analogy of Religion* (1736) by Joseph Butler. The opponents often saw deism as atheism in disguise and a serious threat to common morality and civil society. They used different strategies of argumentation to show the validity of the doctrines of natural religion, as well as the usefulness and truth of the Christian revelation.

III. Conclusion

This chapter has discussed the notions of natural and revealed religion in the context of Early Modern British philosophy and theology. Its main purpose has been to point out the characteristics of natural religion as understood by thinkers of that period. These features included rationality, universality, and accordance to the nature of eternal and created things. The concept of *natural,* when applied to religion, was opposed to *irrational* and *supernatural.*[7]

References

Berkeley, G. (1948–57), *The Works of George Berkeley Bishop of Cloyne.* A. A. Luce and E. T. Jessop (eds). 9 vols. London/ Edinburgh: Thomas Nelson and Sons.

Boyle, R. (1675), *Some Considerations about the Reconcileableness of Reason and Religion, with a Discourse about the Possibility of the Resurrection.* London: Printed by T. N. for H. Herringman.

Burnet, G. (ed.) (2000 [1737]), *The Boyle Lectures (1692–1732): A Defence of Natural and Revealed Religion: Being an Abridgment of the Sermons Preached at the Lecture Founded by Robert Boyle* (4 vols). Bristol: Thoemmes.

Burns, N. T. (1972), *Christian Mortalism from Tyndale to Milton.* Cambridge, MA: Harvard University Press.

Butler, J. (1736), *The Analogy of Religion, Natural and Revealed, to the Constitution and Course of Nature.* London: J., J. and P. Knapton.

Clarke, S. (2000 [1737]), Dr Samuel Clarke's *Demonstration of the Being and Attributes of God Abridg'd* (Burnet, G. ed.), *The Boyle Lectures (1692–1732): A Defence of Natural and Revealed Relgion: Being an Abridgment of the Sermons Preached a the Lecture Founded by Robert Boyle.* 4 Vols. Bristol: Thoemmes.

[7] Research for this paper was supported by the Estonian Science Foundation Grant No. 8715.

Collins, A. (1713), *A Discourse of Freethinking, Occasioned by the Rise and Growth of a Sect Called Freethinkers*. London: Pemberton.

Coward, W. (1702), *Second Thoughts Concerning Human Soul*. London: R. Basset.

—(1703), *Farther Thoughts Concerning Human Soul*. London: R. Basset.

Force, J. E. (1985), *William Whiston. Honest Newtonian*. Cambridge: Cambridge University Press.

Gerrish, B. A. (2006), 'Natural and revealed religion'. In K. Haakonssen (ed.), *Cambridge History of Eighteenth-Century Philosophy*, Vol. 2. Cambridge: Cambridge University Press, 641–65.

Hobbes, Th. (2002 [1651]), *Leviathan* (R. Tuck [ed.]). Cambridge: Cambridge University Press.

Law, W. (1732), *The Case of Reason, or Natural Religion, Fairly and Fully Stated*. London: W. Innys.

Locke, J. (1979 [1690]), *An Essay Concerning Human Understanding*. (P. H. Nidditch [ed.]) Oxford: Clarendon.

Newton, I. (1713 [1687]), *Philosophiæ Naturalis Principia Mathematica*. London.

Stewart, M. A. (2006), 'Revealed religion: the British debate'. In K. Haakonssen (ed.), *Cambridge History of Eighteenth-Century Philosophy*. Vol. 2. Cambridge: Cambridge University Press, pp. 683–709.

Tindal, M. (1730), *Christianity as Old as the Creation; or, the Gospel a Republication of the Religion of Nature*. London: [s.n.].

Toland, J. (1696), *Christianity not Mysterious: A Treatise Shewing, That there is Nothing in the Gospel Contrary to Reason, Nor Above It: And that no Christian Doctrine can be Properly Called a Mystery*. London: Sam Buckley.

Whiston, W. (1696), *A New Theory of the Earth, From its Original, to the Consummation of all Things. Wherein the Creation of the World in Six Days, the Universal Deluge, And the General Conflagration, As laid down in the Holy Scriptures, Are Shewn to be Perfectly Agreeable to Reason and Philosophy. With a Large Introductory Discourse Concerning the Genuine Nature, Stile, and Extent of the Mosaick History of the Creation*. London: B. Tooke.

Index